FELT

FELT

WILLOW MULLINS

BERG

oxford + new york

English edition
First published in 2009 by
Berg
Editorial offices:
First Floor, Angel Court, 81 St Clements Street, Oxford OX4 1AW, UK
175 Fifth Avenue, New York, NY 10010, USA

Berg is the imprint of Oxford International Publishers Ltd.

Library of Congress Cataloging-in-Publication Data

Mullins, Willow (Willow G.)
    Felt / Willow Mullins.
        p. cm.
    Includes bibliographical references and index.
    ISBN-13: 978-1-84520-439-6 (pbk.)
    ISBN-10: 1-84520-439-5 (pbk.)
    ISBN-13: 978-1-84520-438-9 (cloth)
    ISBN-10: 1-84520-438-7 (cloth)
    1. Felt work. 2. Felting. I. Title.

    TT849.5.M85 2009
    677'.63—dc22

                                        2008047666

British Library Cataloguing-in-Publication Data

A catalogue record for this book is available from the British Library.

ISBN 978 1 84520 438 9 (Cloth)
        978 1 84520 439 6 (Paper)

Typeset by JS Typesetting Ltd, Porthcawl, Mid Glamorgan
Printed in the United Kingdom by MPG-Biddles Limited, King's Lynn, Norfolk

www.bergpublishers.com

CONTENTS

INTRODUCTION

From houses to clothing, from car parts to works of fine art, from translucent, cloud-like gossamer sheets to thick, heavy, water-resistant mats to carefully sculpted three-dimensional shapes, felt is one of the world's oldest and most understated textiles. At its most ancient and elemental, felt is simply entangled wool fibers, matted together. No stitches, no seams. Unique among textile structures, felt does not rely on first turning raw fibers into yarn as weaving and knitting do; rather felt harnesses the chaos of tangles. While those of us who weave and knit may look upon the confused snarl of our yarn with frustration, for those who felt, this confusion of fibers is a thing of beauty.

Rooted among the nomadic peoples of the Middle East and Central Asia, felt has traveled the globe. It has been found in tombs and archaeological sites, most famously Pazyryk in the Altai Mountains of Siberia but also in Denmark. When felt first appeared is not known, but archaeological evidence suggests that it has been used in Central Asia for at least 8,000 years (Burkett 1977, 112). Its use in hats and tents was noted by scholars of ancient Greece and China and the famous European travelers of the Middle Ages. Far from being supplanted by new fabrics, felt has not only retained its traditional uses among the peoples of Central Asia, Turkey and Finland, but has also seen a revival of popularity in the last few decades among hand feltmakers around the world, among artists and in clothing and home fashions. Meanwhile, easy to cut and available in a rainbow of bright colors, felt has been the darling fabric of Western kitsch and craft, well stocked in elementary school art rooms and summer camps. This book seeks to follow the journey of felt through time, space and purpose by pulling into focus a series of snapshots of different felting traditions within history, science, art and ethnography.

In writing histories, it can be easy to fall back on a chronological progression positioning the past and the present as opposite extremes, implying a division between old and new, traditional and modern. Such a progression cannot work for felt. Felt has developed in multiple cultures, each adapting it to their own needs, and often its origins are lost. We do not know whether felt spread with the expansion of Central Asian trade routes across Asia and Europe or if it was developed by several different cultures independently. Among some peoples, felt is thousands of years old and honored as an integral part of life. Among others, felt is utilitarian, used but barely considered. Still others are just discovering the possibilities of felt. Thus while chronology prevails within each chapter, the book as a whole is focused on traditions of felt.

The term "tradition" can mean many things, but here it refers to an element of culture that reflects the beliefs, lifestyle or aesthetics of its makers in some way and is passed on, sometimes unconsciously, from one generation to the next. In this sense, traditions are culturally specific – one feltmaking culture may not have the same traditions as another in how they make, use or think about felt. Further, traditions are not fixed. Some aspects change to keep them relevant to the time while others stay the same to provide continuity and assure that there is a coherent tradition. Yet each culture determines which elements can change and which must be consistent. By thinking about felt in terms of traditions rather than chronology, we avoid privileging the new over the old, and technological advance over the handmade or vice versa. By thinking about traditions rather than strict geography or ethnic group, we may see how feltmaking shows both the diversity and the connections between cultures, especially as the world becomes smaller through the Internet and travel, and to see how some traditions are becoming multicultural. Finally, by thinking about traditions, we can better recognize the creativity of everyone who works with felt, regardless of where they are, how they learned or where their felt is seen.

In order to understand what makes felt so unique and versatile, it is necessary to understand how it is made – what makes felt, felt. The first chapter explores the processes that have been used to make felt, both traditionally and through mechanization. "Felt," as used here, describes any fabric made directly from wool fibers that are entangled with the aid of heat, moisture, pressure and friction and without the use of a binder or adhesive. Today, the techniques that produced felt have spurred the creation of an entire class of textiles – the nonwovens – made from synthetics and blends rather than the traditional wool, and the applications of felt have increased by the hundredfold. True felt requires the special properties that wool and some animal furs possess: scaly surface, natural elasticity and the ability to move along the length of the fiber. The term nonwoven, while including felt, also includes textiles made from fibers other than wool, such as bark cloth made of tree fibers; by other means, such as beating or thermal fusion; or by the addition of resins or adhesives (Kadolf and Langford 1998, 246–50; CIBA 1958, 129, 2). Similarly, feltmaking or felting refers specifically to the entanglement of wool or animal fibers, while fulling describes a related process that relies on the same techniques of felting and properties of wool but starts with a woven or knitted fabric rather than loose fibers. The focus of this book is primarily wool felt, but it will also touch on the textiles and techniques that are related to it, as they can offer insight into just how important the technology of felt is.

The second chapter centers on the early history of felt. From the earliest archaeological evidence through the references to felt by Greek and Roman writers, we can begin to track the movement of felt as it was developed in different areas and adopted by neighboring groups. Though pieces of felt rarely last from one century to the next, enough fragments have been found in tombs and bogs to piece together an idea of the textile's most ancient history. Archaeological felts not only prove the long history of felting techniques and motifs, but also give us clues to felt's many uses and its appearance in different cultures at different times. Combining this physical evidence with textual sources and legends of felt helps fill in the picture, but the early writers also tell us something of how people thought of felt. More specifically, these texts show the extent to which the Greeks and Romans associated felt with the peoples of ancient Persia and Central Asia.

Having established how felt is made and an overall timeline for its use, the rest of the book focuses on several felt traditions. Central Asia, the subject of chapter three, is generally credited as the birthplace of felt. Within the Chinese annals of the third century BCE, it is called "the land of felt" (Laufer 1930, 3). Central Asia covers a vast territory, loosely including Mongolia, northwestern China, Kyrgyzstan, Kazakhstan, Tajikistan, southern Siberia, Uzbekistan, Turkmenistan and parts of modern Iran and Pakistan. Among the nomadic and semi-nomadic sheep-herding peoples of Central Asia, felt and feltmaking are a major part of life. Some have argued that felt makes nomadic life in Central Asia possible (Laufer 1930, 2). Here, felt appears in many forms, from the covers of the traditional nomadic houses – the yurt, *bozu* or *ger* – to clothing to ornaments for horses and camels, and is endowed with deep cultural significance. While feltmaking has waned with the settlement of the nomads, felt continues to be an integral part of Central Asian cultures. It has retained its purpose as a utilitarian cloth, lining truck beds and floors, but it has also become a cultural symbol and a way of claiming cultural identity. In 1995, for example, Kyrgyzstan erected a five-storey felt bozu as part of the celebration of the one-thousandth anniversary of the national epic hero Manas. Some Central Asian feltmakers have drawn on tradition and turned it to modern purposes, using the centuries-old motifs of archaeological felts from Pazyryk for high fashion and art on one hand and objects for Western markets and tourists on the other. Today, the ancient tradition of feltmaking in Central Asia is combining with other traditions to make new and innovative felt art.

Moving westward, chapter four investigates the many feltmaking traditions found between the Caspian Sea in the east and Hungary in the west. This region is hugely diverse, but many of the peoples within it have found in felt a textile that helps to keep them dry and warm as they herd sheep or to stay comfortable within their houses. This chapter focuses on the two major felt centers of Iran and central Anatolia in Turkey, both with strong felting traditions that are being practiced less and less. As in Central Asia, felt once flourished in these regions. Today, however, the technique is suffering from lack of documentation and a diminishing number of makers. Some speculate that ornate, floral-patterned felt rugs were once as expensive as knotted ones in Persia (Raissnia 2007). While the rugs of this region help to demonstrate felt's importance and artistry, the felt mantles that served everyone from shepherds to wealthy men are truly what hold this region together. These mantles represent the significance of felt in these myriad cultures and display the specific ways that each adapted this form to suit their own styles and climates. As in Central Asia, the feltmakers of the Middle East, Turkey and Hungary are combining their traditions with their own creativity to join in a global conversation about felt and art.

The story of felt in Europe, dealt with in chapter five, follows two traditions – one that encompasses the history of hats, guilds and industrialism and another, located in northern Europe, that focuses on home production. The first tradition began with the new fashion for felt hats that swept the continent and the British Isles in the fifteenth and sixteenth centuries, not long after feudal society had begun to give way to commercial exchange. It continued with the rise of feltmaking guilds focused almost solely on the production of hats. In fact, the connection between felt and hats was so strong that felt became a general term for any kind of hat made of cloth, regardless of whether it was true felt (Oxford English Dictionary online

2007). Following the course of industrial development, felt was at the center of some of the debates that have led to modern commercial practice. Europe's other felting tradition was restricted almost entirely to the northern areas of Norway, Sweden and Finland, where felt boots helped to keep people warm during the long winters. Until the twentieth century, these boots were almost entirely made within the family or by local women as a way to gain extra income. Today, though hats have fallen out of fashion, feltmaking in northern Europe is on the rise thanks to its increasing use by artists – who see in felt a way to combine their cultural history with their own inspiration.

Despite felt's honorable place in Central Asia and its longstanding history in the Middle East and even the sartorial history of Western Europe, felt has only recently received the attention that it deserves in the tradition of Western art. In much of Europe and North America, feltmaking was predominantly considered a craft rather than an art. Only through the groundbreaking works of fiber arts and sculptors working in felt in the mid-twentieth century has felt become a vital component of art throughout the world. These new felt artists have pushed the boundaries of feltmaking: incorporating other fibers and fabrics, building new structures out of felt and drawing on their own cultures for new influences. The artistic process that creates these new works of felt exists as much alongside tradition as in its perceived absence. Felt has been equally influential in the fashion world. More recently, felt is gaining new interest as trendy shops carry felt bags and pillows. Chapter six investigates these modern innovators of felt in art and fashion and the role that felt played in the breakdown of artistic hierarchies. All of the artists discussed in earlier chapters resonate here, for they are also taking part in the tradition of fine art feltmaking.

The seventh and eighth chapters move from these individual artists to consider felt in wider Western culture. While artists began to draw attention to felt and introduce it into the traditions of fine art, felt was also making a comeback as a home-produced textile through the 1970s crafts movement, fueled by a resurgence of interest in personal expression and natural materials. Yet felt craft must also incorporate the use of felt for children's projects in schools and summer camps as well as for homemade decorations, poodle skirts and Christmas-tree ornaments. Here, felt became the stuff of individual artistry meant not for the gallery or the museum but the home. More recently, in the early years of the twenty-first century, felt is expanding its reach again, appearing in accessories and home décor sold in both boutiques and chain stores. Chapter seven continues by exploring some of the industrial and scientific uses of felt. We use felt and nonwovens every day, often without even being aware of it. Felt continues to be integral to the construction of cars and airplanes and was even used in building the New York subway system. Similarly, its specific properties and lack of distinct yarns have made felt's sister fabrics – nonwovens – ideal for many medical applications.

One note on my methodology before going on. This work stemmed from my master's thesis on Central Asian felt horse blankets. There, I attempted to document felt's use for animal blankets as well as provide an investigation into the specific concerns related to conserving felt in the museum context. Since then, I have been very fortunate to be able to travel and do fieldwork with feltmakers at conferences and symposia in Europe and North America, on two separate trips to Kyrgyzstan, and during a brief visit to Turkey. During these trips, I sought out feltmakers. In Kyrgyzstan, in particular, I was able to get to know some of the artists working in felt not only in the capital, Bishkek, but also some of the members of the artisan networks Altyn Kol in Kochkor and Altyn Oimok in Bokonbaeovo. Much of the information that appears here is based on this fieldwork. Due to practical constraints, I was unable to do fieldwork in Finland, Sweden and Norway as I had hoped, but I corresponded with feltmakers from this region. For the sections on modern industrial felt, I was able to interview Frank Jani, who has worked in the industry for over thirty years, and to correspond with two of the other major felt and nonwoven manufacturers in the United States. The information on retail and felt in the marketplace is largely based on my own observations, Internet searches and discussions with retailers. The historical and art historical sections are the result of more traditional text-based research. The feltmakers and felt scholars I have met around the world, emailed with and talked to, have all been wonderfully generous with their time and knowledge, and this book could not have taken shape without their help.

Felt now encircles the globe from mundane utilitarian cloth to artistic, technologically savvy creations. Felt is often taken for granted, rarely recognized for the lifestyle it makes possible, but what do we in the West really think about felt? What meanings do we attach to it and how do those meanings change over time, between places and with use? The last, eighth, chapter offers some answers to these questions by looking at our assumptions about felt. Feltmaking is probably the oldest technique for producing textiles on earth, and it continues to influence people's lives. What becomes apparent as we look at felt around the world and through history is that it has created a tradition and a culture all of its own. This book owes its existence to all of the feltmakers who spent time talking with me and offering their assistance and enthusiasm. The story of felt is a truly remarkable one – showing how such a humble textile should impact people so greatly and so quietly. The world's feltmakers know the wonder and worth of this textile. My goal is to share it with you.

1.
THE MAKING OF FELT

On a technical level, felt describes any fabric made directly from wool fibers that are entangled by mechanical means without the use of a binder or adhesive. In other words, felt is a lot like purposefully tangled hair. Felt has traditionally been made by hand, through an arduous process of rolling the dampened wool. While it continues to be made in this way by many cultures or for particular uses, a variety of technologies have arisen to speed the process and reduce the amount of heavy labor. The so-called nonwovens, textiles made from fibers other than wool and often with the addition of resins or through thermal fusion, are the modern extension of the ancient felt technology (Kadolf and Langford 1998, 246–50; CIBA 1958, 129, 2). These textiles show both the innovations of industrialization and the usefulness of the felt structure. This chapter will explore just what "felt" is and why its structure is so special. It will look at the range of methods of production, from a basic description of what makes wool felt in the first place through the traditional methods of hand feltmakers around the world to the industrial production of felt and the adaptation of felt techniques to synthetic fibers.

FROM FIBERS TO FELT

> [A] method of working up wool or hair into a species of cloth, independently of either spinning or weaving, with a degree of stiffening sufficient to preserve its figure, and to answer the purpose of wearing. The process of felting is

curious and interesting; it depends on the conformation of all animal hairs and wool, which disposes them to unite with each other in such a manner, as to produce a firm compact substance. (Qtd. in Pufpaff 1995, 25)

A hatmaker wrote this description of making felt in 1829. Put in words that make the fibers seem to want to felt of their own accord, felt is "curious and interesting" indeed. Yet closer investigation reveals a fairly simple process reliant largely on the natural properties of wool. Sheep's wool is ideally designed for felting, more than any other natural or synthetic fiber. This said, most animal fibers can be felted to some degree. A single wool fiber is typically long and tapered towards the tip, just as human hair is. Wool is a staple-length fiber, meaning relatively short, as opposed to filament length fiber such as silk. The length of wool fibers varies significantly depending on the variety of sheep breed. For example, Scottish Blackface sheep have long, coarse wool, while the wool from Merino sheep is known for its fineness but is comparatively short – 3–5 inches in length. What part of the sheep the wool grew on can also have an effect – wool from the sheep's back is finer and longer than belly wool. The fiber thickness and staple determine the quality of the wool. The thickness of wool is typically measured in microns (where 1 micron is one-millionth of a meter). A coarse fiber might be as large as 37 microns, while a very fine fiber measures approximately 17 microns across. Australian Merino, however, can reach just 11 microns. A bale of this superfine wool was sold for a record US$7,500 per kilogram in 2004 (Whelan 2004, 21). Although most wool will felt to some degree, fine fibers not only make fine yarns for weaving but also produce particularly smooth and pliable felts. Many feltmakers prefer one kind of wool over others, often favoring the product from their regional and traditional sheep breeds, such as the fine-wooled Finn in Scandinavia or the double-coated fat-tailed mountain sheep of Kyrgyzstan. That said, Merino is popular worldwide.

Each fiber consists of a medulla, a cortex and a cuticle. The medulla forms the core of the fiber and has a comblike structure that helps provide the insulation for which wool is famous. Around it, the cortex consists of two components that react differently to moisture and heat and cause the fibers to have crimp – the spiraled coil that appears as waviness in locks of wool (Kadolf and Langford 1998, 53). In the early 1800s, crimp was considered to be the primary reason for wool's ability to felt (Smith and Walker 1995, 15). It can be measured according to the number of twists per centimeter or inch, or the frequency, though many feltmakers think of it in terms of the amount of extension, or how much a fiber gains in length when the crimp is pulled out straight. The amount of crimp often increases with the fineness of the wool fiber.

A higher quality fiber, i.e. finer and with higher crimp, will tend to felt faster than a thicker, wavier fiber, since the fineness allows the fibers to move through smaller spaces between other fibers while the higher crimp makes it twine around other fibers more easily and thus makes it more difficult to extract (Smith and Walker 1995, 51–5). A simple way of thinking about this is the difference between unknotting very fine, lumpy yarn such as a bouclé (or curly hair) and untangling thick, smooth pieces of nylon rope, which by comparison seem simply to fall apart.

Crimp is caused by the two different types of keratin cells in the cortex. In one set of cells, the paracortex, the keratin is matured and hardened and the cells are larger but, in the smaller orthocortex cells, the keratin is soft and pliant. The two bundles of cells lying next to one another cause the fiber to both bend back and forth and to twist on its axis, with the paracortex generally on the inside of the bends, forming the characteristic coil of wool fibers (Kadolf and Langford 1998, 53). The cross links between the keratin molecules in the orthocortex and paracortex allow the wool fiber to be stretched and then return to its original length when released, making it naturally elastic (Johnson 2002, 12). The shape of the crimp coils helps the fibers twine around each other during the felting process. Moreover, both the crimp and the elasticity are increased with moisture and temperature, exactly the two elements added during feltmaking. Yet it is the surface of wool fibers that makes them so well suited for felting.

The cuticle of the fiber is covered in scales, and it is these scales that turn wool into felt. The scales on a single fiber of sheep's wool are attached at the base to the fiber's core and have jagged, free edges, overlapping much like roof shingles. On the sheep, these scales help to direct rain and other moisture away from the sheep's body and make it more difficult for dirt and vegetal material to work into the fleece (Smith and Walker 1995, 11). Once shorn and washed clean of the protective grease, termed "lanolin," the wool fibers can be joined together by enmeshing their scales through heat and moisture creating felt.

The felting process is aided further by wool's tendency to shrink under these conditions, something anyone who has mistakenly washed a wool sweater or socks in hot water in a washing machine knows firsthand. This shrinkage is caused by "creep" – the ability of the fiber to move towards the root when pressure is applied (Burkett 1979, 1). The direction of creep is caused by the orientation of the scales, so that they provide friction when rubbed from the tip towards the root but creep when pressure is applied in the opposite direction. Machine-washable wool fabrics were developed by coating the scales with a silicone-based polymer to limit creep and the fibers' ability to link together, effectively making the fiber surface closer to cotton (Smith and Walker 1995, 12). Like crimp, the elasticity and creep are both augmented by heat and moisture, which cause the fiber to swell, thus spreading out the scales and allowing them to enmesh more freely. Once enmeshed, the scales cannot easily be pulled apart.

The process of feltmaking can be summed up as the entanglement of haphazardly arranged wool fibers through the introduction of heat, moisture, pressure and friction, which may be supplemented with a weak alkaline solution (Burkett 1979, 1; CIBA 1958, 129, 2; Emery 1966, 22). The weak alkaline solution is typically soap. Soap helps to reduce the surface tension of the water, which in turn allows the water to soak more easily into the wool fibers. This process builds on the distinctive qualities of wool, using heat and moisture to increase the crimp, elasticity and creep while opening up the scales to make a coherent textile. Even a small difference in the moisture level or temperature can affect the felting process. One American felt manufacturer produced large rolled batts and stored them in the cellars below the factory until they would be felted several days later. This system worked fine until the company built a new factory and moved from their old location, which had stood on top of a stream. At the new location, they followed the same procedure, but the wool refused to form into a good, solid felt as it had at the old factory over the stream. Discovering that the relative humidity had been substantially raised in the old cellars by the stream, allowing the batts to be permeated before they reached the felting machines, the company ultimately had to build conditioning rooms in the new factory to replicate the environment produced by the stream and give the wool enough moisture to produce the strong felts they were known for (Jani 2007).

Applying pressure and friction puts the creep into action, forcing the fibers to intertwine and the fibers to shrink together. Felt is best achieved by first carding a fleece into batts to separate the fibers. This allows each fiber to act individually and increases the potential for the scales to enmesh and for movement of the fibers to take place. The batts are layered to ensure that the tip–root orientation of the fibers varies, so that creep will occur in multiple directions as the fibers are felted together, making for a stronger fabric with no specific orientation, unlike woven fabric with its distinctive warp and weft. This lack of orientation means that felt has the same strength regardless of how tension is applied to it. Woven fabric, on the other hand, does not have even resistance to tension. If you pull it in the warp direction, it will be considerably less flexible than if you pull it at a 45° angle to the warp along the bias. Since batts for felting are layered, pressure in one direction activates the creep of one layer of fibers, moving them through the other layers. Applying pressure in other directions activates other layers. This process is clear when hand felting, since consistent pressure in only one direction, vertically from the top to the bottom of a square for instance, will cause shrinkage in only that direction while the horizontal dimensions will remain unchanged, rapidly turning the square into a rectangle. For even felting, therefore, pressure must be applied in a circular movement across the whole felt or rolled from multiple directions (Smith and Walker 1995, 13).

The ability of wool to felt is particularly impressive. While other natural animal fibers, such as rabbit and beaver hair, can be felted, they first require a process called carrotting. Carrotting uses a solution of hydrogen peroxide and nitric acid to create scales on the fibers so that they can then be felted. This process can create very fine felts and has been used for centuries in hatmaking. Because sheep's wool felts so readily, it can be combined with other fibers — animal, plant, or synthetic — in a blended felt that contains as little as twenty percent wool (Johnson 2002, 13). These blended felts are common for industrial uses. Mixtures of wool and cotton are very common for producing the *namda* embroidered rugs of India and Pakistan, while many artists working in felt have experimented with a wide variety of fiber mixtures, including silks and synthetics. Yet as different fibers are added, the felt loses strength, since those fibers will not enmesh. Wool must be at least half of the mixture to provide adequate strength (Johnson 2002, 13).

With this basic understanding of how wool is able to become felt, and more to the point is specifically adapted to the purpose, we can look at how felt has been made throughout history. As we have seen, feltmaking essentially uses moisture, heat and friction to mat wool fibers. How the heat and moisture are added, whether an alkaline agent such as soap is used and if so what kind, and how the wool is prepared into the batts to be felted have changed over time and between cultures. Although we have historical evidence of feltmaking for millennia, the exact components and process before Greek and Roman times and among peoples who did not leave a written record is largely speculative. Each group of feltmakers has relied upon the materials they have to hand, so while feltmakers in olive-growing regions may prefer olive-oil-based soaps and the wool of the local fat-tailed sheep, feltmakers in the United States might prefer the more readily available Merino wool and liquid dishwashing detergent. Similarly, Kyrgyz feltmakers roll the large *ala-kiyiz* rugs with their felt-in designs in canvas rolls, tightly tied, that are slowly pulled and stomped on; Mongolian feltmakers tie these rolls behind camels or horses, who pull them across the steppe. The remainder of this chapter will look first at one description of traditional feltmaking, as a place to start, and then follow the industrialization of felting to see how that process has become mechanized, before turning to how to make felt three-dimensional and add design elements.

TRADITIONAL FELTMAKING

All felt is made by first cleaning the wool to remove the lanolin that the sheep produce along with any dirt and debris that may be stuck in the fibers. The fibers must then be separated to ensure optimal felting, before forming them into thick, fluffy batts that look much like clouds. These batts are then moistened with hot water and gently rubbed to initiate the interlocking of the wool fibers. More moisture or soap may be added as needed to keep the wool damp – but not soaking – and warm. As the fibers mat together and shrink, the felt begins to become firmer and stronger, so that the friction and pressure can be increased. Throughout this process, the feltmaker must pay careful attention to make sure that distinct layers are not forming between the piled batts of wool and that the piece is being felted evenly in all directions to maintain the desired shape. The feltmaker must also watch for any weak or thin areas, where the fibers were not evenly distributed in the batts. If they are caught early in the felting process, many of these issues can be fixed as the piece is felted. In the final stages of felting, the piece is rolled and pounded from every direction to help shrink the felt as much as possible, hardening it and smoothing out the surface. Once done, any remaining soap is rinsed out of the felt and it is left to dry. These steps are the rudiments of feltmaking, but they are nonetheless the process used for making all felt in one form or another. Several authors have produced excellent in-depth instructions for hand felting, explaining how to keep edges straight and dimensions exact, and giving ideas for projects. For now, however, this description serves as an introduction to felt itself, from which we can see both the tradition and innovation of feltmaking.

Traditional feltmaking is still carried out throughout Anatolia and Central Asia using primarily sheep's wool, although goat or camel hair may also be added, and it has been taken up by hand felters the world over, stretching all the way to the United States and Australia (Burkett 1979, 2). The cultures of the Middle East and Central Asia, which loosely include everything between Hungary in the west through Mongolia in the east and from southern Siberia in the north into northern India and Pakistan, have been making felt for millennia. While feltmaking has been more or less important to these cultures at various times, they nonetheless have a continuous tradition, passed on orally and by example from one generation to the next. For this reason, these cultures serve as a perfect example of traditional feltmaking. One of the best step-by-step descriptions of traditional feltmaking was recorded by Veronika Gervers and Michael Gervers in Anatolia in the 1970s (Gervers and Gervers 1974). Their account provides a good basis for understanding the process of traditional feltmaking, from which variations between cultures can then be explored.

The wool is shorn from the sheep in either spring or fall. In Anatolia, the wool may be cleaned by running the sheep through a stream prior to shearing and then removing debris by hand from the shorn wool (Gervers and Gervers 1974, 16; Burkett 1979, 2). In Mongolia, where the sheep are shorn twice a year, at the beginning of summer and the beginning of fall, the sheep are run through the stream *after* shearing to get them used to the cold and to invigorate new wool growth (Batchuluun 2003, 57). The wool fibers are then separated and any remaining debris is removed. Separating the wool is an arduous task and may use any number of tools. The carding bow is probably the most common throughout Central Asia and into Europe. The bow is a long piece of wood with a string attached. The string is plucked or hit with a mallet and its vibrations help to loosen the fibers from one another and release the debris. The wool can also be fluffed and separated by using wooden, rake-like forks or with wool cards. Cards consist of two wooden paddles covered with small tines, which can be scraped against one another to loosen the wool and release any dirt. The wool is moved from one card to the next, back and forth, until sufficiently clean.

Once cleaned, the wool is laid out on a reed screen in a thick batt (Burkett 1979, 3; Gervers and Gervers 1974, 16; Sjöberg 1996, 24). Sometimes an older felt, called the "mother felt," is used in place of the reed screen, in which case the felt being made becomes the son or daughter felt. Generally, the felt is laid so that the fibers in each layer are perpendicular to those of the layer below. The batt of wool fibers may be thirty to forty centimeters thick (Burkett 1979, 3; Gervers and Gervers 1974, 16). Old felt may be incorporated into the center of the new felt for added strength or uncleaned wool may be added in the center (Gervers and Gervers 1974; Sjöberg 1996, 25). The amount of wool used depends entirely upon the end purpose of the felt. For the thick rugs of Kyrgyzstan, over a kilogram of wool is used for each square meter of the batt – the final size of the felt rug after shrinkage being much smaller. For a lightweight hat, only a hundred or so grams might be needed. Once the batt is laid, the wool is dampened by sprinkling hot water over it (Burkett 1979, 3; Gervers and Gervers 1974, 16; Sjöberg 1996, 25). Then the felting begins in earnest.

First, the felting process may be started by gently rubbing the dampened wool by hand to provide the agitation necessary to interlock the scales on the surface of the fibers. Once the felt is holding together as a single fabric, it is formed into a roll along with the cloth or screen on which the wool was originally laid out. As the roll is turned, it pulls against the outside fibers, which in turn move against one another, thereby further intertwining the fibers and tightening and shrinking the felt. In Mongolia, this step is done by pulling the roll containing the felt behind a horse or camel across the steppe. Horsehide soaked in water is preferred as a covering for the felt roll since it retains water well and continues to keep the felt moist as it is dragged along. According to tradition, the horse dragging the felt should be a grey or dun (light brown with a dark mane and tail) stallion or gelding. The felt will be dragged in straight lines between 15 and 20 kilometers long, back and forth up to twenty times, meaning the felt has traveled close to 400 kilometers before it is finished. That is roughly the distance from Boston to New York or London to Newcastle! Different peoples within Mongolia and Siberia travel this distance differently: back and forth among the Khalkh, in a large circle among the Tuvans, Buryat and Kazakh, while the Uzemchin Mongols use either an oxcart or a pair of horses rather than a single animal to pull their felt (Batchuluun 2003, 75). In the Kyrgyz Republic, the felt is rolled into a reed screen, which is wrapped in canvas and tightly tied. The roll can either be kicked along and stomped on by a line of feltmakers, or a long loop of rope cast around the middle of the roll can be pulled slowly along the ground by one feltmaker walking backwards to guide it. Large pieces of felt require approximately forty-five minutes of rolling for their first felting.

Once the felt is firm and fully enmeshed, the mat is unrolled and the felt is rolled by itself on top of the reed screen to harden and shrink it to its final size and even the edges and surface. During this process, the felt is continuously unrolled and rewound in different directions to assure even shrinkage (Burkett 1979, 3; Gervers and Gervers 1974, 22). As a final step, the surface of the felt may be smoothed by rubbing – either using the hands or with a wooden block – and any soap that was added is rinsed out (Burkett 1979, 4; Gervers and Gervers 1974, 22). From laying out the cleaned wool to a finished piece of felt, the process can take anywhere from an hour to half a day, depending on the size of the piece and the process used. Cleaning the wool can double that amount of time.

Felt can be dyed after it is made or the wool can be dyed after cleaning and before felting. In Kyrgyzstan, both methods are used, while in Mongolia, the wool is often left in its natural color. Natural dye techniques are still in use and favored by some, though recipes can be closely guarded secrets. Turkish feltmaker, Mehmet Girgiç, prefers natural dyes for their variability, although he insists that the dyes must use a mordant of metallic salts to both achieve the depth of color and help the dye stay fast. In Kyrgyzstan, many feltmakers will use walnut and chamomile in their dye baths to help preserve the felt from insects. Most often, though, they use synthetic dyes from Russia to obtain the bright colors. Many of the felt artists around the world similarly use synthetics for ease.

Feltmaking tends to be done either by men as a primary profession in towns among settled peoples or by women in their villages among the nomadic peoples, although this division is mostly dictated by regional tradition (Gervers and Gervers 1974, 22). In Anatolia and among the tribes of the southern Middle East, feltmaking is mostly a man's job, and feltmakers may travel around a larger region making felt for families or villages in their homes with locally supplied wool in much the same way that weavers once traveled in the colonial United States. These male feltmakers tend to specialize in the larger, heavier felts, such as the mantles worn for shepherding from Hungary to Iran and the large, embellished rugs. Women in these regions may also make felt, but it is more likely to be lighter weight and for more utilitarian padding. While this is a general division of labor, it should also be noted that who makes the felt is culturally specific. In much of Central Asia, feltmaking is mostly a woman's job, although the men may help during the primary rolling stages, thus where Kazakh and Kyrgyz people have settled in countries further west, they have brought their feltmaking traditions with them. So it is not uncommon to find one village of ethnic Pashtun, for instance, with a designated male feltmaker, while in the next village of ethnic Kyrgyz, the women make the felt at home.

Local culture determines much of the procedure followed. In Mongolia, the making of felt is surrounded by tradition. Blessings are said at each stage of the process that are meant to bring good luck to the feltmakers and to the felt itself. These blessings often elaborate the qualities that are sought in a good piece of felt, such as evenness, whiteness, durability and softness (Batchuluun 2003, 84). In accordance with felt's sacred status, strict rules govern traditional feltmaking. The felt comes first in Mongolian feltmaking and is made for the good of the community, thus any activity that places the needs of the individual before those of the felt is taboo. There should be no arguing during feltmaking, and the process should never be disrupted in any way. Whistling is also prohibited among some groups since it is seen to call the wind, which might cause problems if the wool has just been laid down and not yet felted (Batchuluun 2003, 93–4).

FELT HATS

Outside the lands of felt in Asia, by far the majority of felt has historically been found in hats. Making felt hats, however, requires some special techniques and the craft has acquired many of its own terms. Fortunately, as a skilled trade that developed into a mechanized industry, hatmaking is relatively well documented through letters and manuscripts, primarily from the nineteenth century. Moreover, hats provide a good illustration of how felt can be made three-dimensionally without seams, unlike most other textiles, as well as the range of processes that have been developed to make felting easier and faster and to attempt to use fibers other than wool to make felt.

Hats are made not only of sheep's and goat's wool, like most other felted products. Instead, they are more likely to contain furs, such as beaver, rabbit, nutria and even historically seal and monkey, all of which may be blended to provide the best mixture for a smooth yet sturdy hat. Because fur does not have the same natural crimp as wool, the furs had to be processed to make them suitable for felting through carrotting, so-called because it turned the tips of the fur fibers reddish yellow like a carrot (Harrison 168). The carrotting process consisted of layering the fibers in a box and dampening them with "a mixture of about one part nitrous, or nitrous and sulphuric acid, and six parts water," turning the box occasionally to make sure that all of the fibers were dampened without any of the liquid pooling in the box (qtd. in Pufpaff 1995, 27). The box full of fibers was then left overnight to soak. The nitrous referred to was, in fact, mercury nitrate, and while it did help to raise the scales on the fibers, it also slowly drove the hatter insane with continued exposure, leading to the Mad Hatter of *Alice in Wonderland* fame. In the United States, where much of the hatmaking trade was centered in Danbury, Connecticut, the symptoms of mercury poisoning – paralysis and loss of memory leading to eventual death – were called the "Danbury shakes" (McDowell 1992, 53).

While the recipe above was given in an 1829 manuscript, in 1868, the hatter John Thomson wrote in his *Treatise on Hat-Making and Felting* that the carrotting process was a recent invention. Thomson gave the following procedure:

> The method pursued to accomplish this result is, to dissolve 32 parts quicksilver in 500 parts of common aquafortis, and dilute the solution with one half or two-thirds of its bulk of water according to the strength of the acid. The skin having been laid upon a table with the hair uppermost, a stout brush, slightly moistened with the mercurial solution, is passed over the smooth surface of the hairs with strong pressure... In order to aid this impregnation, the skins are laid together in pairs with

the hairy sides in contact, and put in this state into the stove-room, and exposed to a heat in proportion to the weakness of the mercurial solution. The drying should be rapidly effected... No other acid or metallic solution but the above has been found to answer the desired purpose, although sulphuric acid without the quicksilver has a limited effect... (Qtd. in Pufpaff 1995, 89–90)

Mixing mercury with nitric acid was apparently deemed preferable to older methods which required more direct exposure to acid. Thomson lauds this method of carrotting as not requiring liquids other than water during the rest of the felting process and allowing the maker to use "boilers other than those of lead" (Thomson qtd. in Pufpaff 1995, 89).

Carrotting may take place either before or after the fur fibers have been cut from the skin and trimmed, depending on the chosen method. If only sheep's wool is used, then scouring may be necessary (McNulty qtd. in Harrison 1960, 171). Once they are carrotted or scoured and loose, however, they are blended with other fibers to achieve the desired mix of wool and fur.

1 Hatmakers at Ayer, Huston Company in Portland, Maine, c.1893.

After mixing, the fibers are blown to remove any long, coarse hairs that might be in the mix. These hairs, called kemp, are common on many varieties of sheep as well as many fur animals with double coats, but they are stiff and do not felt well (McNulty qtd. in Harrison 1960, 169). The blowing machine was already in place by Thomson's period and has not changed much since. It consists of a fan that blows the fibers from one chamber into another through a series of screens and across brushes so that the fibers are graded by fineness as they are blown through the box, while any dirt is loosened and falls through the screened bottom of the box (Thomson qtd. in Pufpaff 1995, 96). A revolving copper cone inside a glass box collects the useable fibers until enough has been gathered for a single hat (McNulty qtd. in Harrison 1960, 169). The fibers on the cone can then be dampened to hold it together and removed as a single piece (called a "Dunce's Cap"), ready for felting. J.M. McNulty, writing on behalf of the British Felt Hat Manufacturers' Federation, reported the average Dunce's Cap measuring "about 24 inches high by 30 inches wide" (McNulty qtd. in Harrison 1960, 169).

From this point, the felting process closely resembles traditional feltmaking. The wool is hardened into felt through rolling it in canvas to form hoods. Some of the terminology, however, is specific to hatmaking. Planking refers to the process of shrinking the initial loose felt down into a good hard fabric:

> As the hat approaches its proper size, it is scalded and belabored with determined importunity, coiled, rolled, pressed, and pinned, backward and forward till the size of the hat is reduced to nearly half of its original dimensions, and the tension of the several fibers becomes so great that the hat will felt no farther. At this stage it is impossible for it to be torn asunder... (Thomson qtd. in Pufpaff 1995, 103)

This is, of course, the very same process used by feltmakers everywhere to shrink and strengthen the felt. Given this, one can see where Thomson might have preferred carrotting since at least the hatmaker was not obliged to work with acid-laden wool. McNulty, however, does recommend that the felt be kept boiling hot throughout this stage and that sulphuric acid may be added to help with the shrinkage (McNulty qtd. in Harrison 1960, 170). After being felted and dried, hats are shaved with a knife or sandpaper to remove any loose fibers from the surface. The hat can go back to the planking table again at this point if a napped finish is desired, not dissimilar to the hairy finishes found on some of the archaeological felt masks from Germany. This finish is produced often through a "plating" technique that lightly felts the napped surface to the underlying felt (Thomson qtd. in Pufpaff 1995, 104–5).

Hats made of wool were rarely dyed before they were felted. Instead, dyeing took place either during the planking process, for soft felt hats, or much later after the felt had been shellacked, for hard felt hats (McNulty qtd. in Harrison 1960, 171). Thomson notes that ordinary black hats were dyed with a solution of chipped logwood, green sulphate of iron and French verdigris (qtd. in Pufpaff 1995, 110). Although it can be stiff, felt on its own does not have a hard surface without the application of some sort of stiffener. In order to make the tall top hats and hard derbies, hatters developed the proofing process to impregnate the felt with shellac mixtures. McNulty reports using a solution of shellac dissolved in water and borax, applied to both sides of the felt with rollers. The felt was then steamed to dissolve the shellac and soak it into the felt (McNulty qtd. in Harrison 1960, 171). Thomson offers the following recipe:

> 7 lbs. of orange shellac
> 2 lbs. of gum sandarac
> 4 ozs. Gum mastic
> 1 lb. of amber resin
> 1 pint of solution of copal
> 1 gallon of alcohol or of wood naphtha
> (Thomson qtd. in Pufpaff 1995, 94)

All of the ingredients are mixed and the copal solution added last. Another of Thomson's recipes calls for black shellac and borax but is closely related, although Thomson notes that although it is cheaper, it requires a bit more delicacy in mixing.

Finally, the hat is steamed into shape on a hat block and allowed to dry. The surface is again rubbed with sandpaper to smooth it out and remove any loose fibers before it is ready for the brim to be shaped. The exact finishing technique from this point on seems to have depended on the type of hat being made, since smooth hats required sanding, napped hats required brushing and trimming the fibers to an even length, and silk hats, popular after the mid-nineteenth century, were covered in fabric (Thomson in Pufpaff 1995, 111–19). Shaping the brim appears to require a deft and well-trained hand, but the basic shaping of hats seems to have become mechanized fairly early. The hatmaking process shows how felt can be shaped once the initial felting stage binds the fibers together. By working on a wooden form, felt can be made three-dimensional as it shrinks and dries without requiring cutting and stitching like other textiles. As the recipes for carrotting prove, however, making hats was a complex and risky job. Flat felt did not require as much processing but the acid method of feltmaking, common in industry, and the arduous labor involved made technological developments desirable.

MODERN INDUSTRIAL FELT

The cotton gin revolutionized the cleaning of cotton to make it ready for spinning, and the spinning jenny greatly speeded and improved the process of spinning raw wool and cotton into yarn, eventually allowing cotton to replace wool and linen as the standard fibers for clothing. While these technologies had huge effects on the way that woven cloth was made, felt required its own technologies to move the process from the traditional household courtyard into the factory. Some of the first industrial advances in feltmaking arose not around true felt, the intermingling of loose fibers into a cohesive fabric, but in the process of "fulling" woven textiles to give them a felt-like finish.

This technique of fulling woven or knitted fabrics has been in existence at least since the Roman period and followed much of the same process as the later stages of felting loose wool fibers. Like felting, fulling was a difficult task carried out with hot water and intensive rolling and scrubbing. By the end of the Middle Ages, however, fulling machines were beginning to be used. These machines generally consisted of a long tub into which a roll of fabric wrapped in canvas was set. The roll was wet with hot water, which collected in the trough. As the roll was turned, a large beater, the length of the roll, would hit the fabric from above. Each time the roll was turned, the beater would hit it, over and over until the fabric's surface was felted. The roll would need to be unrolled and rerolled in different directions to keep the fulling even. During the eighteenth and nineteenth centuries, people began to mechanize these machines, powering them by steam so that the roll would be turned and the beater pressed down mechanically. Such fulling machines have changed little since that time, but they are still widely used today, particularly for fulling the surface of wool fabrics for winter coats. Their motors are stronger, they are often made of steel rather than wood, and they hold much larger rolls of fabric, but the mechanism remains the same.

The fulling machine only gives us a way to speed up the middle and end of the felting process, however. To felt wool from the beginning, from the loose batt of fibers, other techniques are needed. First, the loose wool had to be made into a consistent batt. While traditional felting relied on bowing the wool or using a large rake to loosen the fibers by hand, industry based its designs on traditional European wool cards. Needless to say, it took a substantial amount

2 Eighteenth-century fulling mill from Bockler's *Theater of New Machines.*

of time to card enough wool for a batt large enough for felting. By putting the tines onto two cylinders, however, more wool could be carded at once, especially as the cylinders were made increasingly wider and longer. In modern processing, the wool can either be clean virgin wool or else recycled from old felts and other woolen items (Jani 2007). Many companies prefer to use wool from South Africa to make felt, arguing that the climate there seems to produce the most consistent fibers with the best felting properties. By contrast, many of the woolen yarn spinners favor the Falkland Islands wool (Jani 2007).

Once the wool is carded, a comb removes the finished batt. On large industrial machines, the batt is removed alternately with a cross-lapper and a vlamir. The cross-lapper rolls the batt perpendicular to the fibers, while the vlamir rolls it in the same direction as the fibers. Industrial felt is made with multiple carded batts, layered so that the fibers alternate in direction, thus allowing them to enmesh more easily during the felting process. The cross-lapper and vlamir make the task of layering easier, since they can alternate gathering the batts from the carder and layering them in preparation for the felter. Four layers are considered the standard for a single piece of fabric, but more may be added to increase the thickness (Bryk 2007). With the addition of cotton or, more commonly, synthetic fibers into wool for making felt, as well as the use of recycled fibers, carding becomes an important stage in industrial feltmaking, since fibers are blended and evenly distributed through the carding process. Today, carding machines are able to produce long rolls of fiber batting that can then be fed into the felting machines, though often multiple carding machines are used, each with finer tines than the last to produce a clean, even batt.

The earliest felting machines simply reproduced the process of felting by hand – they provided hot moisture, usually in the form of steam, pressure and agitation to lock the fibers together and shrink them into a strong fabric. The fiber batt first rolls over a steam table to become hot and damp. Attaining the proper level of moisture is crucial as the workers at the American felt factory located over the stream discovered. Once the felt is damp enough, it enters a plate hardener. The plate hardener does the initial job of felting the fibers together. The batt is placed on a large, flat bed. A plate drops onto the top of the batt, pushing it down while the machine agitates back and forth, thus adding both pressure and agitation (Felt Association 1943, 11). Further hardening and shrinking is accomplished in the fulling machines, which press the felt between two sets of rollers while soaking it with a hot sulphuric acid solution, not much changed from the solutions used by the hatter described above. Due to environmental regulations aimed at protecting the water in rivers, the acid solution may be replaced with a solution of acetone. Scientists have tried to develop more efficient dry felting processes, but these generally have not been as successful (Jani 2007). A single piece of felt may shrink about twenty-five percent during this process. After the first fulling, the acid is neutralized by running the felt through a solution of soda ash and then fulled again. Felt typically is dyed as a finished textile after it is made rather than as fibers before felting, although much felt for industrial use remains undyed. Fire retardants and other aqueous-solution finishes may also be applied at this stage. The felt now only needs to be dried, which can be done either by placing a roll of felt into a centrifuge to spin the water out, by tentering it through large driers, or even by simply hanging it to dry (Jani 2007).

The plate hardening method is not the only way to produce good felt. As time passed, people began looking into producing fabrics that had all of the useful properties of felt but could withstand much higher heat than wool, which becomes brittle with exposure over time or in temperatures of about 200°F (about 93°C). In the mid-twentieth century, new synthetic fibers, such as polyester, began to be developed. These fibers did not have scales and thus could not be felted with traditional methods, requiring new techniques to turn them into a nonwoven fabric. The most common of the new methods of felting also comes out of older technologies. Felters have known how to use needles to make felt for some time. A single felting needle is a long, thin, usually round needle that contains several barbs near its point. The barbs pull fibers from the surface of the batt as the needle is inserted, tangling them into the other fibers. By combining hundreds of needles on a large plate that can be punched down onto the batt over and over, a good, sturdy piece of felt can be made in a relatively short time without the need for the steam and sulphuric acid of the plate hardener method. Furthermore, needle-felting works better on batts that have a high proportion of non-wool fibers, since it does not rely on the natural scales of the wool to interlock and draw the fibers closer together.

For creating feltlike fabrics without any wool at all, scientists made use of the melting capabilities of the synthetic fibers. Nonwoven fabrics can be made by extruding the hot, liquid synthetic solution so that the yarns mingle together and interlace. Since they are laid down while still warm, they stick to one another as they cool. This fabric can be further bonded by pressing hot metal styluses onto the fabric, creating "stitches" almost like the quilting stitches that hold the quilt face to the batting inside and the backing fabric. Many mattress pads demonstrate the result – a nonwoven, heat-bonded fabric, resembling felt but made of nylon or polyester. The range of synthetics that can be used for both needle-felting and in nonwovens is impressive, including polypropylene, Teflon and even Kevlar, as well as natural cotton fibers and cellulose fibers, such as rayon (www.aetnafelt.com). Nomex was developed specifically to withstand higher temperatures than wool in a nonwoven form. Other nonwovens are good for resisting particular chemicals, mildew or other environmental problems (Jani 2007). Wool felt still has some advantages, however – it is homogenous throughout its structure, so that it can be cut at any angle, and the inside is as sturdy and looks the same as the outer surfaces, which is not always the case with nonwovens. Needled felt, because it pushes fibers through in specific places and not in others, can look corrugated when cut, like the edge of a cardboard box.

According to Aetna Felt, one of the largest American manufacturers of woven, pressed and needled felt, each process has its own benefits, depending on end-use. Woven felt is the strongest, since it uses two different methods of binding the fibers together. However, woven felt cannot be made very thick without decreasing the strength of the fabric – 0.5 inches is Aetna's maximum thickness – and cut edges can still fray. Pads for musical instruments, such as drums or horn-stops, and blankets used in printing to help protect the etched surface are often made of woven felt. Pressed felt typically has the highest wool content and can be made into the thickest and densest fabric. It commonly reaches 3 inches thick. Its edges can be cut and will not fray, but it is not as strong as woven felt. Pressed felt is perhaps the most traditional of the felting methods, but its modern uses include air filters and gaskets for advanced machinery and even lifesaving equipment in hospitals. Needled felt can have the highest synthetic content, making it less expensive to produce, but it is not as easily cut as pressed felt. Craft felts are typically produced through the needle process and upon examination the pattern left by the needle can sometimes be seen (Aetna 2007). Felt is regulated for hardness and thickness in the United States by standards produced by the Society of Automotive Engineers, because of its use in cars and aerospace technology. As yet, however, no standards have been developed for synthetic nonwovens (Jani 2007).

Once the felt has been made, usually in large rolled sheets, it is sent to a cutter. These cutters work with the companies that need felt parts for their own products, such as auto companies or medical equipment makers. The die-cutter uses large presses to stamp out the felt into almost any needed shape. If necessary, woodworking lathes and grinders can be used to help shape the felt. One of the great benefits of felt as a fabric is its thick density and lack of directional orientation. These qualities allow felt to be worked in thicker sheets more like wood and in thinner ones like paper, opening up the range of tools available. In fact, much of the equipment used for cutting felt was originally developed for cutting metal. Although many cutters still keep machines manufactured in the Second World War up and running, the modern machines are computer-driven and operate on hydraulics (Jani 2007). At the die-cutters, the felt might also be printed with designs before being cut or have an adhesive coating applied. Superior Felt, a die-cutting company in northern Illinois, employs a large range of felt, which is cut to specification for a wide variety of purposes. Although the company specializes in filtration, it has also made gasket seals and printing pads, athletic lettering and school pennants (Jani 2007). Another die-cutter in the United States, Sutherland Felt, states that it specializes in "BSR applications" – "buzz, squeak and rattle" (www.sutherlandfelt.com). At one time, much of the felt-cutting was done in small operations. One woman in Chicago ran a very successful cutting business out of the basement of her home for thirty years. She had manufactured her own strip cutting machine from razors and employed one other person (Jani 2007). Other companies date back to the American Civil War, making and cutting felt for use in soldiers' uniforms. Despite all of these technological advances, felt remains a relatively simple fabric, yet it need not be a plain one.

ADDED DESIGN AND PATTERN

While plain felt is used plentifully, for the walls and roofs of yurts for example, feltmakers have developed a wide range of methods for embellishing felt. Some of these methods are part of the traditional craft of feltmaking in cultures like those found in Central Asia; others are new developments that build on felt's unique properties and combine it with new innovations in textiles. What follows is by no means a comprehensive list of embellishment techniques, but it will serve as an introduction to gain familiarity with some of the more commonly used methods. Some of the techniques are particularly associated with a certain culture, which has perfected them to a high art form. This is especially true in Central Asia, and thus the techniques that have been so important in the Central Asian cultures will be touched on here but described in more detail in chapter three. The ways of embellishing felt can be divided roughly into processes that take place before the wool is felted or during felting and processes that are applied after the felt is made. Obviously, one need not restrict oneself to a single method of embellishment, and feltmakers have shown great creativity in how they choose to decorate the felt they make.

First, a design can be felted into the background using different colors of wool during the production of the felt, thus providing a quickly finished product. This method forms a single continuous piece of felt, since the embellishment is added before the wool batt is even fully dampened to begin felting. Felted-in designs are common throughout the feltmaking world and can become highly intricate in the hands of a master. Felt can also be made on another base fabric, such as a loosely woven lightweight silk or synthetic. This process, known as Nuno felt, was developed about 1994 by Australian feltmaker Polly Stirling and Japanese feltmaker Sachiko Kotaka. By felting onto another fabric, the feltmaker takes advantage of the differences in how the two fibers react to heat and moisture. This process can create interesting texture and color combinations, since the wool is soft, muted and fuzzy next to the silk or synthetic fabric, which puckers as the wool around it shrinks into felt. The resulting textiles can have a range of properties that distinguish them from either traditional felt or the fabrics on which the felt is built. Nuno felt in particular can be made much lighter in weight and with greater drapability than traditional felt (Stirling 2007). This idea of layering felt with other textiles has become extremely popular, because of its creative possibilities, and has been taken up by feltmakers around the world and even by fashion designers, such as Issey Miyake.

The second set of techniques relies on producing one or more pieces of wool and then adding ornamentation, usually by needle-felting or sewing. One method involves cutting pieces of felt of different colors and piecing them together with sewn seams in a mosaic or patchwork technique. In Central Asia, the abutted seams are often then covered with embroidery to help strengthen them. This method is often used by the Kyrgyz and Kazakh to make their famous *shyrdak* carpets. Felt or other fabrics can be applied by appliqué, with one piece of felt forming a ground fabric as on the Noin Ula and Pazyryk felts. Finally, embroidery can create the design (Turnau 1997, 105–6). Needle-felting, as described above, allows for felt to be made without moisture or heat, and can be as effective, if not more so, as stitching pieces of felt together.

Heat, moisture, pressure, agitation and wool – with these ingredients, humans have been making felt for at least 8,500 years. A Turkish feltmaker once showed me how to make felt in the palm of my hand, the wool pulled fresh from the bale, not yet cleaned or scoured, and the only moisture a few drops of water from a teapot. Felt requires no specially carved needles or hooks, no spinning wheel or loom. The way that women in Mongolia or men in Turkey make felt, carrying on the traditions of their ancestors, differs only in mechanics and scale from the way that it is made in factories in the United States or Germany. Nonetheless, felt has been the source of infinite inspiration. We have developed technologies to process it faster, including carding machines, reed screens and electric-powered plates. We have harnessed felt's sturdiness and found ways to apply its special properties to other fibers through needle-felting and heat-bonding synthetics. We have found ways to sculpt felt, to make it into three-dimensional shapes through the felting process or through carving it with woodworking tools. We have used it to depict our cultures and our dreams, to cover and house us. The rest of this book is dedicated to the variety of form and function that felt has taken and the ingenuity of those who make and use it, but as we travel the world exploring felt, we must always return to the basics of heat, moisture, pressure, agitation and wool.

2.
THE HISTORY OF FELT

Felt keeps people warm and protected from the elements. It has served the purposes of industry and artistry, but to understand exactly how important felt has been, it is helpful to know some of its history, from the earliest findings of felt in archaeological sites to the recent resurgence of interest in felt by artists and craftspeople around the globe. This chapter is concerned with the first half of that story – the early history and mythology of felt. The history of felt is largely centered in Central Asia, where people have not only perfected feltmaking over centuries but have put the textile to such an array of uses that it has supported the nomadic lifestyle there. But this is only one part of the story. The history of felt is also, to a great extent, a history of hats and socks and boots. While felt has been used for a great many purposes, it seems to have naturally found a place on people's heads and feet.

At least 8,500 years old, felt is among the oldest textile forms made by man after fashioning cloth from animal skins. Since it relies only on moisture, heat, friction and the natural properties of wool fibers, felt is also the least reliant on technology of all textiles, requiring neither needles nor looms. Only bark cloth, made of pounded plant fibers, compares in simplicity of manufacture. Despite its ancient history, felt remains one of the least noticed and most used textiles in the modern world, especially in the West. Nonetheless, felt has been found in archaeological sites from Mongolia to Scandinavia. References to felt appear in Greek and Roman texts, describing both local and foreign felt production, particularly among the

Scythians. Scandinavian texts dating to around 1000 CE remark on the use of felt, particularly in the form of boots, which continue to be made today throughout not only northern Norway, Sweden and Finland, but across much of Russia and Siberia. On the other side of Asia, Chinese writers mention the use of felt by the Mongolians for clothing and tents, later commented on by Marco Polo, Plano Carpini and William of Rubruck during the Middle Ages (Burkett 1979, 18–21; Johnson 2002; Polo 1958, bk. 1, ch. 52). Felt has even been found in British bog sites, although no firm date has been established (Burkett 1979, 100). Feltmaking has continued to be important beyond these early findings. Some of the appearances of felt in this history are fleeting, a scrap found or a single reference in a larger text. Some we will merely mention here to discuss in more detail later. Yet by drawing together the many diverse histories of felt, its overall importance in the history of Asia and Europe becomes clear, and through providing such a wide-ranging history, we can get a larger sense of the true impact of felt as a unique textile structure.

ARCHAEOLOGICAL FELT

The history of felt is largely based on physical remains and on the cultural traditions of places where it continues to be produced. While we know felt and feltmaking to be among the oldest textiles and ways of producing textiles, unfortunately the archaeological evidence is scant compared to woven or knitted textiles. Felt tends not to survive well through the centuries, partly due to its structure, which, while sturdy, is susceptible to breaking down over time through use, exposure or insect damage, and partly due to the environments in which it has flourished. When felt first appeared is not known, but archaeological evidence suggests that it has been made and used in Anatolia and Central Asia for at least 8,500 years (Burkett 1977, 112). Early felt objects have been found both in Turkey and at the other end of the Central Asian steppes in the Altai Mountains in tombs at Pazyryk, Noin Ula and in the Tarim Basin (Barber 1999, 33–39; CIBA 1958, 129, 25; Harvey 1996, 62). Some scholars suspect that felt is actually much older than these modest dates, because of the relative ease of its manufacture, but physical evidence remains to be discovered.

The earliest archaeological evidence for felt is found in Turkey at Çatal Hüyük. The site was excavated in the mid-1960s by James Mellaart, who was intent on finding the lowest, thus oldest, level at the site, labeled Level VIII. Çatal Hüyük is dated to approximately 6500 BCE, putting it soundly in the Neolithic age. At that time, the site was a bustling settlement, and the animal remains suggest that a wide variety of wool-bearing species passed through, which would have provided the materials for feltmaking. Samples of felt were found at Level VI, dated to around 5800 BCE, but Mary Burkett has argued that the older wall paintings at Level VIII suggest that felt was known during this older period as well. The paintings adorn the interior wall of what appears to be a shrine and consist of "five panels [divided] by parallel vertical lines. Within each panel there are whirling curvilinear motifs ... strongly reminiscent of felt appliqué" (Mellaart qtd. in Burkett 1977, 112). Burkett convincingly argues that these designs replicate the designs found on both historic and contemporary felts made in Anatolia. Indeed, the resemblance is striking, both being based on lozenge shapes with curled ram's horn motifs emerging from each point. This early date – 6500 BCE – for felt has since been generally accepted.

The next archaeological evidence of felt dates from a few centuries later and hundreds of miles to the east of Çatal Hüyük. The Tarim Basin in the Xinjiang region of China, Noin Ula in western Mongolia and Pazyryk in the mountainous areas of Siberia's Altai region (at the point where it briefly borders northwestern China between the western tip of Mongolia and the eastern corner of Kazakhstan) have all revealed early use of felt. The high desert climate of these Central Asian areas has been particularly suited to the preservation of ancient textiles, but excavators were unprepared for the extent of felt usage by the historic inhabitants of this area and their high level of skill. No history of felt and feltmaking would be complete without these finds, yet in this chapter we will deal with them only in their archaeological context.

The earliest of the Central Asian finds – from the Tarim Basin – are also the most recently discovered. The mummies that are now in the museum at Ürümchi were found in a set of sites along the eastern edge of this basin, a stretch of desert between the Tien Shan and the Kunlun Mountains in the far northwestern corner of China. Approximately 3,000–4,000 years old, the mummies were especially notable for both their combination of felted and woven materials and for their distinctly Caucasian features. The first images most Westerners saw of these mummies came in 1994, through an article in *Discover* magazine, which was followed by articles in *Archaeology* and *National Geographic*, but the local Uyghur people had known about them for decades if not centuries, and the Hungarian explorer Sir Aurel Stein and the Swedish explorers Sven Hedin and Folke Bergman had found the mummies that now lie in the Ürümchi museum nearly a century before the recent excavation (Barber 1999, 18–21).

Yet it was not until the mid-to-late 1990s that the textiles on the mummies came to be analyzed – by a group of scientists from China and the United States including Victor Mair of the University of Pennsylvania and Elizabeth Wayland Barber from Occidental College. All of the mummies' clothing was made of wool, indicating that it was probably the most accessible fiber available to people at the time. The wool was spun and woven into large rectangles that were sewn together to make garments or interlocked for certain caps and bags through a technique similar to *nalbinding* – a form of knotless netting using a single needle with a large eye to work yarn in loops through the previous row of loops (Bush 2001, 28). (True *nalbinding* was developed in Scandinavia during the Iron Age, but the technique, which is similar to knitting in structure but made through a different process, has been found in other cultures around the world.) The mummies showed that wool was also wrapped around the legs and placed inside shoes, becoming felted with walking – it appears not to have been felted beforehand. However, felt was also made by these people, primarily for hats. Aurel Stein noted such a felted hat on one of the mummies he saw in the early twentieth century about fifteen miles northeast of the Chinese encampment at Loulan. Most of the mummies were discovered at this Loulan site on the far eastern edge of the Tarim Basin. Stein found several graves containing mummies and commented on "the peaked felt caps decorated with big feathers and other trophies of the chase" (Stein qtd. in Barber 1999, 94). Barber similarly remarked upon the felt hats worn by many of the Ürümchi mummies:

> A third headpiece was molded from two sheets of white felt into a simple helmet shape, then decorated in front with a curving roll of felt that looks remarkably like a pair of horns.
>
> The largest and most arresting hat, also plumed, looks like something that might have belonged to Robin Hood. The dark brown felt of its body curves up to a high, rounded peak at the top and flips over at the bottom to form a small cuff around the wearer's face. Around the edge of the cuff, thick but neat buttonhole stitching in light tan contrasts decoratively with the dark felt; similar tan stitchery continues up the center front and down the back, holding the two halves of the hat together. Partway down on one side, several big feathers were attached. (Barber 1999, 33)

Clearly, felt was the preferred material for hats among the Loulan people. What may be more interesting is that they relied on stitching to shape the hats rather than shaping the hat during the felting process as is more common in the West, especially much later in the medieval period. Today, traditional Kyrgyz *kalpak* hats, however, are still made through stitching together flat pieces of felt.

Barber argues that the shape of the second hat described above is related to the Phrygian cap, with its high point and cuffed bottom, that was described by Greek and Roman authors

(1999, 34). The Phrygians moved into Anatolia from the steppes sometime around 1000 BCE, replacing the Hittites. This history makes it possible that the people in Loulan were either somehow related to or trading with the Phrygians, especially since the peoples of the steppes were spreading out during this period. That the Loulan people probably came out of the steppes is likely, and Barber offers their use of felt in support. The steppes were largely inhabited by nomadic groups. Felt is especially suited to nomadism, requiring relatively little time to make and no cumbersome tools, and providing excellent shelter from wind, rain and snow as well as padding for pack animals' saddles (Barber 1999, 37). A direct link between the Phrygians and the Loulan people, however, is purely speculative as no physical evidence has been found.

Nonetheless, Loulan and Ürümchi both lie on the ancient trade routes that linked Turkey and the Middle East with China, routes that would later become the Silk Road. Through linguistic analysis of borrowings between ancient Iranian and Chinese, Victor Mair has suggested that these routes were in place by 1000 BCE and are referenced in the Shang Dynasty, from 1500 to 1100 BCE, so a trade connection is possible. The felt provides some further evidence. Felt-producing cultures, however, certainly existed throughout the steppes and the mountain ranges of Central Asia from the early finds around Loulan through to the present. Archaeological sites point to a fairly consistent culture in the area between Loulan and Ürümchi. For example, a site near the present-day town of Turfan, dating to around 700 BCE, revealed a woman wearing a tall felt hat in dark wool and a "felt-hatted man" (Barber 1999, 198–200).

Yet perhaps the most famous find of felt came from the fifth century BCE sites at Pazyryk. This find, located in the High Altai Mountains of Siberia, offers one of the most comprehensive and fascinating collections of archaeological felt. Pazyryk lies about 400 miles north-northwest of Ürümchi, some 100 miles from the far western corner of Mongolia where its borders intersect with those of China and Russia, and Kazakhstan begins to widen out to the west. The site consists of a set of barrows, first investigated in 1924 and excavated in 1929 and again in the late 1940s by a group from the Institute of the History of Material Culture of The Academy of Science in the USSR and the Hermitage Museum in St. Petersburg (Rudenko 1970, xxxiii). These tombs date from sometime around 400 to 500 BCE and are believed to have been built by the Scythians. Like the Phrygians, the Scythians were another of the peoples who moved out of the steppes into the surrounding areas at the beginning of the Iron Age. Unlike the Loulan people, who may be related to the Phrygians, the Scythians are related to the Mongols genetically but are linguistically linked to the Iranians. The Scythians originated in western Turkestan and replaced the Cimmerians as the dominant tribe controlling the lands east of the Black Sea and into what is now western China around 750 BCE. During the third century BCE, the Scythians were pushed out of the northwest by the Sarmatians, another Iranian tribe, while Alexander the Great entered Persia in the southwest (Grousset 1970). Certainly other groups were also present in the area around Pazyryk at the time the tombs were made, including the Hsiung-nu, but scholars have tended to accept the site as Scythian because of the similarity between the art and objects found at Pazyryk and those of other known Scythian sites.

Sergei Rudenko's book *Frozen Tombs of Siberia* (1970) provides the most comprehensive catalogue of all of the objects found at Pazyryk during the 1940s, along with their interpretation. The list is impressive, including a wide range of textiles and metal objects. The textiles range from knotted carpets to fine woven silks, indicating trade with a variety of peoples stretching from the Iranian plateau into China. The felts, however, are particularly interesting, and it is these felts that helped make the Pazyryk site famous. The people who are buried at Pazyryk used felt for multiple purposes. Rudenko and his team found felt tents, similar to the yurts still made and used by peoples in the region, felt socks, felt ornaments tied into hair, and felt saddle blankets and bags. The saddles and saddle covers showed intricate designs in the animal style associated with the High Altai peoples – the bodies twisted organically and often locked in combat. Felt was also incorporated into harnesses and bridles. Furthermore, the felts were embellished using a variety of methods. Most were appliquéd with leather or multicolored felt, showing knowledge of dyes, while others were embroidered. Both the range of designs and the methods used for their application suggest the skills of specialized feltmakers in the community (Rudenko 1970, 276).

Of course, there are also hats at Pazyryk. Men's felt hats were found in barrows two and three. Like the hats found near the Tarim Basin, one of these was tall and made of stiff brown felt. The other was stitched from two pieces of white felt, which were covered by leather, cut and stitched in the same pattern. Both hats have flaps that covered the ears and nape of the neck. Yet they show some technological advancement from the simple sewn hats of the earlier finds, since they have been shaped over a block. Rudenko speculates, "Evidently the sodden, sewn-up shape had been placed over a spherical wooden block and pulled and pressed on it, so that it took the required form and, when dried out, could be removed" (90). This would be one of the earliest known uses of a form for shaping three-dimensional felts, beginning a tradition that would circle the globe and last through the centuries, still to be used today. The Pazyryk hats are embellished with cut-out pieces of leather and gold leaf, as well as braids. Interestingly, only the men were found to wear felt hats; the women's hats were made of fur and wood. The Pazyryk site's importance cannot be underestimated in the history of felt. It provides both some of the earliest surviving felt and some of the most complete, its complexity hinting at a long history of feltmaking in Central Asia. What is important here is its connection to the finds around it, the earlier Ürümchi and Loulan sites to the south and the later Noin Ula sites to the east.

Completing the major Central Asian archaeological finds of felt is the site at Noin Ula in Mongolia. This site was first officially excavated by the Mongol-Tibetan Expedition organized under the auspices of the Russian Geographic Society at the same time as the Pazyryk finds in 1924–5, although many of the tombs had been robbed in antiquity. The site is named Noin Ula, "the valley of the dead," for the Noin Ula mountains surrounding it in northern Mongolia in the upper Selenga River basin, about 700 miles east of Pazyryk and halfway between the Mongolian capital Ulaan-Batur and Lake Baikal in Siberia. Three groups of tumuli, 212 tumuli in all, were found nestled against the sides of the hills around the Sudzuktè and Tzurumtè passes (Trever 1932, 9). Unlike the tombs around Ürümchi and Pazyryk, where the aridity of the mountain desert air helped to preserve the objects in the tombs, the Noin Ula tombs were completely submerged in a watery bog like those found in northern Europe. The site is believed to have been developed by the Hsiung-nu people, probably a Turkic group who moved west out of northern China during the second century BCE. The Hsiung-nu split during the first century BCE into a Northern or Western group that pushed all the way to the Aral Sea and a Southern group that officially submitted to Han Chinese rule. The Southern Hsiung-nu continued to raid throughout northern China, providing at least one reason for the building of the Great Wall (Grousset 1970).

Unusually, the tombs at Noin Ula, particularly Tumulus 6, can be dated fairly exactly in the first century CE. The Noin Ula tombs contained a variety of objects imported from China and the Iranian peoples as well as of local manufacture. The Iranian items mostly consisted of kilims as well as embroideries most likely from western Turkestan. The Chinese objects include signed silk scrolls and lacquered bowls, one of which provided the clue for dating the site. The bowl found in Tumulus 6 is incised with Chinese characters around its base that give the name of the maker and the date: "September of the 5th year of the Chien-p'ing" (Trever 1932, 15). This date, taken in conjunction with the style of the writing, placed the bowl in the

Han Dynasty (206 BCE to 220 CE), which would mean the bowl was made around 2 CE. For the Hsiung-nu, this would be during the reign of the Southern Shang-ui, between the eighth century BCE and the thirteenth century CE, and some scholars have argued that Tumulus 6 is the chief Uchdzolu-dzoti's royal tomb (Tsarev 2001, 95).

The many felt objects found at the Noin Ula site were mostly made by the Hsiung-nu themselves. The tombs all consisted of two chambers made of logs with a connecting corridor. The inner chamber, where the body lay, was covered in a felt rug, while other felt rugs decorated the corridors and the walls and ceilings of the outer chambers. Nikita Tsarev describes the felt rugs:

> All Noin-Ula felt carpets have a complicated multi-layer structure. They have a thick felt foundation, covered with felted woolen reps [ridges] on the front, and plain silk textile on the back. The edges are finished with a broad stripe of decorated silk attached by sewing. All decorative elements are sewn on, thus the carpets get heavy additional stitching, which is made of sinew threads. The field decoration is formed by sewn-on woolen cord; while that on the borders is applied by a beautifully executed felt appliqué technique. (97)

These rugs, then, are edged and backed with woven silk fabric while the tops are covered with woven wool that has then been fulled, and are embellished with appliqué depicting spirals, trees and scenes of combat in a similar animal style to those found at Pazyryk. The combat scenes focus on images of wolves and yaks or elk and gryphon. While the Hsiung-nu felt rugs are clearly related to the Pazyryk felts, Tsarev points to several differences. Most obviously, the Hsiung-nu used felt as a base fabric that was then covered with woven goods, while the people of Pazyryk used felt by itself or embellished with other fabrics, but did not totally cover the felt before ornamenting it. Both groups used cut-out felt designs for appliqué work and both embroidered their felt carpets, but the people at Pazyryk kept their connecting stitches as fine as possible while the Hsiung-nu turned these lines into embroidered motifs (Tsarev 2001, 97). For all of their use of felt, the Hsiung-nu did not seem to have invested as much worth in the felt as did the earlier people at Pazyryk or the later Central Asian peoples. They used felt predominately for utilitarian purposes, as padding underneath other textiles or leather, rather than embellishing it on its own. Also, Noin Ula remains one of the few sites yielding felt only in the form of rugs and not in hats or socks. The finds at Pazyryk and Noin Ula are perhaps more compelling since felt remains an important textile throughout this region today. Because these sites reveal much about Central Asian culture and tie closely to that area's history of pattern and motif and contemporary use of felt, we will revisit them in the next chapter in terms of their regional significance.

Although felt was not typically a native product of China as far as we know, and no archaeological felt has been found in China except in the northwestern areas of Loulan and Ürümchi, felt was known to have been used by the Chinese for mattresses as well as in military uniforms. Sturdy and thick, felt provided good protection not only from the cold on winter marches and from the chafing of the tanned leather and metal used as outer armor, but also as an inner layer of protection against the spears and arrows of war. We know that the Chinese military used felt as part of their armor from possibly the most famous Chinese archaeological site of all – that of the terracotta warriors in Emperor Qin Shi Huang's mausoleum near the modern town of Xian in central China. The site contains over 7,000 life-sized figures of soldiers, each with its own features and military dress, arranged in battle formation with carts and horses accompanying them. The figures themselves are constructed entirely of carefully sculpted terracotta, but the particular style of dress they depict shows their use of felt clothing underneath their breastplates as well as felt shoes. Their connection with the Central Asian tribes from the lands of felt gave them a distinct advantage for winter warfare.

Felt may be most famous in the sites of Central Asia and China because of its long continuous history there and its use to this day, but felt has also been found in archaeological sites in Europe. Unlike the Central Asian finds, much of the felt in Europe is not true felt but rather woven wool fabrics that have been fulled after weaving. Fulling attempts to impart the special characteristics of felt, particularly its sturdiness, warmth and water resistance, to woven fabrics. Fulling helps to make woven textiles sturdier by interlocking the fibers in more than one way. Fulled textiles may be easier to form into three-dimensional objects, such as hats, than purely woven fabrics. Since fulling relies to a great extent on the same technology as felting, they must be considered together.

Some of the earliest potential evidence of feltmaking in Europe was found around 1935 in burial mounds in Jutland and North Slesvig in Denmark. Here, several caps were discovered that dated to the Bronze Age, around 1500 BCE (CIBA 1958, 23). As Irena Turnau points out, however, while these caps were initially believed to be true felt, it is also possible that the felting is a result of mineralization and the environment of the bog in which they were found, rather than intentional on the part of the original artisan (1997, 21). In the late 1930s, a horse bridle with felt straps was uncovered near Hesse, Germany that dated from around 1400 to 1200 BCE. Another piece of felt from the late Bronze Age was found in a tomb at

Behringen in Hanover (CIBA 1958, 23). Both were preserved in the Berlin State Museum but disappeared during the Second World War, leaving no European felt that was made before the fourth or fifth century CE. Bjorg Hougen reported two small pieces of felt from that period in archaeological finds from the 1930s in Norway. The felt was found wrapped around a man's leg, possibly the remains of a sock (Sjöberg 1996, 17). Sheets of felt only 3 millimeters (about 0.12 inches) thick were found dating from the seventh or eighth century CE in northern Germany.

After the Norwegian felts, however, most of the early European felts date from around the eleventh and twelfth centuries and into the Middle Ages (Turnau 1997, 21). Several felts were also discovered in Lübeck, near the Baltic coast of Germany close to Hamburg, dating from around the thirteenth century, among them at least two hats. Inga Hägg documented one of the largest finds of felt pieces, which were excavated at Haithabu near Schleswig at the base of the Jutland peninsula in what is now Germany. The city was an important port for the Danish Vikings between 900 and 1200 CE. Twenty-one pieces of felt were found at Haithabu, all either dense, thin, heavily felted fabrics presumably used for hats and hoods or else thick, softer fabrics with a napped finish used as part of animal harnesses and saddle coverings (Turnau 1997, 22). Evidence suggests that the Vikings also used felt for making shirts and caftans. One of the Vikings' more unique uses for felt was as caulking between the planks of boats and ships – several strips of felt at Haithabu appeared to have been cut from larger pieces and were covered in pine tar, which would have increased their water resistance (Turnau 1997, 22). Such tar-covered felt would continue to be used for waterproofing in construction, if not necessarily in ships, into the twentieth century.

The set of felt artifacts found in northern Germany also contained some that were finished to look like animal fur. Pieces of spun threads had been added to the wool during the felting process, so that when the felt was napped, the texture and length of the napped fibers varied, creating a shaggy appearance. A similar technique can be used in weaving and was common during the eleventh and twelfth centuries in Iceland, Sweden and Wolin, a large island off the coast of Poland. The German archaeologist Karl Schlabow found a fourteenth-century felt cap in Friesland that had been finished in this way. The cap is remarkable since it is true felt rather than fulled woven fabric. The yarn was sewn into the felt after it was finished at around an impressive 210 pieces of yarn per square inch. Turnau suggests that many of these felts finished to resemble fur were used for masks, either for religious or military purposes (Turnau 1997, 22).

Other European finds of felt have been scant and most date to the medieval period. Felts have been found from the thirteenth century onwards in sites in the Netherlands, Russia and Poland. The Polish findings are, in fact, somewhat earlier – from the eleventh century – and include a small toy animal with four paws, ears and a tail (Turnau 1997, 24). In Russia, felt appears to have been used for making hats, gloves and boots during the early Middle Ages. Felt was also in use in southern Europe along the Adriatic and into the Balkans by the thirteenth century. In addition to the usual hats and caps, people of this area also manufactured felt blankets and mattresses. While the oldest known felt in England is dated to the 1550s and was found among castle artifacts near Newcastle-upon-Tyne, in northeastern England, Mary Burkett remarks on six felt hoods found in 1867. Only one survived excavation from the ground, and no firm date was ever established. Burkett suggests that feltmaking may have been known during Roman times in Britain, either from the Romans or natively. A carved stone from the third century CE found at Housesteads Roman fort, half way along Hadrian's Wall, shows three figures wearing hooded cloaks that could have been made of felt. The felt hoods from 1867, however, could as easily have been from the Middle Ages as from this earlier date (Burkett 1979, 100–1). After this point, much of the feltmaking industry is well recorded in the records of the hatmaking and fulling guilds of the Renaissance. While the archaeological record suggests that felt has been known for 8,500 years, the textual evidence shows feltmaking firmly established by the time of the Greeks and Romans.

THE WRITTEN RECORD OF FELT

The word "felt" itself is closely tied to its history. The English word comes straight through from the Old English or Anglo-Saxon "felt." The word derives from Old High German *filz*, which persists in modern German, and the Old Dutch *vilt* (Oxford English Dictionary online). These forms are also related to *filt*, found in Danish, Swedish and Norwegian, which seems to come from the Old Scandinavian root *floki*, meaning "to stamp," although Mary Burkett remarks that in Norway and Sweden the old word for felt was *tova* (Burkett 1979, 97; Turnau 1997, 7). Some linguists have related felt, *filz* and *filt* to *plusti* in Old Slavic (Laufer 1930, 18). Finnish, being part of a different linguistic family than these other European languages, employs the word *huopa*. Although the classical Latin word for felt is *pileus*, developed from the ancient Greek *pilos*, the Romance languages did not follow their forebear. Instead, their words are similarly related to the Old High Germanic *felt*. Italian and Portuguese offer *feltro*,

French *feutre* and Spanish *fieltro*. Romanian employs *fe'tru* (Turnau 1997, 7). Even the Latin itself had changed to *filtrum* by the Middle Ages (Laufer 1930, 18). Historian Berthold Laufer suggests that the overwhelming use of the Germanic word instead of the Roman implies that the knowledge of feltmaking came from the Germanic tribes. These peoples may have learned it from the Slavs to their east, who in turn were taught by the Scythian and Turkic peoples of the steppes with whom they traded (Laufer 1930, 18).

The Russian word for felt is *voilok*, which Turnau suggests may have come from the Turkish term *oilik* (1997, 7). It is related to the Polish *wojlok*. However, this term only arises in Middle Turkic. The Old Turkic root is *kidiz*, which continues to be found in some dialects as *kijiz*. This older form is the one that remains throughout the Central Asian languages, almost unchanged from the Uyghurs of China to the Turkmen in the west. Turkish dictionaries often specify *kijiz* as felt and *oilik* or *oima* as boots made of felt, while Russian dictionaries seem to use *voilok* for both (Starostin 2005). Although Laufer's assertion that the Germanic peoples learned feltmaking from the Slavs, who learned it from the Scyths and other Turkic peoples, does seem possible, the linguistic split between the Turkic *kijiz* and the Germanic *felt* or *filz* does not support it. Given this rather convoluted history, Turnau's belief that feltmaking is a simple enough technique for it to have been discovered by several different groups independently of one another seems more likely (1997, 7). Another option combines the single origin theory with the multiple origin theory: felt technology may have been discovered independently by some cultures while other cultures learned it from their neighbors. Similar debates about whether ideas and technologies spread from a single point or are invented concurrently by multiple groups are at the root of some of the geographic schools of folklore scholarship, but they have rarely been decided definitively, and there is little reason to suspect we will ever know exactly how, where and when felt was developed (Zumwalt 1998, 79). What is clear is that it has been an important part of life for many cultures across Eurasia for a long time.

Many of the written references to felt describe its use by the people of the Middle East and Central Asia yet come from the peoples who surrounded them, from the Greeks and Romans to the west and the Chinese to the east. By proximity, it is not surprising that the Greek and Roman writers, including Homer, Hesiod and Herodotus, should comment largely on the tribes of the western half of this region, including the Persians, while the Chinese annals document felt production among the eastern groups. Some overlap does occur, as both remark on feltmaking among the Scythians and in northern India. This is not to say that the Greeks, Romans, and Chinese did not make or use felt, for they certainly did, as the many written resources and some archaeological evidence can attest. Berthold Laufer argued that felt was purely utilitarian for these peoples, however, whereas it was a vital fabric for the nomads who occupied the land between them (1930, 18). While the extent of this argument is debatable, certainly the written record of felt supports that the textile found its primary importance in the Middle East and Central Asia, while nonetheless continuing to be prized for hats throughout the centuries.

Homer provides the first known reference to felt, and though only fleeting, this helps to establish felt as a known textile in ancient Greece by the seventh century BCE. In the tenth book of the *Iliad,* the poet remarks that Odysseus wears a "headpiece the midst of which with felt was lined," possibly a helmet made of leather but lined with felt, not dissimilar perhaps from those found in the later tombs of Noin Ula (*Iliad* book X, line 262, qtd. in Laufer 1930, 16; Forbes 1964, 92). Slightly later, Hesiod also remarks on the use of felt for caps as well as for shoes. He links felt into mythology by placing Phineas in a felt-covered yurt, where he was taken by the Harpies as punishment by Zeus for revealing too much of the god's plans (Laufer 1930, 9). Generally, felt appears to have been a common material for hats and caps as well as for cloaks and waistcoats throughout the classical world. Certain styles of felt hats were associated with particular professions in Greek imagery. Artisans were often depicted wearing felt caps, such as the blacksmith god Hephaestus, who watched over craftsmen, and Daedalus, the architect who built King Minos' labyrinth and also constructed wings so he could escape it. Odysseus may have gained his felt cap either as a sailor (Charon, the boatman who guides souls across the River Styx, also wears a felt hat) or as a soldier (Laufer 1930, 17). In Rome, a felt cap was given to slaves upon attaining their freedom, resulting in the phrase *ad pileum vocare*, "to call the felt cap," which referred to promoting rebellion among the slaves (Laufer 1930, 17).

Around the same time, Herodotus reported that Xerxes the Great of Persia wore a felt hat, and most of the soldiers accompanying him to Greece, including the Lycians, also wore felt caps. Xerxes distinguished himself from his soldiers by the style of his hat. Xenophon writes that the king's hat was tall and stiff, while his soldiers folded theirs forward. Herodotus bizarrely suggested that the Persians' felt caps led to their having thin skulls, presumably because the felt gave too much protection and prohibited the bones from fully thickening (Burkett 1979, 18). Aristophanes later used this image of the king in his tall felt hat in his comedy *The Birds*, calling the comb of the cock a "Persian cap" (Laufer 1930, 10). The Persians and peoples to their north and east, including the Medes and Bactrians, were well known for their use of felt not only in hats but also for bags and rugs, like the *namad/namda* rugs made today in Iran, Pakistan and northwestern India. The felt hats of the Medes are even inscribed on the stone reliefs in the Achaemenian palaces at Persepolis (Johnson 2002, 61). Yet the Persians were far from the only people to use felt for armor. Thucydides, writing in the late fifth century BCE, noted the efficacy of felt armor against arrows and remarked that siege-towers could also be covered in felt to provide greater protection (Forbes 1964, 92).

Herodotus continued his discussion of the peoples of Central Asia by describing the Scythians' houses as felt tents resting on carts (Laufer 1930, 9). His description suggests a felt-covered wooden frame that could be removed from the cart and set up on the ground, similar to the yurts that remain in use throughout Central Asia today. Herodotus' description suggests that Hesiod may have been referencing the Scythians when he spoke of the "milk-fed nations whose houses are wagons" (Laufer 1930, 9). Aeschylus wrote similarly of the "wandering Scyths who dwell in latticed huts high-poised on easy wheels" in *Prometheus Unbound* (Laufer 1930, 9–10). It is possible, of course, that the poet Aeschylus got his information on the Scythians from the historian Herodotus, as they lived around the same time. More importantly, however, these texts offer documentary evidence of the Scythians' use of felt that coincides with the archaeological evidence provided by the finds at Pazyryk, providing a clear portrait of the importance of felt in Central Asian life during this period.

The Roman writers also commented on felt use in other regions. Writing at the very beginning of the first century CE, Strabo offers this testament to the skill of the Indian felt-makers: "when they saw sponges in use among the Macedonians they made imitations by sewing tufts of wool through and through with hair and light cords and threads and that after compressing them into felt they drew out the inserts and dyed the sponge-like felt with colours" (Forbes 1964, 92). This technique for making sponges from felt is quite fascinating and shows particular ingenuity in turning feltmaking to any purpose. By Strabo's description, the Indian feltmakers must have sewn cords randomly through a bat of wool prepared for felting. Once the wool was felted, the cords could be removed to leave a series of holes, replicating the air pockets in a natural sponge.

At roughly the same time as Xenophon and Thucydides were commenting on the use of felt by the Persians, the annals at the end of the Chou Dynasty in China also remarked on the use of felt, primarily for rugs and mattresses (Laufer 1930, 3). The Hsiung-nu, the Scythian-related tribe that had built the barrows of Noin Ula and filled them with their felt furnishings, had been in contact with the Chinese since around 1400 BCE. Laufer suggests that it was through military and trade contact with the Hsiung-nu, among others, that the Chinese gained their knowledge of felt (1930, 4). In order to hold the Hsiung-nu at bay, the Chao emperor Wu-ling adopted the nomads' clothing and use of the horse for warfare in the early third century BCE. The Chinese annals record the use of felt by warriors for shields, hats and boots as early as 230 BCE (Johnson 2002, 66). The next emperor, Shih-huang-tai, would order the building of the Great Wall in 215 BCE to help keep the felt-clad nomadic tribes out of China. Despite the consistent use of felt for the next several centuries by the Chinese, the textile continued to be associated with the nomadic tribes to the west, known as the "land of felt." Felt clothing was remarked upon among the Jan-mang people of what is now Szechwan during the Han Dynasty, which lasted from around 206 BCE to 220 CE (Laufer 1930, 5). Either the Jan-mang or the descendents of the Hsiung-nu brought about a fashion for felt girdles around 280 CE, which was met with a certain amount of scorn by the annalist because of their nomadic associations.

Starting what would prove to be a long line of travel writers who mention felt, Fa Hien journeyed as a Buddhist pilgrim from China into India through Central Asia around 399 CE. He gives the earliest written account of the people who lived at that time in the eastern Turfan valley – an area just south of Loulan, where the mummies of the Ürümchi museum were found. Fa Hien remarks:

> The clothes of the common people are coarse, and like those worn in our land of Han (China), some wearing felt and others coarse serge or cloth of hair; this was the only difference seen among them. (Qtd. in Laufer 1930, 9)

Although it is tempting to think that these were descendants of the people of Loulan, there is little doubt that they were an Iranian people and thus related to the tribes who flourished throughout Central Asia until the sixth century and whose western relatives were written about by the Greeks and Romans.

Chinese records of felt both at home and abroad continue fairly consistently through the next several hundred years. The T'ang Dynasty annals comment on the use of felt for plates, clothes and large squared tents in Tibet in the seventh and eighth centuries CE. Like feltmaking peoples everywhere, many Tibetans continue to wear felt hats and boots. Felt blankets worn by the men of the Nan-chao people of modern Yunnan province were noted in 860 CE by the writer Fan Ch'o, who also wrote that white felt was worn in P'iao, which corresponds roughly to Prome in ancient Burma (Laufer 1930, 5). Felt clothing continued to be worn in Yunnan through 1148 CE, when Chou K'ü-fei remarked on it. Chou recorded the difference in the types of felt manufactured in China – "thick and solid" in the north, while large, thinner pieces were constructed in the south, "to a length of over thirty feet and to a width of [*sic*] sixteen to seventeen feet" (Laufer 1930, 6). These large pieces were then doubled and the ends stitched to form a continuous piece that was then wrapped around the body and belted much in the manner of a sari or a great kilt. Laufer notes that the Lolo and Moso peoples of southern China still wore a similar felt coat at the time of his writing in 1930 (6).

The West is unlike China in that, after the early Greek and Roman period, felt does not seem to appear again in written texts for several centuries. The oldest textual reference to felt in English is found in an inventory written by the monk Ælfric of Eynsham, near Oxford, and dates to around 1000 CE (Oxford English Dictionary online). This listing of felt puts the material soundly in Great Britain by this date, though as pointed out earlier, whether it came to British shores through Roman soldiers or the Vikings of northern Europe or through native manufacture is unclear. From this time on, felt makes regular appearances in inventories and more particularly through the craft guilds of the Middle Ages.

In the thirteenth century CE, however, several Europeans traveled in Central Asia and wrote about their experiences there. What is important here is the documentation of felt and feltmaking among diverse peoples across Central Asia and Europe at this time in history. We will investigate in more detail what these writers had to report in later chapters. While trade routes along the Silk Road had been established for centuries by this point (Grousset 1970, 37), Plano Carpini was among the first of this later group to record culture among the Mongols in 1246 in his book *Historia Mongalorum*. Also known as Friar John of Pian del Carpiné, Carpini (in his role as an ambassador from the pope) attended the funeral rites of a Genghiside khan and the election of the next khan near Karakorum in modern-day Pakistan. He remarked on the use of felt as part of the ceremonies as well as in several other aspects of Mongol life (Olschki 1949, 11–13). Approximately eight years after Carpini's travels, Friar William of Rubruck was also traveling in the Mongol empire and commented on the use of felt, particularly for religious purposes (Ruysbroeck 1900, 83). The last of these thirteenth-century travelers is also the most famous. Marco Polo recorded the use of yurts and other tents and coverings made of felt and used by the Mongols at the end of the century. Unfortunately for felt scholars, Polo's writings have come under fire in the last few decades. Much of what he reports was either already in print at the time or, perhaps more interestingly, existed in the oral accounts of merchants who traded with the East. It may never be resolved how much of his writings are true to what he saw or how far east he really went in his travels; nonetheless, felt's appearance in his work shows the strong connection that medieval people made between the peoples of Central Asia and their reliance on this simple and sturdy woolen textile – a connection that remains to this day.

THE FOLKLORE OF FELT

Several myths have arisen to explain how felt originated. Rather interestingly, those that have survived in Europe and America have largely been based in Christianity. In Central Asia, where felt is so much a part of everyday life, such origin myths do not seem to have been widely recorded. While a large body of beliefs pertaining to felt have been recorded by missionaries, merchants and travel writers in Central Asia from the thirteenth century to the present, they seem to revolve around the use of felt in various ceremonial and religious contexts rather than any kind of origin tale. With these reports, it can be much more difficult to separate exoticism from ethnography, since we must rely heavily on the accounts of European explorers who often have their own agendas. Part of any mythological system is providing an explanation for the way the world works, particularly the more mysterious parts of it. In that context, the seemingly spontaneous moment when wet wool becomes an integrated fabric does appear adequately mysterious to warrant its own stories, especially the first time one sees and feels it happen.

According to one legend, felt appeared without any human aid. The sheep on Noah's Ark, kept in the confines of the ark's hold, shed their wool. The wool was urinated on and trampled by the sheep and other animals in the heat of the hold. When the Ark landed at Mount Ararat in eastern Turkey and the animals all disembarked, Noah found the felt rug left behind (McGavock 2000, 9). This story clearly links feltmaking, and felt rugs in particular, to the very geographic area where they have enjoyed a long history and are still found today.

A more common story tells that St. Clement, the fourth pope, is responsible for felt. The legend varies, but in essence St. Clement wrapped his sore feet with wool and walked on to his destination. When he arrived and removed his shoes, he discovered that the wool had felted (McGavock and Lewis 2000, 9). In some versions, he is on a mission; in others, on the run from persecution; in still others, he simply had particularly painful feet that were prone to getting blisters (Laufer 1930, 3). Oddly, in several variations, he wraps his feet not in wool but in tow, the short fibers of flax used in making linen, which rather defeats the purpose of the story, since flax cannot be made into felt. The dates of Clement's papacy vary between sources – from his being the last pope ordained by St. Peter in Rome to his living sometime in the Middle Ages. Occasionally, the tale continues beyond his discovery of felt. In these, St. Clement returns to Rome, where he sets up a feltmaking workshop and employs monks as the first feltmakers. Historical evidence is against Clement here, since both Greek and Roman writers commented on felt manufacture, and images of feltmaking appear on the walls of Pompeii, implying that the craft was well established by the time Vesuvius erupted in 79 CE.

A few authors attribute the creation of felt to St. Christopher rather than Clement or even to Moses. Regardless of which saint may have found felt first, both Christopher and Clement are considered patrons of hatters, who are generally associated with the production of felt. St. Clement is also a patron of fullers, which may include feltmakers. Here he is joined in his patronage by St. James the Lesser, who was beaten to death and therefore retained the club as a symbol, which by association linked him to fulling since clubs can be used for pounding the cloth. The most direct reference to felt among the saints is Anastasius the Fuller, who was martyred in the fourth century but about whom very little is known (www.catholic-forum. com 2007). The linking of feltmaking and fulling to a saint demonstrates the importance of these technologies, at least during the Middle Ages when many of the patronages were established.

A third legend attributes the first felt to one of Solomon's sons. According to this legend, the boy was a shepherd who was trying to make a waterproof mat out of sheep's wool, having seen water shed off the sheep themselves. After several failures, he burst into tears in a fit of temper and stomped on the loose fleece where it lay on the floor, turning the wool into felt (Westfall 2005, 55). This legend, like the one associated with Noah, would place the first production of felt in northern Iran – an area, like Turkey, that continues to have a tradition of felt production to this day. While the characters may be apocryphal, it is possible that felt was first developed in this region. As with all legends, what is more important is that, at least for the legends' tellers, felt was strongly associated with the Middle East and Central Asia, as it remains today.

While some of the gods of ancient Greece and Rome, such as Hephaestus and Charon, were depicted wearing felt caps as marks of their professions, the Gemini twins Castor and Pollux are the most closely associated of the Greek and Roman pantheon with felt. The Dioscuri, as they are sometimes called, are often symbolized by either a pair of felt caps that are attached to one another or else a single felt cap covered in stars. The conjoined caps are believed to represent the two hemispheres of the single world or, conversely, the single egg from which

3 Roman Statue of Castor or Pollux wearing a felt hat.

the two twins were born (Olschki 1949, 44). The star-covered felt cap may be a reference to the Gemini twins' appearance as constellations in the sky. Leonardo Olschki points out, however, that Castor and Pollux came fairly late into the world of astronomy, appearing as constellations only after the fourth century BCE. Their story goes further back, however, since they turn up in Homer's *Iliad* fighting alongside the Greeks. The twins are said to be the sons of Leda and therefore Helen of Troy's brothers. Olschki goes on to suggest that the myth of the starry hat, which became the twins' icon, came from Central Asian religions and was transmitted into Rome through Greece. Some evidence for this exists, since a similar pair of brothers known as the Aswin Horsemen existed in mythology in the Middle East.

The twins were particularly popular in Rome during this period, as protectors for both sailors and craftsmen as well as for the middle class – "all men entitled and accustomed to wear the undyed felt cap as a mark of their rank and privileges, and as a symbol of their civil liberties" (Olschki 1949, 45). Headgear was a primary marker of rank, since noblemen wore none at all, and the slaves were indicated by their Phrygian caps. "The felted mob," then, were that very middle class distinguished by their felt caps, which were celebrated not only in the sky in the constellation of Castor and Pollux but also on coins and other representations throughout Roman art and culture.

From the walls of Çatal Hüyük through the writings of Marco Polo emerges a story of felt that stretches across Asia and into Europe. In this 8,500-year-old history, felt has dressed kings and commoners, been on hand for funerals, coronations, through wars and in peace. Felt has made appearances in the far-flung empires of the Persians, the Romans, the Scythians, the Mongols and various Chinese dynasties, stretching this single, simple textile halfway around the world. Felt has become an icon not only of the peoples who used it for clothing and houses throughout Central Asia but also of the "felted mob" of Rome and their twin deities Castor and Pollux, of Medean troops and the kings of Persia. This story offers an intriguing pedigree for such a simple mass of matted wool to bear, and yet if ever a textile were up to the job, it is certainly felt. What is outlined here offers only a glimpse of the many hats and boots and mats in which felt has put in an appearance, the sketchy images provided by fragments of archaeological fabric and references in ancient texts. We can only guess at the true extent to which felt was used. What is clear from this story is that felt has been important in Eurasian history into the thirteenth century.

From the Middle Ages on, the story of felt becomes much more culturally rooted. In Central Asia, the tradition of feltmaking has continued uninterrupted from the time of Pazyryk to the present, yet it has also continued to show innovation and creative adaptation. In Turkey, the Near East, and southeastern Europe, felt continued to serve its traditional purposes for the next several centuries, yet also put in appearances in the Crusades and later battles. In Europe, the tradition of feltmaking is tied to the rise of the craft guilds and to the Industrial Revolution. Felt moved outward across the globe, become indispensable in industry, a marker of kitsch, and a medium of beautiful artistry.

3.
FELT IN CENTRAL ASIA

Centuries ago, the Chinese referred to Central Asia as the "land of felt"; the name is as true now as it was then. If any culture has built its lifestyle around felt and turned this simple textile into an entire way of life, it is the peoples of Central Asia. So strong is this connection between Central Asia and felt that Berthold Laufer remarked in his 1930 work on felt as follows:

> Eliminate felt from the Chinese, Greek, and Roman civilizations, and they would still remain what they are, not being in the least affected by this minus. Eliminate the same element from the life of the nomadic populations, and they would cease to exist, they would never have come into existence. With these people felt is a fundamental of culture, an absolutely essential feature and necessity of life, while with the highly civilized nations like the Chinese, Indians, Greeks, and Romans it is a side issue, an incident, an element of occasional and minor importance. The use of felt, therefore, has reached its maximum intensity and its climax among the nomadic tribes of Asia. (Laufer 1930, 2)

While weaving and other textile technologies have certainly been known throughout Central Asia since at least the Scythians and perfected in some areas, as exemplified by the knotted carpets of Persia or the Kyrgyz and Kazakh woven tent-bands, many of the groups of the region have laid their lot with felt. The idea that cultures are "more" or "less" civilized has fallen into question since Laufer wrote this famous statement, but the unqualified importance of felt to peoples from Mongolia to Turkestan continues to be true.

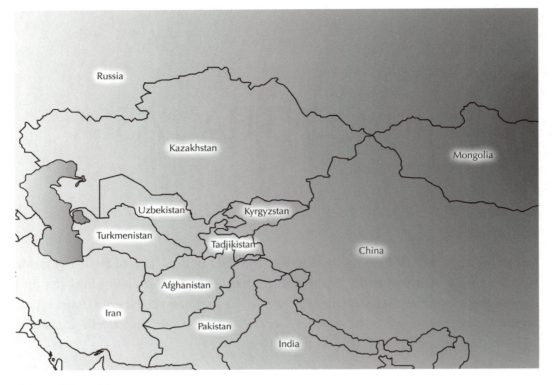

4 Map of Central Asia.

Central Asia covers a vast territory, stretching roughly from China to the Black Sea, and its people have traditionally been nomads whose lives are based on herding sheep and horses. For these peoples, whose lands cover the steppes, the mountains and the high desert, felt provided the strength and insulation needed to keep warm in the winters and cool in the summers, to pad what was hard and to hold everything together. The tradition of feltmaking has continued, seemingly unimpeded, from the Scythians to the present day and while some of the forms and functions that felt has taken in the intervening centuries have changed, sturdy felt remains an integral part of Central Asian life.

AMIDST THE -STANS

First and foremost, what is meant by Central Asia? The term is a loose one, primarily defined by the people who inhabit it. Geographically, Central Asia refers to a large area of land, sometimes historically called Turkestan, which lies between the Caspian Sea on the west, the steppes of southern Siberia on the north, India and Tibet to the south, and the hills of Mongolia and central China to the east. It includes the Takla Makan, Kara-Kum and Kyzyl-Kum deserts, parts of the Pamir, Tien Shan, Altai and Kunlun mountain ranges, as well as the Hindu Kush. This area incorporates part of ancient Persia (modern Iran and Pakistan) and all of Afghanistan, Turkmenistan, Uzbekistan, Kazakhstan, Tajikistan, Kyrgyzstan, part of southern Siberia, and the Chinese region of Xinjiang (Harris 1993, 91; Harvey 1996, 8–14; Leix 1941, 1434–36). Some scholars, especially regional historians such as Rene Grousset, include Mongolia, Manchuria and the Caucasus region north and east of the Black Sea. To help focus this work, only certain parts of these areas are included. For our purposes, Central Asia will incorporate Mongolia in the east but stop at the Caspian Sea in the west. The felt traditions of the people in the Caucasus, in places such as Georgia and Armenia, certainly are connected to the Uzbeks, Turkmen and Kazakhs to their east and north, but they also share felt ties with the Iranians, Pashtun, Turks and Kurds to their south and west, and so they will be discussed in more detail in the next chapter.

The Central Asian tribes are largely Mongol-Turkic, with the exception of the Tajiks, and historically nomadic (Leix 1941, 1440; O'Bannon 1974, 13). The people can be broadly divided using the names and political–geographic areas of the former Soviet Union states, although it must be noted that none of these states either contain the entirety of any ethnic group or are limited to a single ethnic group (Mayhew et al. 2000, 51). The Tajik require special mention, being the largest and one of the few ethnic groups of Iranian-Caucasoid descent rather than Turkic. The Tajik are also believed to be the oldest ethnic culture in Central Asia, being descended from the Persians and Samanids (Mayhew et al 2000, 56).

Within the larger ethnic groups are a number of smaller tribes. The Kyrgyz and Kazakh are culturally similar and closely related to the Karakalpak, a smaller ethnic group inhabiting parts of both Kyrgyzstan and Kazakhstan (Bacon 1966, 47). The Turkmen tribes are probably the best documented in current literature. Rug scholar George O'Bannon reports twenty-four Turkmen tribes before the Mongol invasion, and at least twenty-three surviving to the nineteenth century, including "Turkomanized Arabs," or tribes of Arabic descent linked linguistically and culturally to the Turkmen (O'Bannon 1974, 23). Another rug historian lists nine Turkmen tribes as inhabiting the Soviet Republic of Turkmenistan (Justin 1980, 90). Among the better-known tribes are the Salor, Saruq, Tekke, Yomud, Goklan, Ersari, Chaudor and Kyzil Arak. The region also contains several other ethnic groups, such as the Pashtun, centered predominantly in Afghanistan and Pakistan, and the Uyghur, who have historically inhabited the far western edge of China and eastern Kyrgyzstan. Here, it is enough to know that these groups exist and nearly all of them have some kind of felting traditions, although few have been well documented. Due to limited information, much of this chapter centers on Mongolian and Kyrgyz feltmaking, although other groups are discussed.

The Central Asian peoples may also be divided by their level of nomadism, although this designation is less valid since the questionably successful Soviet attempts at promoting settlement and collectivization of land. Historically, the Kyrgyz and Kazakh tend to be nomadic, ranging between summer and winter camps, while the Tajik have mostly been settled in towns. The Turkmen and Uzbek have varied between settled and nomadic lifestyles depending on the specific tribe or family group and the current political situation. In some of the sixteenth-century khanates, and extending into the eighteenth century, the Uzbek often controlled the towns, especially in western Turkestan, using their Turkmen allies for military support, the Tajiks for agricultural products, and trading with Europe, India and China for other goods (Sumner and Feltham 2000, 13). In some cases, certain tribe members may be nomadic while others follow an agricultural lifestyle. Often in this situation, nomadism is preferred, since ownership of animals symbolizes wealth (Harvey 1996, 7–14; Mayhew et al. 2000, 53). By far the lion's share of feltmaking has been done historically by the nomadic peoples, since felt does not require moving specialized equipment between summer and winter pastures and makes use of the most readily available fiber – wool.

A BRIEF HISTORY OF CENTRAL ASIA

Historically, Central Asia has been an area of great flux and tribal migration, as the result of – and causing – innumerable small wars. The nomadic lifestyle led to the search for new pasture, causing encroachment on the land of other tribes and more movement. The use of felt for tents and house coverings helped to make much of the movement possible. People have inhabited Central Asia since at least 2000 BCE. The Cimmerians controlled the steppes east of the Black Sea and into the area around the Caspian Sea from about 1100 BCE until approximately 750 BCE, when they were replaced by the Scythians. The Scythians were an Iranian people who had originated in western Turkestan and are particularly known for their aesthetic style in both gold and felt. During the third century BCE, the Scythians were pushed out of the northwest by the Sarmatians, another Iranian tribe, when Alexander the Great entered Persia in the southwest (Grousset 1970).

In eastern Central Asia, several Turko-Mongol peoples vied for control with the Chinese. Like the Scythians, they were known for their use of felt. The Hsiung-nu first appeared in Chinese annals at about the time the Scythian culture began to migrate and break down. The Hsiung-nu later evolved into the Huns and swept across Asia and eastern Europe in the fourth century CE. During the sixth century CE, the Turkic tribes allied and routed first the Huns with the aid of the Sassanians and later the Sassanians with the aid of the Byzantines. In the eighth century CE, the southwestern area of Central Asia was invaded by Arabic peoples, partly fueled by the spread of Islam (Grousset 1970).

The next large empire after the Hsiung-nu was formed by the Mongols under Genghis Khan at the end of the twelfth century and covered most of Central Asia. The descendents of Genghis Khan were to rule for the next several centuries, with Tamerlane revitalizing and expanding the empire in the second half of the fourteenth century. During the sixteenth to eighteenth centuries, much of Central Asia gradually subsided into small but powerful khanates, mostly led by the Uzbek. Russia expanded throughout Siberia and began to move into Central Asia during the eighteenth century, sparking off the "Great Game" with Britain, who controlled India and was expanding northward. The two countries spent the next century skirmishing and spying on one another. Eventually, both Russia and Great Britain lost their control in these regions, leading to today's host of young nations, which are only loosely divided along old tribal and ethnic lines (Grousset 1970; Harvey 1996, 7–16; Herodotus 1958; O'Bannon 1974, 14; Polo 1958; Sumner and Feltham 2000, 8–20).

Despite the to-and-fro movement of various peoples throughout Central Asian history and the large expanse of land on which these many migrations took place, the making of felt has remained fairly consistent, and more interestingly, some of the methods and motifs found in the felt have continued through it all. Now that we have a rough idea of where Central Asia is and who is making felt there, we will let the felt itself be our guide. Much of the ancient and early historic evidence for feltmaking has already been discussed, yet so far we have focused on the forms these felt pieces have taken. The questions of felt's larger role within the ancient cultures of Central Asia and that history's influence on the present day remain.

ANCIENT FELT

A site at Pazyryk, dating from the fifth century BCE, forms the earliest evidence of felt's vital role in the cultures of Central Asia, and so the story of felt in this region must begin again with a closer look at a few of the highly sophisticated felt pieces found in these ancient tombs. The Pazyryk find was notable for the large number of intact felts and other textiles that displayed a coherent cultural aesthetic which was both in keeping with the Greek reports of the Scythians and yet also contradicted them. From the evidence found at Pazyryk and Noin Ula, a picture emerges of a culture that has brought feltmaking to its height and was relatively consistent across Central Asia. As Rudenko states:

> Surveying the Pazyryk finds and those akin to them we can see that in the steppe and foothill area of southern Siberia and central Asia [sic], as well as eastern Europe, there lived in the middle of the last millennium B.C. numerous tribes, distinct in origin and language, but sharing in material culture and to some extent at the same social level, and with similar customs. Such a uniform way of life arose not only from a similar livelihood but also as a result of varied, but often close, inter-tribal connections. (Rudenko 1970, xxxiv)

Pazyryk thus becomes a sort of portal into the culture of this period. More importantly, however, the felt pieces found there point to a continuum of culture and a cultural aesthetic that reached out not only geographically but through time.

As stated in the second chapter, the people who buried their dead in the barrows at Pazyryk were probably related to the Scythians. They used felt for a wide variety of purposes including several articles of clothing, rugs and wall hangings, sculptured animals and saddle blankets and head covers for horses. The last of these categories deserves some special attention, for the people of Pazyryk were a culture of horsemen and their respect for their horses is demonstrated in the care they gave to saddlery. The saddles themselves were made of wood, often ornately carved in some of the same patterns as the gold jewelry found at the site and sometimes covered in patterned or embellished leather. Since wood hardly provides a comfortable journey for either horse or rider, the people produced felt saddle blankets to go between the saddle and the horse and saddle covers to cushion the rider from the saddle – this system of pads and blankets is still in use throughout Central Asia, as we shall see later. While both are embellished, saddle pads, which could be seen on top of the saddle, tended to receive more attention than the saddle blankets, which are generally covered up by the saddle and pad on the horse.

Certainly, no discussion of either early saddlery or Pazyryk would be complete without addressing its felt saddle covers. Most of the decorated saddle covers consist of fine felt and are embellished with appliqué in either felt or leather, sometimes covered in gold or tin foil (Rudenko 1970, 229). At times, the leather has been carefully painted or scored, and often the felt ground is dyed blue or red. The covers fold along the center where they would lie on top of the horse and hang down on either side and thus are decorated with two sets of images, typically depicting a tiger or griffin attacking an elk. These motifs are the images of the Scythian animal style, twisting through curvilinear forms and marking musculature with commas. Some of these animals also appear on the felt wall-hangings of the tombs (Rudenko 1970, 234). The Scythians are celebrated for this style, which is repeated throughout their works and in the tattoos found on human remains in the tombs.

Possibly the most famous of these was found in Barrow One. Saddle covers were also found in barrows Two and Five, though these were not decorated. The Barrow One saddle cover shows a large sheep or goat being attacked by a winged griffin. The edges are embellished with three large, round felt tabs that extend on the sides. On each of these tabs, the artist appliquéd a ram's head of red felt with blue horns containing red rosettes. Each ram is surrounded by the heads of two horned lions of red, blue and yellow felt. Eyes gleam with gold and the whole tab is trimmed in blue and red fur (Rudenko 1970, 238). This saddle cover contains some of the best of the Pazyryk feltwork and is an archaeological treasure. The animal style it represented died out with the Scythians but the Pazyryk felts contain the beginnings of design motifs that would continue to be used into the present. The seemingly lowly saddle blankets bear the marks of felt artistry to come.

Sergei Rudenko, one of the lead archaeologists at Pazyryk and the chronicler of the site's excavation, refers to the felt blankets that went under the saddles as *shabrack*s, after both the Russian and Turkish terms. While some of the blankets were thick and clearly intended to provide the necessary cushioning for the saddle, others were works of art, meant to enhance the beauty of the horse and possibly to show off the wealth of the rider. The majority of the shabracks found at Pazykyk consisted of large pieces of felt measuring as much as 70 by 236 centimeters, and often made of fine white felt. Appliqué in felt provided the primary means of embellishment. One shabrack found in Barrow Five, for example, has a strip in the middle that has been left plain where it would not show under the saddle. The rest of the blanket is covered in fine, appliquéd motifs depicting five deer antlers surrounding a red four-petal rosette in a blue circle. The edges of this shabrack are embellished with a border of more antlers in a running wave pattern in blue and grey and finally bordered with a rim of red (Rudenko 1970, 169).

Another shabrack in the same tomb has a pattern reminiscent of a *mille fleurs* carpet, with a large red and white lattice containing four-petal rosettes in blue on a yellow ground and marked at the interstices with red rosettes in blue circles. The border in this shabrack is also notable for its pattern of antler motifs in red on a white ground connected with a curving line, again forming a wave (Rudenko 1970, 173). Far from the sea, however, waves may not be such a common source of imagery for the many peoples of Central Asia as the animals that form a part of everyday life. With the extra curl seen on the edge of the curves in the border of the second shabrack, these forms seem like antlers, yet if that extra curve is removed, the remaining single curl closely resembles the curve of a dog's tail, a common border motif for modern felt rugs. In the edges of these shabracks from Barrow Five, we begin to see elements of designs that will be carried through the next 2,500 years. These decorative borders resemble some of the patterns that continue to be used by Kyrgyz and Kazakh feltmakers in their pieced shyrdak (felt rugs), and may provide early evidence of the historical basis for those motifs.

Yet the Pazyryk felts show the foundation not only of designs that will be carried into the present, but also of construction techniques. The third shabrack found in Barrow Five is embellished with a pattern of shield-like shapes that resemble fish scales, each containing one of two different stylized antler motifs, which alternate in rows. The alternation is between both motif and color, so that the first pattern appears in red on a yellow ground as well as yellow on a red ground, while the second pattern interchanges blue and orange (Rudenko 1970, 170). This use of negative images shows not only a creative way of economically using all of the available felt cut within the overall design, but also makes that design quite complex, since it provides four full rows before the pattern is repeated. This use of negative color patterns is the hallmark of the shyrdak, and precisely what makes them so visually arresting. This process allows for the maker to cut out two shyrdak or two panels of a single piece, as in the third shabrack, at the same time. While Rudenko has remarked that the culture was fairly consistent geographically across Central Asia during the fifth century BCE, finding evidence for the beginning of the shyrdak technique in Pazyryk points to a relatively consistent culture of feltmaking from this early period to the present.

THE CULTURE OF FELT IN THE MEDIEVAL PERIOD

During the medieval period, several Europeans traveled through Central Asia for reasons that varied from curiosity to religious mission to the opening of new trade routes and agreements and, as we have already seen, several of their accounts exist. Evidence here is scant, making a few leaps of several centuries, but the picture that emerges helps to highlight the importance of wool and felt for the Central Asian cultures. Unfortunately, it is much more difficult to separate exoticism from ethnography, since we must rely heavily on the accounts of European explorers. For this reason, it seems more appropriate to look at how these writers, from Homer through Marco Polo, describe the uses of felt both at home and abroad. There can be no doubt that felt was, as it continues to be, extremely important to the Central Asian peoples, and thus the likelihood that it was linked with mythology or considered to have magical properties is high. Yet without evidence from the cultures themselves, we must take our sources for what they are – outsider perspectives written by men who often had motives other than pure anthropology. It should also be noted that the peoples encountered by these travelers were generally called Mongols, since the great Mongolian khans were then in control of Central Asia; however, multiple ethnic groups were living in the area at this time.

Felt in the medieval culture of Central Asia was noted for both its utilitarian role and its ceremonial one. Marco Polo commented on the round felt houses, the yurts, in which the Mongols lived and on their ability to move the yurts on large carts. Marco Polo's comments support the evidence of the early Greeks on moveable felt houses and are seconded by Plano Carpini, writing in 1246 CE. Carpini was able to attend the election of Guyuk Khan on July 22, 1246, near Karakorum, and so was able to see the use of felt in at least the external part of the ceremony, as the staffs surrounding the event were tied with red wool (Olschki 1949, 11). Felt likely appeared in other forms during the ceremony as well. Berthold Laufer quotes a speaker at Chingiz Khan's coronation as using the white felt on which the new khan sat as a touchstone for his comments on how to rule. Laufer continues that white felt remains sacred among the Mongols. It is used for ceremonies from weddings to animal sacrifice and is also connected with wealth, since a newly made yurt will look whiter than an older one (Laufer 1930, 15). The importance of white felt is also given voice in the oral traditions of Mongolia. One oral poem associates white felt with totems, possibly related to shamanic totems, while red felt is linked to idols (Batchuluun 2003, 153).

All of the medieval travelers remarked on the use of felt idols by the Mongols. Both Carpini and William of Rubruck, also called Ruysbroeck, noted instances of felt being cut out in the shape of a man and then this man-shape being considered as the elder brother of the male head of the house. The figure was hung in the yurt either near the door or opposite to it. Sometimes a second felt figure was present, as the elder brother of the woman of the house, while an abstract form resembling the udder of a sheep was set above the figures as a guardian for the flocks (Laufer 1930, 15; Batchuluun 2003, 32). Marco Polo referred to the human felt figure as Natigay, who he claimed was the "god of the earth, who watches over their children, cattle, and crops" (Polo 1958, bk. 1, ch. 52 qtd. in Laufer 1930, 15). He goes on to describe whole families of felt people being rubbed with grease from the family's meal. By the fourteenth century, the Christian missionaries were burning these figures in an attempt to gain converts and exorcise what they believed to be devils, but John Smith, who more famously was involved with the early settlement of Virginia, described their use by Turkic peoples in southern Russia at the end of the sixteenth century at some length (Laufer 1930, 16). The practice certainly did not entirely die out. In modern Mongolia, these felt forms often resemble foxes and are hung above children's beds to bring good dreams, while a felt horse might be hung over the hearth of the yurt as a totem of the sky. In 1986, two brothers in their eighties were still known to be making traditional felt totems and figures whose form, they said, had been passed down by previous generations and connected to the tombs of Pazyryk (Batchuluun 2003, 34). In the Kyrgyz Republic, felt animals and people are still made, though often as toys for children or for sale to tourists.

The traditional connects the ancient to the modern, providing a link between past and present that shows both continuity and development. In tradition, the different ways in which the separate cultures throughout Central Asia have made felt their own through technique and form, color and pattern come to the fore. With the breakup of the Soviet Union into independent nations, many of the cultures in these new countries have turned to the traditional as a way of asserting their national identity and connecting to their cultural past. In this modern context, then, Central Asian feltmakers are both revitalizing traditional forms as well as drawing on those forms to create innovative new textiles and images.

TRADITIONAL FELT

Create by the book
A cover just like wool
Felt sprinkled
With the waters from one hundred rivers
Felt laid out
By our daughters like paintings
Perfect like porcelain
Even like snow
Felt as white as a shell
Felt with a back like silk
Unmeasurable

Treasured Fabric
Unbreaking permanent felt
Unwearing resilient felt
May you become an ornament on the ten-walled ger
A carpet for all
An ornament on the eight-walled ger
An autumn carpet for all
An ornament on the six-walled ger
A shield against the winds of summer
Headed by the old gray-haired grannies
Happy, unending fortune each day
Abundant felt.

(Namjildorj 1992 qtd. in Batchuluun 2003, 68)

Central Asia's veneration of felt as the fabric that has made life there possible is summed up in these lines from a traditional Mongolian blessing. Felt is a tradition in and of itself, made around the seasonal movement and shearing of the sheep, and endowed with a thousand small traditions – affecting each step in its making and embellishment and codifying its use. As the blessing shows, felt is treasured for its strength as well as its simple abundance, and for many of the Central Asian cultures, felt can be sacred. From the early finds of Pazyryk and Noin Ula, these cultures have continued to base their existence on felt, developing regional variations in method and design. Moving through the ages from Pazyryk to the present, however, requires not only understanding of the motifs and techniques of feltmaking but a look at the whole ecology of cultural beliefs that surrounds felt. John Miles Foley uses the term ecology with reference to verbal art, as a way of describing how all of the aspects surrounding the performance of an oral poem interrelate (2002, 188). An ecology of feltmaking might include not only how felt is made in a culture like the one at Pazyryk and the images portrayed in the felt, but also how the culture's visual aesthetics, cosmology, folklore and craft all influence one another.

The tradition of feltmaking continues to thrive in Central Asia both as an important expression of culture and a link to the past. As much of Central Asia begins to emerge from Soviet rule and form new independent nations, the peoples who live there have chosen felt as one place to assert their sense of who they are culturally and historically. As the examples above show, felt has continued to have relevance not only as part of everyday life in Central Asia but as a tradition passed down from generation to generation. Despite large-scale settlement of nomadic peoples under the Soviets and the rise of the full range of consumer goods and technologies available to modern people everywhere, which might seem to reduce the necessity for felt, feltmaking in its traditional forms has continued to be both vibrant and relevant, perhaps all the more so in the midst of that very modernity. As many of the Central Asian countries struggle to define themselves within a global context, felt can serve as an important reminder of cultural identity.

Felt expert Stephanie Bunn has suggested that the traditional feltmaking techniques and styles of the former Soviet Union can be divided roughly into three groups: the Kyrgyz and Kazakh tradition, the Uzbek tradition, and the Turkmen (Bunn 2004). Each of these styles shows distinct variations in what is made, how it is made, and how it is embellished. The last of these groups merges in style with the felts found throughout the northern part of the Middle East and into Anatolia. For that reason, most discussion of Turkmen felts will be covered later. Oddly, given their habitation of western China, the Uyghur people make felts very similar to those of the Turkmen, despite being surrounded by peoples with much more pervasive feltmaking traditions. In expanding this list to the rest of Central Asia, we can add the Mongolian felts, which make up their own group with some relationships to the Kazakh. Probably the most well-known felting traditions are to be found among the Mongolians and the Kyrgyz and Kazakhs, all peoples who have dwelt, or continue to dwell, in the felt houses remarked upon by the medieval travel writers – therefore, we will spend the most time with them. The yurt, as the most iconic of felt objects, deserves special attention.

YURTS

The word "yurt" derives from Russian and is a general term for any circular felt-, or increasingly canvas-, covered dwelling. The Mongolians refer to a yurt as a *ger*, and the Kyrgyz call it a *bozu*. For our purposes, yurt will suffice as the most common term in English, though the others are important to know and will also be used. The yurt is probably the largest use of felt in traditional cultures, and much of the large-scale felt production is aimed at supplying the walls, floor coverings, cushions and bags that make up the yurt's covering and interior. Yurts are most common in eastern Central Asia, particularly among the Kazakh, Kyrgyz and Mongolians, with many of the Turkmen peoples preferring black tents. However, they are used by peoples throughout the region. Given the windy, treeless plains that make up much of Central Asia, the yurt is immensely practical. Its shape allows much of the wind to curve around it easily. The thick felt provides shelter from sun, rain and snow and gives enough insulation to keep the interior warm in winter, with the help of a small stove, and cool in the summer. Few things are more relaxing than sitting in a cool yurt on a hot summer day drinking tea on the felt rugs and cushions.

The Mongolians construct their ger somewhat differently from the Kyrgyz' bozu, but both essentially consist of the same components. A round crown, made of wood, forms the top, from which long wooden poles act as roof rafters. These rafters connect to an upright wooden lattice that serves as the frame for the walls. The crown of the yurt is extremely important in all of the cultures. Not only is it the centerpiece on which the rest of the yurt hangs, but it also symbolizes the center of the world and the sun that shines through it during the day. The lattice wall forms a circle and ties at each end to a door frame, also of wood. These pieces are all laced together with long, woven bands, which are an art form of their own, and then felt sheets are used to cover the frame. All of the wood in a yurt is usually painted red, both to protect the wood and for good luck. Yurts can be anywhere from 4 meters in diameter to 30 or 40 meters, depending on the number of lattice pieces used. The Kyrgyz even constructed a five-storey yurt in honor of the 1,000th anniversary of their epic poem, *Manas*, in 1995. At the other extreme, some yurtmakers now make mini-yurts for children, with diameters as small as 60 centimeters.

The Mongolian ger has a noticeably different silhouette from a Kyrgyz bozu. The lattice walls, *khana*, stand straight and perpendicular to the ground. The door is typically made of carved and painted wood. The *toono*, the centerpiece that holds the roof together, is carved of heavy pieces of wood that are jointed together. Large wooden poles may hold the toono upright from the ground. Though still noticeably sloped, the roof has a much lower pitch than a Kyrgyz bozu and is comparatively flat. The *tuurga* are large pieces of felt used to cover the khana. These are thick, often with cording along the exposed edges or at the corners to help reinforce them. They may be placed on the wooden frame of the ger in several layers to provide enough shelter and insulation. The *deever* felt pieces cover the roof poles. Until the mid-twentieth century, the wooden door was also covered with a piece of felt, called the *üüd*. As the entry into the ger, the üüd was considered of great importance and thus made of two layers of fine felt, embroidered with symbols of protection and fortune. When the wooden door took the sole place of the üüd, it began to be carved with similar symbols (Batchuluun 2003, 166–167). The *örkh* is the square of felt that covers the toono. Like the üüd, it is symbolic of home and safety and is always closed at night.

The Kyrgyz bozu looks rounder from the outside than a Mongolian ger. The lattice walls, *kerege* in Kyrgyz, are made of bent wood so the walls curve out in the center and then back in to where they are tied to the üük (the rafterlike poles). The Kyrgyz claim that the bowed shape of the walls gives more room inside the bozu, since the bags that are hung from the kerege now rest inside the bow. Because of this bow, the felt wall-pieces can be gathered slightly at the top and bottom as they are sewn to the cording to provide a closer fit. The pitch of the roof is steeper than a Mongolian ger making for a more pointed top. The crown, or *tunduk*, is also constructed of bent wood. A large, flat piece is bent into a hoop and then four or more poles are bent across the hoop in two perpendicular sets. These sets cross in the middle of the tunduk. This image of the crossed wood in the tunduk is so much a part of Kyrgyz culture and symbology that it forms the center of their national flag.

The other major difference between the Mongolian ger and the Kyrgyz bozu are the reed screens, called *chiy*, used by the Kyrgyz. The chiy consist of thin reeds bound together into a large mat. They are made to the same height as the kerege and tied to the outside of the lattice under the felt. In the warmer plains of Kyrgyzstan, the felt covering can be rolled up to allow the wind through, while the chiy provides protection and privacy inside the yurt. These screens also perform a number of other functions. *Ashkana chiy* are used as walls within larger yurts to divide the space. Plain chiy are used to help provide the friction for making felt and are used underneath the felt rugs on the floor of the yurt to help protect them from dirt and damp. The Kyrgyz also embellish the screens with patterns similar to those used on felt rugs by wrapping each reed with dyed wool before placing it in the screen. These embellished chiy are used for yurt doors, often with a piece of heavy felt embroidered with welcoming patterns and stitched to the outside for insulation (Sommer 1996). The use of some kind of reed screen or bundled reeds is common through Uzbekistan and Kazakhstan as well, but the Kyrgyz are particularly known for their intricate embellishment of them.

The use of space within the yurt is similar between cultures. Traditionally, the elders of the family or the guests sit opposite the door, in the warmest (or coolest) place. To the left inside the door is the men's area, where saddlery and hunting equipment is kept. To the right, the women and children keep their goods and equipment for cooking, weaving and feltmaking. In a traditional Mongolian ger, the interior carpets are laid out according to their symbolic associations with shamanism and the zodiac. Since the door should always face south, time can be kept by marking where the light falls within the ger, and the felt rug, which is made to carpet the back part of the ger, is sometimes embellished specifically to aid this purpose, by incorporating time markings into the motif like the numbers on the face of a clock or sundial (Batchuluun 2003, 175–6).

As the nomadic peoples of Central Asia have settled into permanent housing, yurts are no longer as common as they once were. Nonetheless, they remain an important form of housing, particularly among people who still keep flocks of sheep and horses that may travel with them into summer pasture. Even in towns, yurts may be set up in the courtyard of the house to provide a place to have summer meals and gather with guests. Villages of yurts placed next to one another are also found throughout the region, though they are probably more common in Mongolia and southern Siberia, where they may be used year-round or erected for festivals, including those featuring feltmaking. A large yurt festival is held each summer in the town of Kyzyl in Siberia with prizes given for the best yurt. Yurts are particularly important for special events, and the Kyrgyz believe that funerals must be held in the yurt. Despite the advent of new materials to cover the yurt and the increase in settled populations, the yurt and its furnishings remain one of the most iconic images of felt in Central Asia. The yurt has also been exported with some success. People around the world have espoused yurts for their practicality and low impact on the environment. These new yurts are often covered in canvas to withstand different climates, though some have become essentially yurt-shaped homes made of wood. Several yurt hotels can be found in the United States, though perhaps the most surprising yurts I have encountered were along a sparsely inhabited section of the coast of Belize in Central America. These canvas-covered structures were shaped like Mongolian yurts and covered in canvas, complete with vinyl windows sewn into their sides. Yet despite their high mountain desert pedigree, they seemed perfectly at home on stilted wood platforms surrounded by dense tropical jungle and with boats rather than horses tied up alongside of them.

MONGOLIAN FELT

In Mongolia, felt is a way of life. It forms the basis for the traditional style of living, holding everything together: the society figuratively and the yurt quite literally. The Mongolians tie their tradition of feltmaking all the way back through the Hsiung-nu to Pazyryk. Felt has often served as a symbol of wealth and abundance in Mongolia, as seen in its use in the thirteenth-century coronation ceremonies described by Plano Carpini (Olschki 1949, 11–13). Felt would not lose its status as time went on, and during the seventeenth and eighteenth centuries, felt was the preferred currency for the payment of taxes in Mongolia, to be substituted with a horse only in the case of non-payment (Batchuluun 2003, 36). Feltmaking is both the source and the venue for an entire ecology of Mongolian folklore and beliefs. Much of this feltmaking falls into two categories, each with its own customs, techniques and products.

Small-scale feltmaking is carried out year-round by individuals in the home. This type of feltmaking is fairly casual, done as necessity dictates, and is intended to produce the smaller items used in daily life: predominantly bags, hats and boots. These are all lighter in weight, relatively thin and typically of finer quality than the large, sturdy felts that are produced at other times. Hats and boots may be made on wooden molds that help to give them a more rigid shape, while most of this kind of feltmaking is carried out on a small reed screen. These felts depict the artistry of the individuals that make them, such as the religiously based appliqué patterns including Buddhist mandala-based motifs, which reached their height in the nineteenth century but are not often seen now (Batchuluun 2003, 81).

Large-scale feltmaking occurs in the autumn and is a communal event, the basis for celebration as well as an important ritual. Batchuluun separates the actual making of the felt from the felt festival, though both are cause for celebration and cultural expression. Here, the feltmakers join together to make the large, heavy, thick felts that form the walls of the ger and the rugs to carpet them. While the making of felt is a form of material culture itself, it includes a wide range of other folklore forms, from beliefs expressed in blessings and taboos to riddles and storytelling. These festivals, then, encompass a microcosm of Mongolian culture, showing the full range of folklore centered on felt.

By looking at the ecology of feltmaking, we gain a much clearer idea of the importance of felt to the entire culture. According to folklorist William Bascom, folklore serves one or more of four social functions: to entertain, to reinforce social norms, to educate and to control (Bascom 1954). For example, a legend may be told chiefly for entertainment but it also contains models of what is considered good social behavior, such as truthfulness or charity, and teaches listeners about larger cultural, religious or historical beliefs. A proverb, like "there's no use crying over spilled milk," serves as a reminder to the listener to keep perspective and maintain an appropriate response, thus exerting social control. As a special event rich with multiple expressions of culture, Mongolian large-scale feltmaking displays all of these functions through both the oral folklore that surrounds and refers to felt and through the passing on techniques for making this important textile.

The feltmaking events and festivals are hosted by a specific family, though all of the participants will receive felt in the end. The same family may use the same site in a large, open area, ideally near a river, for generations (Batchuluun 2003, 63). The hosting family is responsible for ensuring that the felt is well made, and for providing a feast for the feltmakers who have come to help, though they may employ an *egsii khötlögch* to direct the process (Batchuluun 2003, 99). The egsii khötlögch makes sure that the proper procedures are followed for making a good, sturdy piece of felt, including supervising its technical construction and maintaining appropriate behavior. The felt is laid out, in the manner described in chapter one, on a large "mother felt." Sometimes two mother felts are laid side by side to achieve the desired size. The host family's proprietary sign is made in the bottom corner of the new felt in dark wool before the rest of the wool is laid so that it will be felted in (Batchuluun 2003, 69). The felt is slowly worked by hand until sturdy and then wrapped into a roll and dragged along behind a horse or camel for the prescribed period.

As a special event, feltmaking entails certain blessings and taboos, and the egsii khötlögch is also in charge of offering many of the blessings. Each stage requires its own blessing, from shearing the sheep:

Khaich n'khurts	May your scissors be sharp
Khagd ungas n'khövsgör bolog	And your dandruff-filled wool fluffy
Khaichilsan süref n'	May the shorn herd
Myanga tüm khüreg	Number ten million

(Batchuluun 2003, 58)

To the final rolling of the felt behind the horses or camels:

Bukhun magnai shig	Become hard
Khatuu bolooroi	Like the head of a bull
Buuryn khüzüü shig	Become stiff
Khöshüün bolooroi	Like the neck of a camel

(Batchuluun 2003, 71)

While these are short blessings, some are quite long, but regardless of length all impart the qualities desired for the felt, such as strength or whiteness. Tea may be sprinkled on the felt as part of the final blessing. Blessings may also be said before using felted objects. Such blessings help to reinforce the sacredness of felt and the occasion for making it.

Feltmaking is seen as a community activity that only succeeds through the collaboration of several makers. To this end, various cultural taboos are in place that stress the importance of working together. The interests of the group must come before those of the individual, so the egsii khötlögch must give leave for feltmakers to take breaks for whatever reason and be notified of the maker's return (Batchuluun 2003, 94). Such a system allows the egsii khötlögch to make certain that each part of the felt is laid out and worked evenly. Working on such large pieces of felt, if one feltmaker has to leave, then either another must take their place or the remaining makers must be aware of the absence and fill in the needed wool or pressure. Many of the other taboos function similarly, to ensure the strength and quality of the felt. Negative comments should not be made about the felt and no arguments should take place during its making, since these may result in a lack of attention being paid to the felt. The wool should not be touched once laid out except to felt it, and the horse or camel drawing the felt should not be startled, since both of these acts could result in uneven or thin areas (Batchuluun 2003, 94). Dogs and drunk people are prohibited from the site as they may disrupt the process. Since feltmaking is of such importance to the culture and lifestyle of Mongolian nomadic peoples, the felt must be treated with respect. Some of the taboos are less obvious in their function. Buddhist lamas are not welcome at feltmaking, possibly since they could be offended by the crushing of insects and plants under the rolling felt, although shamans are encouraged to participate. As mentioned earlier, whistling is also forbidden, since it may call the wind (Batchuluun 2003, 95).

Once the felt has been made, the family offers tea and food to the feltmakers as part of the *egsiin ötög* or felt celebration. In making felt, tea is important both for blessing the felt and the feltmakers. Tea made with ghee or butter is offered to the feltmakers as they lay out the felt, and also when they are finished (Batchuluun 2003, 98). This tea accompanies the final blessings said over the felt and the feltmakers and serves as a way for the family who hosted the feltmaking to thank the egsii khötlögch and the makers who helped them. A piece of the new felt or a particularly good piece of older felt must be given to the egsii khötlögch. If no good felt is available, then a sheep is an acceptable substitute. The other makers receive smaller gifts and trimmings from the new felt. A sheep is slaughtered and cooked to serve the feltmakers after their day of work (Batchuluun 2003, 99).

While the large-scale feltmaking described above is one place for celebrating felt, the *egsiin khutaar* shows the full ecology of the folklore of felt and feltmaking. *Egsiin khutaar*, the autumn felt festivals, are highly ritualized and usually take place in the last month of summer or the first month of autumn, around August or September. The egsiin khutaar is both a serious event and a place for much relaxation and enjoyment. After the herds are brought in for the night, the guests will assemble at the home of the hosts. A large feast is laid out and tea is shared among all the guests. Once everyone has eaten, the hosts and elders make speeches, which are reciprocated by the guests. Such speech-making, akin to a series of toasts, is an integral part of host–guest relations in much of Central Asian culture. After the dictates of etiquette have been fulfilled, then the festival can begin in earnest, and everyone is encouraged to participate in singing, dancing and recitations of poetry.

A favorite component may be a competition of riddles, in which typically the people seated in the western half of the ger challenge the eastern half with riddles until they cannot come up with an answer, and the eastern half offers riddles for the western half. Many of the riddles are centered on elements of the feltmaking, such as drawing the rolled felt behind the horse:

> *Zuum khoniny guidel*   The running of one hundred sheep
> *Zurgaan moriny joroo*   The ambling of six horses
>
> (Batchuluun 2003, 74)

The ger itself appears in some:

> *Narand n'gurvaljin*   A triangle under the sun
> *Sarand n'dörvöljin*   A square under the moon
>
> (Batchuluun 2003, 74)

This riddle refers to the örkh – the large square flap that covers the hole in the top of the ger, which is folded back during the day for smoke to escape but is always closed at night. A more difficult riddle makes an analogy between an old practice of sending a piece of wrapped silver to China in exchange for goods that would be sent back, like early mail order, and the way that felt is drawn in a roll behind the horse.

> *Tsalin tsagaan möngöö*   The pure white silver
> *Tsaasand boogood*   Is wrapped in paper
> *Dotor orond yavuulsan*   And sent to China.
> *Ter yuu bolj irekhiig*   No one knows what it will be
> *Medekhgüi*   When it returns.
>
> (Batchuluun 2003, 74)

The white in the first line also refers to the white felt. The extent of these riddles shows the great inventiveness and creativity given to describing fairly ordinary things in new ways. Illustrating both the popularity of riddling and the importance of sheep and felt in Mongolian life, Batchuluun comments on a woman he interviewed in 1987 who, at the age of ninety-three, knew more than one thousand riddles, including seventy about sheep (Batchuluun 2003, 102–3).

Late in the evening, after the light has gone, the chores are done and everyone has had their fill of songs, dances and riddles, the *ülgeriin khutaar* may begin. This, the sacred night, is the time for telling epics and legends (Batchuluun 2003, 103). These form an important part of the oral traditions of many Mongolian peoples and help to pass down their history and beliefs to younger generations. Some believe that if an epic is particularly well told, it will bring the rain. As Batchuluun points out, the legends and epics, like the riddles, proverbs and other forms of folklore, serve not only to entertain the listeners but also to educate them in the social norms and expectations of the group, fulfilling some of the important functions that folklore performs in all cultures (2003, 104; Bascom 1954). Felt's centrality to Mongolians can be seen in this celebration, which incorporates multiple cultural expressions from the felt itself to riddles to epics.

It is unsurprising that felt is so much a part of Mongolian life when so many everyday objects are made of felt. Not only does felt create the walls and carpets for the ger, and hats and boots for its inhabitants, it is also used for cushions, mattresses, padding for saddles and packs for camels and horses, and bags for almost every conceivable use. Perhaps the most well-known of the Mongolian felts besides the ger are the *shirdeg* and *olbog* – the embroidered rugs and cushions. The shirdeg rugs are constructed of two layers of felt that are basted together and then embroidered using running stitches, backed with cotton and trimmed with blue or brown woven fabric. The resulting rug somewhat resembles American whole-cloth quilts, whose pattern is primarily formed by the quilting.

The patterns typically consist of a large central motif, the *ör*; a wide border called the *emjeer khövöö*; and geometric corner motifs, the *öntsög bulan*; although these terms vary somewhat by ethnic group (Batchuluun 2003, 107). Once the felt has been made and the thread spun, the pattern will be outlined in ochre on the felt. The designs are derived from circles and series of interlocking motifs based on circle axes. Straight lines are obtained "using a string which has been threaded through a leather pouch made from the intact skin from the lower part of a sheep's leg" (Batchuluun 2003, 110). First the horizontal axes are marked, followed by the vertical and diagonal axes. Then the external outlines of the larger motifs – what Batchuluun refers to as modules – are inscribed, containing the smaller motifs. Finally, the smaller lines of the motifs themselves are drawn in, with any extraneous lines erased by simply rubbing the felt, and the felt is ready to be embroidered (Batchuluun 2003, 110–11). All of the stitching is done in a tight running stitch or a back stitch.

The motifs embroidered into Mongolian felt rugs are generally symbolic rather than strictly representational; in other words, they are focused on the cultural significance of the signs rather than trying to depict a scene or show the image of a specific animal. These symbolic meanings tend to be related to spiritual functions, similar to the way in which a Roman cross is symbolic of Christianity. In Mongolia, the symbols' meanings center on the desired qualities of life: longevity, happiness, family and abundance (Batchuluun 2003, 145). For example, the wavelike motif found in embroidered felts and pieced felt rugs represents both the water and the skyline of the mountains, and symbolizes prosperity by encompassing the worldview of the Mongolian peoples. The *ölzii* or knot motif, shown by interlocking squares, is connected to happiness. Many of the geometric motifs found in modern felts are abstracted from earlier animal motifs, such as the wolf, deer, bat and sheep's horn. The repetition of the motifs into the interlocking patterns described above symbolizes the unending life of multiple generations and the movement through life typical of nomads. Certain motifs, especially those with religious or political significance, can only be used by or for particular people. The *khas* or swastika cannot be used on anything that will be underfoot, since this symbol, which dates at least to the fourth century BCE, represents the sun and harmony with the natural world (Batchuluun 2004, 112 and 148). Needless to say, many more motifs exist and many are shared between groups throughout Central Asia, though at times with different meanings or in different configurations. Mongolia has perfected its felt to a fine and beautiful art over the centuries, and it remains one of the most well-known felt cultures, yet felt is a common link between many of the Central Asian peoples, and so we will now travel to the west across the lands of felt.

KYRGYZ AND KAZAKH FELT

The culture of Mongolia is closely related to those of the Kyrgyz and Kazakhs and their uses of felt are likewise similar. For decades, if not centuries, the Russians considered the Kyrgyz and Kazakhs to be a single ethnic group separated by dialects of the same language. Later, they were recognized as different cultures that had much in common. Kazakh people roughly inhabit modern Kazakhstan, though groups of Kazakhs exist throughout Central Asia; they are one of the largest ethnic groups of far western Mongolia. The Kyrgyz, while smaller in numbers and territory, are similarly spread, though they dominate the modern Kyrgyz Republic. The two groups are further divided into distinct tribes and family groups, but their feltmaking traditions are held in common.

Since making felt is relatively simple, reliant on friction, heat and moisture applied to wool, the method for making it by hand does not vary tremendously between different ethnic groups, especially those who have shared borders, pastures and trade for centuries. The biggest difference between Kyrgyz and Kazakh feltmaking and Mongolian feltmaking is how the large pieces of rolled felt are turned. The first few steps of making felt remain the same: the wool is carded to loosen the fibers and laid down in a thick batt on top of a reed screen. Usually a bow is used for carding, although more and more often, mechanized carders might be employed to speed up this part of the process. As mentioned above, the Kyrgyz are famous for the reed screens, and these are used to provide the necessary friction for felt.

Once the batt has been sprinkled with water and partially felted, it is rolled tightly in canvas or hide and bound, just as in Mongolia. Rather than hooking the roll up to a horse or camel, however, a large loop of rope is placed around the center of the roll. One person holds the other end of the rope and uses it to guide the roll slowly backwards. A group of people stands shoulder to shoulder facing this leader. As the leader moves back, the group stomps down hard on the rolled felt with one foot. The roll is drawn again and stomped again, this time with the opposite foot. The group must move and stomp together to make the felt strong and even, and so sometimes songs are used to help maintain a good rhythm. A leader may or may not be used to guide the felt. Traditionally, this style of feltmaking may be carried out in any large, flat area. Today, with many Kyrgyz living in permanent houses, it is typically done in the large courtyard near the front of the house. For a large felt rug, like an *ala-kiyiz,* the roll must be pulled and stomped for about forty-five minutes. Once it is hard enough, it is unrolled and rerolled, but this time without the reed screen. The felt must still be hot, since the heat is needed to help full and shrink the felt, and more hot, soapy water can be added if need be. The second rolling is done on top of the reed screen. The women kneel in a line and roll the felt out under their forearms, again pounding it with each roll, until it is the desired strength. To rinse the felt, it is unrolled and folded in thirds lengthwise and clean water is pushed through it using the same rolling method with the arms, then unfolded and refolded again in thirds from the top down, and finally again from the bottom up, rolling and rinsing each time.

The types of felt objects made by the Kyrgyz and Kazakh are similar to those made by the Mongolians: hats, boots, bags of all kinds, horse and camel blankets, and furnishings for the yurts (or bozu, to the Kyrgyz). The Kyrgyz are known for their tall felt hats, called kalpak. These hats are made of two or four wedge-shaped panels of felt, sewn together to form a tall, pyramidal shape, with a flattened top. The seams are covered with velvet or cord and the panels are embellished with embroidery, typically in black or red. This embroidery is very different from that used on the Mongolian felt rugs. Not only is it done in color to show up brightly against the white of the felt, but it also typically uses individual, curling horn or tree motifs, so that a single motif is centered in each panel. The lower part of at least one seam is left unstitched for a couple of inches to allow the bottom of the kalpak to be turned up to form a sort of brim.

Felt rugs fall into two categories among the Kyrgyz and Kazakh: shyrdak and ala-kiyiz. Both are large and thick, but the way in which they are embellished is very different. Neither can be made alone, since both require large pieces of felt and intensive work. For this reason, the women may organize feltmaking celebrations and competitions called *kiyiz ashar*, much as in Mongolia. Shyrdak are considered one of the pinnacles of felt art because of their bold colors, large patterns and visual impact. The shyrdak generally consists of a large central area that may be divided into segments, like the Mongolian embroidered rugs, surrounded by a narrow border and then a larger border. Another narrow border may be used on the outer edge, or segments within the large central area may be marked off with a similar narrow border. The central area and large outer border are typically made using the same two colors, while the narrow borders may employ one or two other colors. The Kyrgyz also make a kind of patchwork out of felt squares, but I have only seen it a few times.

Shyrdak require two large pieces of thick felt in contrasting colors for each area. A pattern is marked onto the felt using chalk. Like Mongolian embroidery, the patterns generally consist of motifs that are mirrored and repeated along horizontal and vertical axes, so first the axes are determined and the motif is drawn freehand onto one segment of the felt. The felt is then folded along the axes and pounded to transfer the chalk outline from one segment to the next to provide an exact mirror image. For long border motifs, the same procedure is used, only along a vertical axis that can then be repeated as many times as necessary. Only the master feltmakers draw the designs, while everyone may be involved in making the felt and sewing it together.

Once marked, the two pieces of felt are then laid on top of one another, basted in place and cut along the drawn pattern lines at the same time. By tradition, the cutting always begins in the center of the felt rather than at an edge. The pieces are taken apart, and the areas removed from one color are replaced with the matching piece from the other to form two whole rugs with identical patterns but in contrasting colors. The Kyrgyz are known for their use of bright colors and contrasts in large designs, while the Kazakh tend to prefer more muted colors and smaller designs (Bunn 2004). The pattern should show equal amounts of each color on each rug. These pieces are then stitched together using a back stitch and the seams are covered by stitching tight cording along them. The whole shyrdak is then stitched to a large piece of felt for backing to protect the seams and cover the stitches. The back may also be covered in woven cloth. Finally, the edges are bound with cording. This technique is employed not only for large rugs and the band that is used around the top of the lattice inside the yurt, but also for cushions and some bags.

While the shyrdak requires intense cutting and sewing, the ala-kiyiz acquires its design through the felting process. A Kyrgyz proverb states that while an ala-kiyiz has only half the lifespan of a shyrdak, it also requires half as much work (Maksimov et al. 1986). A shyrdak is expected to last around 30–40 years; an ala-kiyiz, 15–20 years. The name ala-kiyiz translates as "striped felt," and it is made by laying down three layers of wool, typically white for the background. Approximately 5 kilograms of wool is needed for 4 square meters. When half the felt has been laid, the water for felting is put on to boil, to be ready for when the batt is fully prepared. The design is made by laying out yarn in the desired pattern on the white batt. The area within the yarn is filled in with loose, dyed wool. Once the pattern is laid down, the yarn is removed and the whole batt is gently felted until it is strong enough to be rolled, first in the reed screen and then with the forearms.

The patterns and colors are determined by regional tradition and the artistry of the maker. Certain areas tend to be associated with particular colors. As noted above, the Kazakh felts tend to have more subdued colors, while the Kyrgyz felts are brighter, but even within these groups, there are differences (Bunn 2004). The felts made around the city of Naryn in central Kyrgyzstan typically use red, yellow and green, while those from the northern Issyk-Kul area feature red and blue. Traditionally, natural dyes were used to color the felt, and some makers still use indigo for blue, walnut husks for browns and greens, madder for reds and marigolds for yellows; however, the practice is quickly fading. Most feltmakers now buy chemical dyes imported from Russia since these provide a wider selection of colors and, many feel, deeper and more vibrant tones. Still, several feltmakers I met insisted on putting *ermen,* or chamomile, in their dye baths to help deter moths from eating the felt. Though dyes have changed, patterns have shown more stability. The wave-like motif found in Mongolian border designs is also commonly found in Kyrgyz and Kazakh shyrdak as a narrow band between the center and the border, again symbolizing the mountains and the water. In northern Kyrgyzstan, around the large lake Issyk-Kul, this motif is said to be the image of the mountains and their reflection in the lake.

The patterns found within shyrdak include more than 3,000 symbols, divided into six groups: people, animals, flowers, sky, household and natural landscapes. These patterns permeate throughout Kyrgyz and Kazakh art. Some of the most common symbols in the large borders include the dog's tail (*im kuirup*), symbolizing friendship, and the ram's horn (*kochkor muich*), for general good wishes and wealth. The large central motifs may include the warrior (*zhooker*), mother and child (*umai*), the tree of life or the tulip. Flowers are often related to spring and fertility, and the type of flower may be determined by a combination of shape and color. White flowers are typically associated with crocuses and early spring, red flowers with tulips and yellow with poppies. White, star-like shapes may be daisies or dandelions, although these are more common in embroidery on Uzbek felts (Harvey 1996, 44).

Each motif may carry more than one meaning, such as the flying bird or *zhagalmai kanat*, which can denote dreams and fantasy as well as great hopes (for a newly married couple for example), or can relate to shamanism. Diadiuchenko states that this image is an eagle or falcon and relates to hunting, representing Akshumkar, the eagle of the great epic hero, Manas. Meanings may be dependent on local culture, however, since Diadiuchenko connects the eagle with Manas on one hand and women and the household on the other, while Janet Harvey suggests that the eagle represents power but also the more typical relationship to dreams and shamanism (Maksimov et al. 1986; Harvey 1996, 43). While each motif is symbolic in itself, the combination of motifs on a single felt rug can be read together: mountains, hearts and flying birds together can be read as a wish on the part of the maker for a good life and a love of life for the recipient. While some of these symbols are more common in shyrdak, others are more typical of ala-kiyiz, particularly those employing fine lines that are difficult to execute in patchwork, such as the swan and the kerege, the lattice that forms the side of the yurt.

UZBEK AND TURKMEN FELT

Felt is not as central to life in the western half of Central Asia as it is among the Kyrgyz, Kazakh and Mongolians, but it is still an important part of life, particularly among the nomadic groups. Many of the nomadic groups in Uzbekistan and Turkmenistan settled during the early part of the twentieth century, and with settlement, the need for felt decreased. The years following settlement also saw an increase in the use of automobiles and their gradual replacement of horses and camels for much travel, which further reduced the role of felt, since two of the three main uses of felt in the west were for saddle bags and harnesses and in horse and camel blankets. The third use was for large, geometric rugs, but these were never valued as highly as the knotted pile carpets for which Central Asia is famous. Feltmaking is still carried out throughout the region, though now it tends to be restricted to utilitarian purposes, as part of women's dowries and, in places, for the tourist market.

In Uzbekistan, most of the felt is made around Samarkand. The felts are made in a similar manner to the Kazakh and Kyrgyz: rolling the felt in a reed screen and then with the forearms. Most embellishment is done after the felt has been made, by heavily embroidering the surface, often with cording. The majority of the Uzbek felts that I have seen have been horse blankets made of sturdy, thick felt – either in white or, less commonly, black. Two types of horse blanket are made, just as at Pazyryk: one for over the saddle and one for under it. The former has two or more large slits in the main part of the body for the stirrup straps and girth to hold both saddle and pads in place. Another slit is left for the saddle horn. These slits are reinforced with embroidery. The blankets for under the saddle may be either minimally embellished or else heavily embroidered, in which case they may also serve for a blanket to be used before and after racing the horse. The blankets are constructed of a single large piece of sturdy felt, and the back part is curved and shaped by seaming so that it bends over the back of the horse. The embroidery is often in red and blue and overlapped in a kind of herringbone stitch so that thick lines are formed. The motifs tended to be less complex than those found among the eastern peoples. Spirals and ram's horns are common, as are tree of life motifs, tulips and pomegranates (Burkett 1979, 24–30).

Throughout Uzbekistan and Turkmenistan, a good horse is kept covered at all times with a thick felt blanket that reaches from the neck, sometimes the ears, to cover the tail. These horse blankets help to keep the horses warm in the winter and protected from the sun and insects in the summer. The Turkmen believe that this system helps the horse to stay lean and allows him to run faster (Kalter 1997, 174). Often several of these blankets will be used simultaneously, piled on top of the horse. The saddle, made of hard wood with a high horn and metal stirrups, is placed on top of these blankets. A pillow-like pad made of leather with a felt lining may be placed on top of the saddle. Above any supplemental padding for the rider is another large felt blanket that covers the saddle and most of the horse. Typically, this felt piece is highly embellished. Finally, a woven silk or cotton or knotted pile blanket may be used as a top layer over the felt (Kalter 1997, 174; Mazzawi 2002).

Felt is used on camels, too. Occasionally, felt may be used for the large pentagonal pair of *asmalyk*, used to drape across the flanks of the lead camel in the wedding procession (Pinner 1998, 106), although knotted pile is more typical. These large, pentagonal felts are made of a single piece that is then embroidered or decorated with appliqué, and the three lower edges are embellished with fringe. Asmalyk are the most common felt animal trapping found among collectors in the West, although they rarely appear in scholarly works or museum collections and are unusual in much of Central Asia itself. Asmalyk are most common among the Turkmen, though they are found attributed to nearly every other people except the Uzbek. Unlike most felt embroidery, which is symbolic, they tend to feature pictorial and representational images, sometimes with motifs resembling those typically found on Central Asian carpets. While horses and camels are not in such great use as they once were, the felt used in their trappings has found new purposes outfitting the cars, trucks and bicycles that have replaced them. One collector said that most of the felt he encountered in Uzbekistan in the last several years was on car seats and lining truck beds for added comfort and padding, though some of his Uzbek friends were shocked that he would want anything so mundane when he asked about buying an embroidered felt to take back to the United States as a souvenir (Scott 2002).

Felt carpets are made throughout Central Asia, although again these are considered more utilitarian in the western regions. The Yomut, who inhabit Turkmenistan and western Uzbekistan and into southwestern Kazakhstan, are known for making felt carpets, similar to ala-kiyiz, that have patterns felted in to both sides. Among the Turkmen, felts for use on the floor nearly always use a felted-in design, while embroidery is reserved for wall-hangings and bags. Composite patterns are more common among the Turkmen, employing a few motifs repeated several times, and typically with a more limited number of colors (Bunn 2004). Perhaps oddly, considering their proximity to the Kyrgyz, Kazakhs and Mongolians, the Uyghur – of the Xinjiang region of northwestern China – make felt rugs similar to those of the Turkmen. While the Georgians, on the western side of not only the Turkmen but also the Caspian Sea, are known for beautiful felt rugs closer to those found in the east, though often with different motifs.

MODERN FELT

Henry Glassie, the folklorist and material culture scholar, offers an open-ended description of tradition as "the creation of the future out of the past" (Glassie 1995, 395). In other words, tradition is no longer a static thing, copied exactly from one generation to the next, often losing meaning along the way; instead, traditions are continuous, bridging generations and time. Traditions succeed at this not by remaining replicas of the past but by taking elements from the past and making them relevant in the present. In the West, we tend to see the traditional as the opposite to the modern, but this dualistic view does not exist in many other cultures and fails to hold up under close scrutiny in our own. After all, we blithely celebrate family holidays by watching football games on flat, widescreen televisions and cook our great-grandmother's favorite recipe using an electric food processor and the latest in kitchen technology. Glassie explains that we are able to carry on traditions in meaningful ways by choosing what aspects of objects we see as traditional. He suggests several options: what is traditional about an object may be the patterns and motifs it contains, the way in which it was made, the way in which the maker learned from other makers of similar objects, the way it is used, or any combination of the above (Glassie 1995, 395–412). Therefore, what is traditional about the holidays is not that we watch television but rather that we gather as a family; the recipe and the food are traditional even if the way we cook it is not. By looking at tradition this way, we can see the new feltworks made by artists in Central Asia and elsewhere as both traditional and innovative. These artists are using felt to celebrate their culture and their cultural traditions, but they are doing so not only by producing yurts and yurt furnishings but also by making intricate, gossamer scarves and beautifully designed wall hangings.

In Kyrgyzstan, the tradition of feltmaking is being turned to new purposes. The shyrdak that women have made for centuries, with their distinct designs, had begun to die out with settlement under the Soviet government. Since the economic upheavals of independence, some women have returned to making shyrdak as part of women's networks aimed at helping to promote economic development. Groups such as Aid to Artisans in conjunction with the Central Asian Craft Support Association have helped to foster these networks and guided them to market their work not only in Central Asia but across the world. The Altyn Oimok (Golden Thimble) group draws on the work of about thirty-five women around the town of Bokonbaeovo in northern Kyrgyzstan. Working mostly out of a building bought with grant money, they make shyrdak as well as slippers and small felt figures of people. Janyl Bayisheva, one of the group's founders, hopes eventually to establish a school to teach traditional felt-making techniques as well as design. Bayisheva herself is an artist and has shown her contemporary work in felt. Another, much larger, network – Altyn Kol – is centered in the town of Kochkor in the mountains. Altyn Kol has around 300 members and another 500 women who bring their work in periodically for sale in a shop in the town. This group has recently begun its own workshop and runs a variety of programs to help women with financial management and planning.

All of these women's networks use traditional ways of making the rugs that have been such an important part of their culture. Yet the women are now being taught outside of their families, and while the work is very much for their own livelihood, they are not using the shyrdak they make themselves. Instead, they are marketing them in new ways and often to people for whom the shyrdak is not at all traditional. Interestingly, I heard from several younger Kyrgyz people that, although they did not make or want to make shyrdak themselves, they did want, one day, to decorate their homes with them to show their connection to Kyrgyz culture. For some buyers, these traditions may be even more remote. The work of one woman, Janyl Alibekova, was featured in the European edition of the fashion magazine *Elle* and was the subject of the short documentary on her work, *Red Butterflies Where Two Springs Meet* (Sydykova 2002). Her work is particularly impressive – not only does she work with other women in her area to produce traditional style shyrdak for sale, but she has also adapted the technique to make pictorial shyrdak.

Many artists in Central Asia have chosen to work in felt, connecting their personal expression with the traditions of their culture. As early as the 1970s, Central Asian artists had begun producing abstract designs in felt. After the Soviet states gained independence in 1991, many artists returned to traditional patterns for inspiration. Though the Soviets had discouraged the making of shyrdak and ala-kiyiz, these forms attracted renewed interest once the Soviet era was over. Postcolonial scholars suggest that such a return to elements of traditional culture after a period of political or social upheaval serves to help "[forge] a collective identity" that acknowledges both the people's long history and their present and future (Shohat 1992, 109). Yet while modern artists have drawn on traditional felt patterns and techniques, they have also engaged in experimentation, creating shyrdak with more geometric patterns or colors that fade into one another. I was particularly struck by a hexagonal shyrdak displayed at the Kyrgyz National Museum as part of a special exhibit of felt in 2007. Divided into six triangles, the repeated abstract motif, almost like an elongated traditional dog's tail, radiated out from the center in rich colors.

The young Kyrgyz artist Altynai Osmoeva learned to felt from her family. As the daughter of an artist who was deeply engaged with promoting traditional Central Asian arts, Osmoeva grew up steeped in the traditions of her culture, yet at a time when that culture was undergoing massive changes as a result of the fall of the Soviet Union. Osmoeva's work reflects her engagement with traditions as well as her own reinterpretation of them. Predominantly interested in fashion, Osmoeva designed a series of garments and hats reflecting the Turkic Sufi tradition. These designs paired the structure of felt with the flow and drape of silks and cottons. One tall felt hat, consisting of coiled felt ropes, seemed to challenge our expectations both of hats and the felt itself. These modern Central Asian feltmakers show the vast possibilities of felt, building on a traditional material but using it to join in global discussions about art.

Central Asian feltmakers have developed their traditional craft as they have sought new forms and new markets. Feltmakers have turned to mechanization to card the wool for their traditionally styled shyrdak, others have found new markets and new economic opportunities by expanding into urban and global markets, and some have turned felt to new forms and techniques, keeping only a motif or a particular way of combining colors that seems like a mere echo of tradition. Modern feltmakers may employ any or all of Glassie's definitions of tradition to produce new and exciting works of art. Central Asia is indeed the "land of felt." From the felt yurts and their furnishings to covers and padding for whatever type of transportation is available to the creative designs of contemporary artists, felt has been a way of life in Central Asia presumably for as long as the land has been inhabited. As Central Asia has developed, so has the making of felt. From the mountains and deserts of Central Asia, felt spreads west across the steppes into Iran, the Caucasus, Turkey and into Hungary and eastern Europe. These regions have traditions of felt just as long, but the people live in slightly different climates and they have developed their felt in different, though related, ways.

4.
FELT IN THE MIDDLE EAST, TURKEY AND HUNGARY

In the land between the western edge of China, with the early felts found at Ürümchi, and the plains of Hungary stretches a wide band of felt cultures. Much of this is made by the Turkic peoples who settled this region, forming a series of cultures linked by language and a traditional society based on herding sheep across the plains and mountains. Some of the felt is made by those who had contact with the Turkic peoples through trade or war. All of the felt is made by cultures that adapted similar techniques to survive in climates well suited to shepherding. While it would be impossible to say whether feltmaking emerged from a single group that spread its knowledge or was developed independently by many groups, felt certainly has supported a way of life throughout the region for millennia. Yet each group of people, from the Mongolians in the east to the Hungarians in the west, have made felt in their own way, suiting the material to their own environment and uses.

On modern maps, we divide Europe from Asia at the Black Sea. Politically, we divide the Middle East, from Iran to the Mediterranean Sea, from Turkey, which

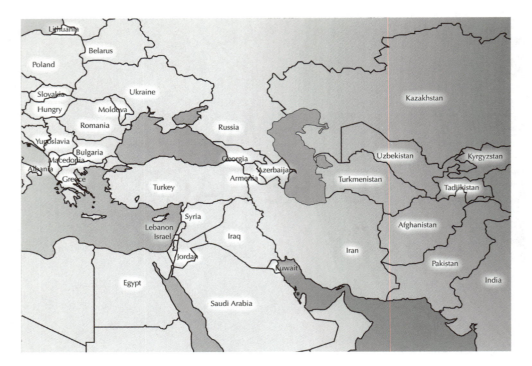

5 Map of the Middle East and Eastern Europe.

is again divided from eastern Europe. For felt, it makes more sense to look at the region between the Caspian Sea and the plains of Hungary together.

In Central Asia, felt remains important as part of everyday life, especially in rural areas; in western Europe, felt has been part of specialized manufacture for centuries, transformed by the Industrial Revolution, and limited in its use primarily to hats and boots. In some parts of the Middle East, the tradition of making felt is closer to that of Central Asia. In Iran and parts of Iraq, felt is made in much the same way as in Kyrgyzstan, though yurts are virtually unknown. In eastern Europe, felt never had many uses and has largely been replaced by other textiles. Between these geographic extremes, however, felt is being made, predominantly in Turkey, the Caucasus and in the plains of Hungary. In these regions, felt remains an important part of traditional culture and continues to be made traditionally. While felt may not be the very fabric of life as in Central Asia, neither is it the industrial product of the west. This chapter focuses on the history and specific traditions of the areas in-between – the felt of the Middle East, the Caucasus, Turkey and Hungary.

EARLY FELT – FROM ARCHAEOLOGY TO THE OTTOMAN EMPIRE

Despite the many archaeological sites throughout the Middle East, little evidence of felt has survived, since like most textiles, it deteriorates more easily than stone and pottery. Nonetheless, felt certainly was used. As discussed in the second chapter, the oldest evidence of felt comes from the Çatal Hüyük excavations, about 100 miles south of the modern city of Konya in central Turkey. Here, patterns were found on painted walls from around 6500 BCE that looked remarkably similar to those found on later felt rugs. Part of what makes this find so striking is not only its early date but also that modern Konya remains a felt producing center today, providing a seemingly uninterrupted tradition of feltmaking for 8,500 years.

The medieval period offers little further evidence. Two fragments of felt were found at Jazirat Fara'un, Coral Island, near Eilat on the Red Sea coast. The site was excavated between 1975 and 1981 and dated to the Early Mamluk period, around the twelfth or thirteenth centuries CE. The fragments both consisted of two layers with the upper layer dyed red, making them similar to other fragments found at Fustat in Egypt from the same period. One fragment had a remnant of leather sewn to it, which might indicate that it was part of a saddle. The Silk Road was flourishing at the same period that this site was inhabited and functioning as a trading center. Felt saddle blankets, padding and cloaks were a major commodity in this exchange, and would have been readily available and well known in the town. Unfortunately, we do not have evidence concerning whether the felt was being made locally all along the route or transported as a specialty produced from one region or another. The latter seems more likely, since felt is known to have been made not only in Mongolia and among the Central Asian peoples during this time but was also produced in what is now modern Iran. Shamir and Baginsky, who reported on the Jazirat Fara'un find, believe felt to have been "among the most commonly traded goods coming from North Africa and the East" (Shamir and Baginsky 2002, 146). It may well depend on the quality and purpose of the felt. Felt was known in the surrounding areas as well during the Crusades, when it provided much-needed padding for armor. While we know that felt has been used throughout this area, as in much of the world, felt's role as a largely utilitarian textile has meant that its history has gone largely unrecorded. Scholars of this region have tended to focus almost exclusively on the eye-catching woven and knotted carpets. We can only hope for more information from sites like Jazirat Fara'un.

The history of felt in Turkey and Hungary is a little clearer thanks to the records of the Ottoman Empire and the work of textile historian Veronika Gervers. The Turkish Ottoman Empire expanded during the fifteenth and sixteenth centuries. In 1526, the Turks defeated the previously prosperous Hungarians in the battle of Mohács, and fifteen years later they took the city of Buda, transforming the plains and Transylvanian mountains of Hungary into the western edge of the Ottoman Empire. The Turks, having come centuries before out of the steppes of Turkestan, brought with them their production of felt. The Hungarians likely produced felt of their own already, but through the Ottoman trading system, felt from across the Empire became available. Felted rugs from Turkey, called *keçe*, were especially popular in the sixteenth century. The rugs were used as either wall hangings or bed covers and could be made with both sheep's wool and camel hair. By the late sixteenth century, keçe begin to appear in inventories of houses as well as lists of purchases made from Turkish towns. One buyer notes a "colorful Italian keçe rug" acquired in Istanbul. Gervers comments that "Italian" refers not to where the rug was made, but rather to the style of the design used to embellish it (Gervers 1982, 30). An inventory from 1629, made in the Hungarian town of Szentdemeter (possibly modern Demeterpuszta near the northeastern border), lists a keçe as the only decoration on the dining room walls (Gervers 1982, 24).

This trade in keçe was large enough for regulations to be put in place by the Ottoman government. The postscript of a letter from Balthasar Sebesi to Prince George Rékószi describes both the fashion for these felted rugs and the limitations placed upon their trade:

> We bought ten colorful *keçes*; ... they are nice and of good quality and as for their size, they are a bit longer and wider ... [than those you ordered]. The ten *keçes* were measured at the Embassy of Transylvania, and were found to be 496 cubits long all together, the price of which, according to the Limitation..., comes to 402 thalers and 15 aspers. [The Limitation] specifies 65 aspers per cubit. This sort of *keçe* from Zelenek is generally highly valued... Had we bought different *keçes*, as those from Edirne, they would have been four cubits wide. Those are different and definitely of lesser quality. In any case, Your Excellency did not specify the kind of *keçe* to be bought, but said that they should be in various colours. We judged that these are better and nicer [than those made elsewhere], though according to their size, their price is rather high. (Qtd. in Gervers 1982, 30–1; brackets added by Gervers)

Written on August 6, 1641, this letter shows a ready market for these felt rugs as well as a state-regulated price on felt. Moreover, felt rug experts of the period are clearly setting standards and certain towns are known to produce better felt than others. Unfortunately, the letter does not tell us what those standards are, but the Edirne rugs seem to be not only of lesser quality but of a different type, either by size or pattern or both, than the ones that were purchased in Zelenek. Edirne still exists as a city in modern Turkey on the borders of Bulgaria and Greece, though Zelenek seems to have disappeared from current maps. Sadly, Edirne is no longer the felt center it may once have been, as much of the Turkish felt production has moved to the Anatolian plateau.

Other felted items were also popular in Hungary during this time. Tents, which were produced and sold by the Turks throughout the Ottoman Empire, were as likely to have been made of felt as woven cloth (Gervers 1982, 8). The Ottomans also made a kind of mantle called a *köpönyeg*, out of felted camel hair that was then covered in broadcloth (a woven fabric, usually mid-weight and made of cotton in plain or twill weave). These mantles were specifically associated with the Sublime Porte, the Ottoman government, although their name derives from the Turkish *kepenek*, the felt mantle worn by shepherds and discussed below. Felted Turkish hats also became a vogue for the Hungarian nobility (Gervers 1982, 15). Although Ottoman power began to wane as early as the seventeenth century, the influence of Turkish culture on feltmaking throughout the former empire lasted until fairly recently, when feltmaking itself began to disappear.

The situation was much the same in the Persian Empire to the south. Felt rugs and horse blankets were widely produced during the Safavid and Qajar periods, extending from around the eleventh century up to 1925. Paintings from these periods depict felt being used particularly in outdoor settings (Diba 1998). During the earlier Safavid period, special felts called *takya namad* were produced for sitting and reclining. They were often depicted in paintings folded into quarters and are recognizable by their pattern and shape. These *namad*, also called *nemet,* or *namda* (more typical in India), appear to have been typically rectangular, made of reddish-brown wool, and often intricately embellished with inlaid designs inside a wide, plain outer border (Thompson 2003, 308). Truly good ones could cost as much as knotted carpet. The best were made from lamb's wool or from *kork*, which at the time referred to the inner coat of fine mountain goats, of a breed related to pashmina. When discovered by Europeans in the 1650s, this wool became a popular material for hatmaking and a source of rivalry between the Dutch and British East India Companies (Thompson 2003, 309).

Larger rugs were also made of felt and could be custom-ordered for specific patterns or sizes, often becoming quite large and consisting of several pieces that were then laid out together. The largest reported namad was 36.6 × 24.4 meters (120 × 80 feet) and had to be carried on fourteen mules. A more typical size was 18.3 × 12.2 meters (60 × 40 feet), requiring only seven mules. Transportation was necessarily a large portion of the cost for such felt rugs, which greatly restricted their export. The feltmakers around Hamadan in northwestern Iran, and Yazd and Kerman in the central part of the country, were especially famous, though felt was made more locally as well (Floor 2003). Such rugs were known to have been used in the Ardabil Shrine in northwest Iran. One of these felts survives in England, at the Ashmolean Museum. The piece shows the characteristic wide, plain outer border surrounding an intricate floral pattern covering the center field and measures an impressive 350 × 177 centimeters (11 feet 8 inches × 5 feet 11 inches).

Feltmaking may have begun its decline but did not stop with Pahlavi's succession to the throne in 1925. The documentary *Grass* (Cooper and Schoedsack 1925) depicts the migration of one of the Bakhtiari tribes across central Iran in 1925. Studying the scenes of the people on the move with their herds, it is possible to spot felt saddle pads and pack covers and at least one felt mantle thrown over the shoulders of one of the men. Felt was still in use twenty years after the film was made. A family friend, Tedford Lewis, came across a woman kneeling on a felt rug while washing her laundry when he was hiking in the area north of Tehran in 1947 (Lewis 2004). He bought the rug from her and later gave it to me, though it had not weathered the years well. The small rug is approximately three feet by five feet. The base felt is natural black wool, and it is embellished with a felted-in design using both thin, partially felted wool and loose wool in white and red. The rug has three borders of white felted wool, each of which is cut in a zigzag pattern on the outer edge and straight on the inner edge. The inner edge is further marked by a thin line of red wool. Inside these three frames, another band of the white felt forms a symmetrical design, this time with the zigzagged edge facing the interior of the rug. The area both surrounding and inside of this fourth border is covered with small white circles, which have a small red spot in their centers. In the very middle of the rug lies another oval of white felt, again with the zigzagged edge facing the interior. In this final border sits a lozenge of red and white, divided into quadrants. The lozenge is not dissimilar from the *gol* patterns found on Persian carpets, showing the aesthetic connection between the two forms. Iranian scholar Willem Floor predicted that, with the increased use of chairs, felt rugs would cease to be used, since they do not survive well under chair legs (Floor 2003). To some extent, his predictions have been fulfilled, but felt continues to be made in Iran as it is in Turkey.

TRADITIONAL FELT

The traditional techniques for making felt are still used by many in the plateaus that stretch from Central Asia to the Mediterranean. Passed down for generations, often within the same family, these methods produce the traditional felted objects that have made the lives of shepherds and townspeople more comfortable for centuries. As in Central Asia, feltmaking is sadly in decline, giving way to synthetic fabrics and store-bought materials. For some things, like the ceremonial hats worn by the dervishes, felt simply cannot be replaced; for some, like the mysterious felt houses of Turkey that will be discussed later in this chapter, felt has been gone for decades. Though diminished, the tradition of feltmaking is still to be found in towns and villages and homes, and felt still plays an important role in the culture and cultural history of the peoples of this region.

TRADITIONAL FELTMAKING

As we have seen, feltmaking follows much the same process everywhere – the matting together of wool fibers through heat, damp and friction to form a single cloth. Yet each feltmaking culture has developed this process in slightly different ways to suit the society and the climate in which they live. In Mongolia, the availability of large, flat stretches of steppe or desert, with little vegetation to get in the way, allowed the people to use their horses and camels – animals they already had in abundance anyway – to pull the heavy roll of dampened wool and provide the necessary friction. In Kyrgyzstan and among many Kazakh people, felt was more easily made by rolling it back and forth and stepping on it. In Central Asia, where the household chores are sharply divided by gender, much felt is made by the women as part of their tasks, though the men may help in the heavy work of stepping on the roll. In Afghanistan, Iran, Turkey and eastern Europe, feltmaking is often considered a skilled craft, and in these cultures, where chores are also sharply divided by gender, making felt is not only in the purview of men but is the work of specially trained artisans. Yet this generalization must be made with great caution, for in an area with so many different cultures, there are certainly women feltmakers, particularly among the various Turkmen tribes (Burkett 1979, 42).

The Turkmen peoples are descended from the Oghuz Turks who came to the regions of northeastern Iran, parts of Afghanistan and what is now Turkmenistan from Mongolia during the tenth century (Burkett 1979, 42). The name Turkmen refers to at least twenty-two different tribes including the Yomud, Salor, Tekke, Atabay and Saryk. Among these peoples, felt is often made by the women in a method closely resembling that of the Kyrgyz and Kazakhs. The wool is laid out on a large mat, dampened and rolled. The tied roll is then pulled back and forth and stepped on to solidify the felt. For the second hardening, the women unroll the felt from the mat and reroll it, kneeling side by side and pushing down with their forearms. Mary Burkett noted that the Atabay Yomud living around Gunbad-i-Qabus were known for making the best felt rugs, but by the time of her visit in the 1970s, the Turkmen believed that feltmaking would be dead within five years. As elsewhere, the women no longer saw the need to go about the difficult business of making felt when they could afford more prestigious knotted carpets (Burkett 1979, 43). Sadly, this prediction appears to have become true, as I did not encounter any recent Turkmen felt, though it seems unlikely that the feltmaking is altogether gone from the region.

Other tribal groups throughout this area also make felt. The nomadic Q'ashq'ai who inhabit areas of Iran and Turkmenistan are known for their feather felting. They cut out patterns from one piece of loosely made felt, feathering the edges and then felting them onto a larger piece of a different color to form the rug. The Baluch people also make rugs but, like the Turkmen, use the method of laying out a pattern and felting the whole rug at once. Their patterns are often very dense and colorful. Patterns in Afghan felt rugs tend to resemble the abstract geometric designs of their knotted rugs. They also make a special kind of felt rug intended to be sat on, with tassels around its edge. Moving south to India, felt has historically been made in Gujarat. Much of this felt is made from wool mixed with cotton and the surface is embroidered with designs. The Kurds in northern Iraq and southeastern Turkey use black wool for the base of their felt and favor birds and flowers in their designs (Bunn 2004).

The feltmakers of Dagestan follow a similar method to the Turkmen. Dagestan lies on the western coast of the Caspian Sea, just to the east of Georgia and north of Azerbaijan and Armenia. Although a republic within Russia, the territory is known for its close cultural and ethnic ties with the tribes of the surrounding Caucasus. While felt is certainly known to be a traditional fabric in these areas – especially in Georgia – there has been comparatively little written about it. The lack of knowledge about felt in this region is due in part to the suppression of private production, including felt, under Stalin in 1929, and at least to some degree because of the difficulty of getting there to do research, since the republic has never had an easy relationship with Russia. Nonetheless, Robert Chenciner documented felt mantles and masks being made by women in the villages in the 1980s and 1990s, despite local assertions that the craft was largely gone (1997).

The women make the felt in Dagestan. They card about four kilograms of wool using a spiked board and then finish the process with a long bow, as found in Iran. The wool is laid out on a large blanket and rolled by a line of kneeling women against a reed screen – called a *ch'um* – just as the Kyrgyz and Kazakhs do. Rolling is an impetus for celebration, as in Mongolia. People tend to gather with drums and balalaikas and sing while the felt is rolled. Once it is firm, the felt is dyed black with willow-bark. Each mantle requires 2 kilograms of bark and 100 grams of iron sulphate as a mordant to help fix the dye to the fibers and darken the color. Finally, the felt mantles are rinsed in a slightly adhesive solution made of cow-bone glue and the surface is brushed to tease out the surface fibers and give it a furlike appearance (Chenciner 1997, 85). The felt mantles of Dagestan are made using methods similar to those of Central Asia, but the need for such mantles places this felting tradition close to Turkey and Iran as well – a perfect mixture for its geographic position.

Michael and Veronika Gervers documented the traditional process for making felt in central and western Anatolia as well as in central Iran in 1972 and 1973, focusing on the felt centers of Balıkesir, Afyon, Konya, Tire and Sandıklı in Turkey and Shiraz, Isfahan and Seh Gabi in Iran. Their description of the felting process provides a perfect example of how felt ties this region together through the methods used and still shows regional and cultural difference. Gervers and Gervers' article provides an excellent in-depth description of the felting process (1974). Following both their lead and the research of anthropologist Louis Levine, I will describe the work of two feltmakers – Mashd Heshmat Bakhtiari in Iran and Mehmet Girgiç in Turkey – in some depth in order to provide a glimpse of some of the techniques particular to these areas.

A detailed description of felt being made by a craftsman in central western Iran named Heshmat, at the Kurdish village of Seh Gabi, was written by Louis Levine in 1977 at the bequest of Veronika Gervers. Mashd Heshmat Bakhtiari, who was Lur rather than Kurdish, lived in a town near Seh Gabi and traveled among the villages on a regular route, as he was needed, making felt and mattresses. He learned the trade as an apprentice to a friend of his father and passed on his knowledge to apprentices of his own, including his sons. The majority of his time was spent making mattresses by stuffing carded cotton into a woven cotton cover, and he preferred this work to feltmaking since it was less arduous. Nonetheless, he was a skilled feltmaker. He would stay for a few weeks in each village making felt from the wool provided by the local villagers (Levine 1977, 203).

Levine commissioned a coat from Heshmat called a *qaput*, bearing traditional designs. The process of making the coat was very similar to that used to make Kyrgyz ala-kiyiz. Heshmat first carded all of the wool with a bow, which took about half of the day, then laid out a pattern in black wool on a piece of canvas. The design depicted a goat in the center of the back, two sun motifs and an outline around the back. The canvas was an adaptation, being easier to carry between villages than the large and bulky rush mats used traditionally, though Heshmat admitted that he would have preferred a mat (Levine 1977, 208). Most of the coat's fabric was made of white wool, laid down over the black. While the Central Asians typically do this step by hand, in both Iran and Turkey, the maker slowly releases the carded wool onto a wooden fork with long, widely spread prongs, which he shakes to distribute the wool onto the batt below. In Iran, the fork is called a *panjah* and typically has four prongs, while I saw five- and six-pronged forks used in Turkey. Only the wool of a lamb in its first year is used for felt (Levine 1977, 203).

Heshmat then rolled the canvas and wool together and tied them. From this point on, the process closely resembled the method used by the Kyrgyz women – rolling and stepping back and forth across the floor. Heshmat did his felting in a kitchen and bedroom on the second floor of the house in which he was staying rather than outside, since it was warmer there. Levine notes that felt is made in the bath house during the winter, which would be ideal for both its heat and humidity (1977, 205). After the first hardening, Heshmat opened the roll and folded the large, cross-shaped felt into the coat it would become, tied it back in the canvas and rolled the felt again. The third hardening was done without the roll of canvas and allowed Heshmat to work the coat from every direction. At this point, soap may have been added to help size the felt, although Gervers noted that, around Shiraz, resin is used in place of soap (Gervers 1974, 19). Unusually, Heshmat also stretched the felt periodically throughout this long, final fulling process, pulling it to elongate the sleeves. The sleeves on this coat are vestigal, tapering to a point and tied behind the back of the coat. To flare the bottom of the coat, he opened the felt up and climbed inside to work the edge out (Levine 1977, 208). Once the coat was finished, the hem was trimmed straight and the front cut open. Heshmat mostly made felt hats and rugs, though during the same trip on which he made the coat for Levine, he also made a vest and a horse blanket – items he had not been called on to make for some time (Levine 1977, 208).

Writing ten years before Levine, Hans Wulff described some interesting techniques being used in Iranian hatmaking. The sheep's wool is often mixed with goat wool and cleaned with potash to remove the grease before it is carded. The wool is then laid in a copper dish over a fire to keep it warm during the first phase of felting. Once the felt is holding together, a cotton pad cut to the diameter of the finished hat is laid on top and another layer of wool is added, slightly smaller than the first. The edges of the first layer are folded up over the second to make a single piece and felting continues on the dish. After the felt is initially hardened by rolling it in a cloth, one layer is torn open and the cotton pad is removed. The torn layer now becomes the hat's brim as it is fulled and shaped over a wooden form. In small towns, the felter will complete the hat himself, but in larger cities, the final shaping and finishing is done by a special hatter rather than the original feltmaker (Wulff 1966).

Certainly felt is still made in Iran, particularly in the northern areas around Isfahan, Shiraz and Golestan Province, and following much the same process as Levine reported. As of around 2000, most Iranians reported that feltmaking is rapidly dying out and felt was difficult to find in the bazaar, but felt saddle blankets and rugs with felted-in designs, and mantles, could still be found with persistence or specially ordered from the maker. Interestingly, in nearby Azerbaijan, feltmaking was largely done by predominantly male professionals in the towns, and they then sold the felt to the Shahsavan people for their domed felt tents – the reverse of many feltmaking groups in Central Asia (Raissnia 2007).

Turkish feltmaking follows much the same method, though recently technology has taken some of the difficulty out of the task. Mehmet Girgiç is a traditionally trained feltmaker in Konya in central Anatolia. I was honored to spend the day with Mehmet and document his feltmaking in 2007. He learned feltmaking from his grandfather and has taught all of his eight children to make felt, too. His technique is similar to Heshmat's. Our first stop was at the wool bazaar. While wool from the local fat-tailed sheep is good for carpets, Mehmet uses lambswool or Merino for making felt and prefers that the wool be shorn from sheep under four years of age. The type of wool he uses depends on the purpose of the felt. For thick felt, the fat-tailed wool is best. Mehmet can tell from the dryness or brittleness of the wool fibers whether it will be good for felt. In Turkey, sheep are shorn twice a year, and feltmakers like the autumn shearing better since the fibers are shorter (Gervers and Gervers 1974, 16). After cups of tea and much discussion, Mehmet agreed on a price for a bale of wool with the merchant, and we all went for a traditional lunch of lamb. Back in the workshop, Mehmet, like Heshmat, uses the fork to lay out and moderate the thickness of the wool. While he has the old rush mats for felting, he now primarily uses bubble wrap or plastic reed screens, since they work well and are readily available. Once the wool is laid, he dampens it by sprinkling water over a small whisk brush and shaking it onto the wool. Mehmet uses a small amount of olive oil soap in the water sprinkled on the felt throughout the process. The mat and wool are rolled up and tied. While Mehmet knows and is skilled at the stepping method of making felt, he now uses a large felting machine for the initial hardening process. The machine turns the roll in a trough as a wooden paddle beats down onto it.

Although this first hardening may be done by machine, Mehmet insists on finishing the felts by hand. He adeptly demonstrated three different styles for fulling: the one used in Konya, Afyon style, and his own. In Konya, the maker kneels on the floor and draws the felt up with his forearms onto his lap then pushes it down and away, similar to the technique used by the Kyrgyz and Mongols but closer to the body. Around Afyon, in western Anatolia, the felt is held even closer to the body, drawn up almost to the maker's chest and then pushed away and beaten down across the body with only one arm at a time. The maker alternates arms to maintain the evenness of the felt. In Mehmet's own style, he worked the felt on a table with his daughter and wife, rolling it with their forearms and occasionally trading places to keep the felt even. This method he said required less work. Mehmet runs a large workshop, employing ten assistants, and mostly makes rugs and scarves for sale, though he did have a traditional Anatolian hooded felt coat on a mannequin with an artistically shaped felt face outside of his shop. He also teaches workshops to felters around the world. He is among the last of the traditional Turkish feltmakers, however, and the lack of feltmakers is noticeable in the dwindling uses of felt.

HATS AND CLOAKS

One of the most important uses of felt throughout the region, from the Caspian Sea to Hungary and south into Iran, is for hats and mantles. While hats are often specific to the culture in which they are found, and carry much more symbolism in Turkey than elsewhere in the region, mantles tie the various cultures together into one region of feltmakers. In Turkey, as in much of the world, felt was seen as the best fabric for hatmaking, and the hat most associated with the Turks is the felt fez. The fez gains its name from the city in Morocco that provided the material for the red dye used on the felt. Despite the North African origins for the dyestuff used in making these felt hats, I did not find evidence of a local feltmaking tradition except for basic utilitarian needs, such as padding for pack animals. Most of the felt in North Africa seems to have been imported through the Ottoman Empire or other trade with the Middle East. With its distinctive slanting sides, flattened top and lack of a brim, the fez is one of the best-known hats in the world. In the early centuries of its popularity, the felt fez had strips of cloth wrapped around its bottom edge – these might have included pearls and decorative ribbons on fez worn by the nobility. In his history of hats, Michael Harrison suggests that this cloth-wrapped felt shows the adaptation of Greek clothing styles by the Turks after they conquered Constantinople in 1453. The victorious Turks took on the everyday headwear of the Greeks – the felt *pilos* – and added the turban, which was required to be worn by all Turkish Muslims (Harrison 1960, 75). Looking at paintings and portraits from the Ottoman period, it is possible to trace the development of the fez from the turban as this band of wrapped strips of cloth becomes smaller and smaller.

The fez took on political dimensions during the fall of the Ottomans and the rise of the modern republic in the early twentieth century. Ataturk, considered the founder of modern Turkey, outlawed the wearing of the fez in favor of brimmed, felted hats. Most sources agree that this new law was due to the fez's symbolic relationship with the Ottoman period and thus with being seen as backward at a time when Ataturk was trying to Westernize the culture. However, some claim that it was linked to the ability of Muslims to pray while wearing the fez, since its lack of brim did not prohibit them from touching their forehead to the ground (Harrison 1960, 75).

Nor is the fez the only symbolic felt headwear found in Turkey or the former Ottoman world. The Janissaries were the elite guard of the Ottoman sultans – a special corps made up of boys drawn from Christian families who were schooled at the palace and converted to Islam. They were under the patronage of the Bektashi Order, a Sufi group who saw as their mission helping dissenting groups become more within the mainstream of Islam. The Janissaries symbolized this relationship through their long white felt hats, which were embellished with a band of angora at the top that folded towards the back, and were meant to represent the felt mantle worn by Haci Bektas Veli, the order's founder.

Only the *sikke* carries as much iconic weight as the fez. The traditional hat worn by the whirling dervishes – the select members of the Sufi order, Mevlevi, founded by thirteenth-century poet Rumi – represents the grave to those who know the Mevlevi's world but symbolizes Turkish culture for those outside. The hat is tall, often close to two feet in height, with a slightly rounded top. Traditionally, they were made from the fleece of a yearling camel, although now sheep's wool is also used. The hats are made from a large, hollow oval of felt. One end of the oval is then turned inside the other to form two layers (Girgiç 2007). These sikke are the first garment given to a man just joining the order. The sikke is of such importance to its owner that punishments sometimes consisted of divesting the wearer of his sikke until pardon, when a special ceremony had to be undertaken to allow him to wear it again (Atasoy 1992, 267).

Three different styles of sikke are made, depending on their purpose. The tallest, with its slightly flattened top, are worn by the dervishes themselves. A slightly shorter, rounder version is placed upon the tombstones of members of the order. The shortest of the sikke, and the only one bearing the wrapped turban cloth along the bottom edge, can only be worn by those above a certain rank (Atasoy 1992, 266; Girgiç 2007). The color of the fabric used for the *destar*, the turban-like wrapping around the bottom of the sikke, determined whether the wearer was a descendent of the prophet. Another felt hat, called the *elife*, is worn by those who have undergone their final training and a 1,001-day-long retreat. This hat, named for the Arabic letter it resembles, tapers into a pointed crown that forms "a high, stiff ridge from front to back" (Atasoy 1992, 265).

The sikke is part of a full symbolic system centered on the *sema*, the religious ceremony during which it is worn. The Mevlevi order was founded in the Turkish city of Konya in central Anatolia by the philosopher and poet Mevlana Celaleddin Rumi during the thirteenth century. His son organized the dervish sect following Rumi's death in 1273. The order grew extensively during the Ottoman period and exerted a significant influence over political and cultural life. The sema is meant to embody humans' connection to god. The dervishes' long white robes, with their full skirts, are their death shrouds; the sikke is the tombstone placed at their heads. As they whirl, they place their arms out, with the right hand facing up towards god and the left down to earth, channeling god's blessing. The dervishes form a constellation between them, which rotates across the space as they whirl. Like the fez, the dervishes were also outlawed by Ataturk in the 1920s as being detrimental to progress. The order was able to reform, however, during the 1950s as a cultural organization and social club. Today, it has adherents throughout the world, and in Turkey exists as both a religious and cultural influence and a tourist attraction.

The rest of the region is hardly short on felt hats. To the west in Hungary, the *süveg* forms part of the traditional national dress for men. The hat is tall with a small brim. Interestingly, like some of the ancient European felts, the surface is sometimes teased to make it resemble fur (Turnau 1997, 102). In Iran and parts of northern Iraq, tall felt hats are still produced and worn. Both naturally colored or dyed black, these conical hats have a smooth finish, produced by rubbing them with pumice and treating them with gum. In 1970, Mary Burkett collected a hat made in Shiraz with two flaps that could be folded up along the crown or down to cover the ears. They could also be pulled out to form a small bill at the front for shade, but she notes that this was a recent introduction to the area (Burkett 1979, 57). Among the many peoples

Plate 1 Felt saddle blanket from Pazyryk fifth-century CE. Copyright: The Hermitage Museum.

Plate 2 Felt swan from Pazyryk, fifth-century CE. Copyright: The Hermitage Museum.

Plate 3 Kyrgyz yurts, Issyk-Kul oblast. Photo: Willow G. Mullins.

Plate 4 Rolling felt in Kyrgyzstan, Altyn Oimok group, Bokonbaeovo, Kyrgyzstan. Photo: Willow G. Mullins.

Plate 5 Red felt marked with a pattern ready to be cut for a *shyrdak*, Altyn Kol, Kochkor, Kyrgyzstan. Photo: Willow G. Mullins.

Plate 6 Kyrgyz *shyrdak* detail. Photo: Willow G. Mullins

Plate 7 *Ala-kiyiz* detail, possibly Uzbek or Turkmen. Photo: Willow G. Mullins.

Plate 8 Horse halter, possibly Turkmen. Photo: Willow G. Mullins.

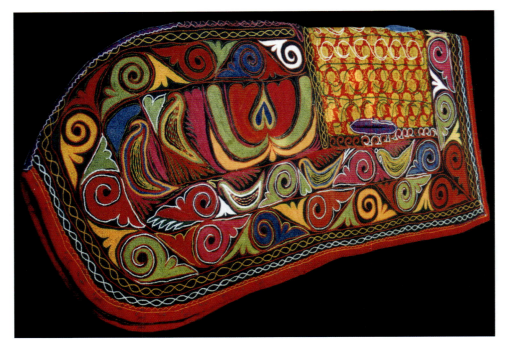

Plate 9 Uzbek saddle blanket. Photo: Willow G. Mullins.

Plate 10 Felt hat by Altynai Osmovea, Bishkek, Kyrgyzstan. Photo and copyright courtesy: Altynai Osmovea.

Plate 11 Detail of artwork by Raikul Ahmatova, Bishkek, Kyrgyzstan. Photo: Willow G. Mullins. Copyright courtesy: Raikul Ahmatova.

Plate 12 Iranian felt rug from Ardebil, age unknown. Photo and copyright: The Ashmolean Museum, Oxford (EA 2002:6).

Plate 13 Mehmet Girgic laying out the wool for felt using a rake. Photo: Willow G. Mullins.

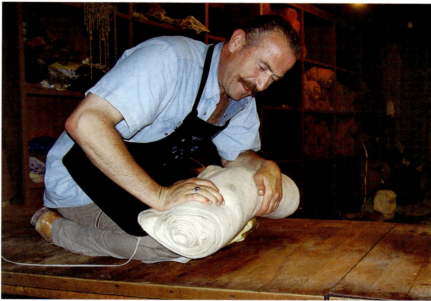

Plate 14 Mehmet Girgic rolling felt in traditional style. Photo: Willow G. Mullins.

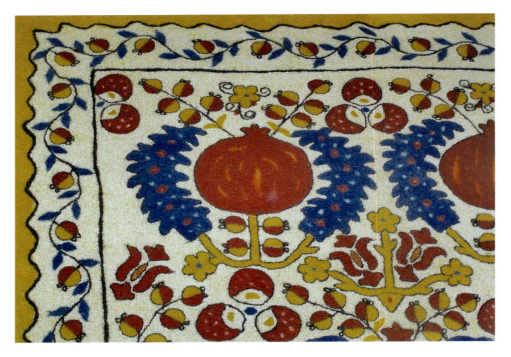

Plate 15 Pomegranate felt wall hanging from Girgic's workshop, Konya, Turkey. Photo: Willow G. Mullins. Copyright courtesy: Mehmet Girgic.

Plate 16 Detail of an Iranian felt rug, possibly Lakai. Photo: Willow G. Mullins.

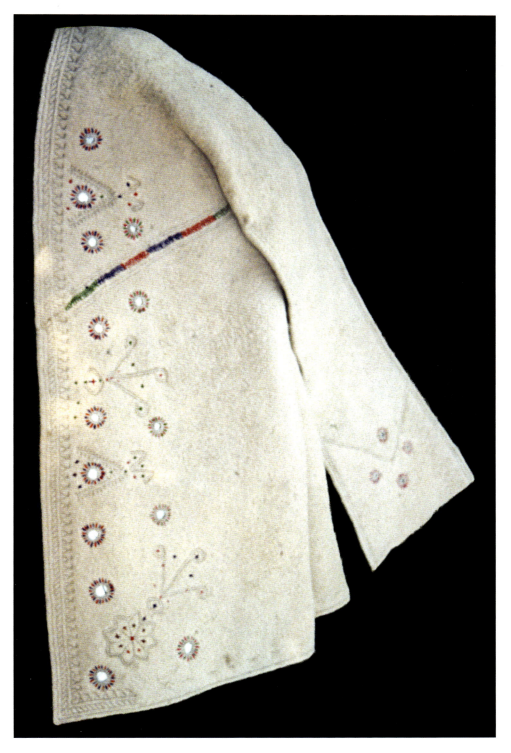

Plate 17 Afghan coat in private collection. Photo: Willow G. Mullins.

Plate 18 Turkish coat by Mehmet Girgic. Photo: Willow G. Mullins. Copyright courtesy: Mehmet Girgic.

Plate 19 Iranian felt mantle with felted in embellishment. Copyright: The Royal Ontario Museum.

Plate 20 Hungarian szur, fulled wool coat with felt appliquéd embellishment. Copyright: The Royal Ontario Museum.

Plate 21 Hats in an Istanbul giftshop for tourists, Turkey. Photo: Willow G. Mullins.

Plate 22 *Vihkihuopa* (wedding felt) "The Holy Rowan is Blooming," by Eija Pirttilahti, Finland. Photo and copyright courtesy: Eija Pirttilahti.

Plate 23 Artwork by Karoliina Lumolommi, Finland. Photo and copyright: Arvilommi.

Plate 24 "Homogenous Infiltration for Grand Piano," by Joseph Beuys, Germany. Photo: Art Resource, New York. Copyright: © 2008 Artists Rights Society (ARS), New York/VG Vild-Kunst, Bonn.

Plate 25 Felt appliqué pullover, c.1970, by Jean Ray Laury, United States. Photo and copyright courtesy: Jean Ray Laury.

Plate 26 "Aurora Borealis Ensemble," by Jorie Johnson, Japan. Photo and copyright courtesy: JoiRae Textiles.

Plate 27 Inge Evers' installation in felt, with the artist on the left, Netherlands. Copyright courtesy: Inge Evers.

Plate 28 "Four Seasons," waistcoat in fine Merino felt. Fabric pieces and stitch incorporated in the felt. Designer/maker Sheila Smith. Photo and copyright courtesy: Sheila Smith.

Plate 29 "Glacier Bay," by Christine White. Photo: John Polak. Photography and copyright courtesy: Christine White.

Plate 30 Flower by Jean Ray Laury, detail from "Houswife's Fantasy" series, felt appliqué, United States. Photo and copyright courtesy: Jean Ray Laury.

Plate 31 Coat by Elsa Schiaparelli, spring 1939 collection. Copyright: The Metropolitan Museum of Art, New York, Gift of Ruth Ford, 2002 (2002.479.4).

Plate 32 Felt appliqué Christmas stocking. Photo and copyright courtesy: Linda Welters.

between the Caspian and the Black Seas, an equal number of traditional hat styles exist, almost all of felt and most without brims (Turnau 1997, 102).

In the Caucasus, while hats may be made of felt, they are as likely to be sewn together from pieces of sheepskin, but felt finds another important role in the masking traditions of many of the ethnic groups. The masks were worn primarily for New Year's parades and other festivals throughout the year, often connected to weddings, although historically they have also been used in battle to frighten the opponents. While many of these warriors' masks were traditionally made of metal, as they have moved from being used in battle to more celebratory occasions, they have also begun to be made in felt. Felt masks may represent birds, bears, sorcerers, old men and a whole cast of characters who appear in the *Cruel Khan* displays put on by the friends of the groom at weddings. Weddings offer numerous masking opportunities – not only through the performance of narrative plays like the *Cruel Khan* but also in processions that provide both buffoonery and wishes of happiness and fertility to the couple, such as the men wearing fools' masks as they carry a young boy in a cradle around the reception (Chenciner 1997, 88–9). Masks may also be worn by boys during the festival that ends the month of fasting, Ramadan, when they visit local houses performing in exchange for treats. In some areas, spring and harvest festivals still include pantomimes with masked participants (Chenciner 1997, 91). Often these masks are made of felt that has been painted and stitched with lines to form the face, have stuffed horns for a Devil or ram mask, or are adorned with wrinkles of stitching and long white beards to represent the *aksakal*, or elder. These felt masks are typically made by the same women who specialize in making felt boots and mantles for daily wear (Chenciner 1997, 88).

As hats have tied the felted world together and have played important roles as much in the symbolic as in the sartorial history of the Ottoman Empire, mantles link the feltmakers from the Caspian Sea through to the Transylvanian mountains. In its most basic form, the felt mantle is a large single piece of thick, dense felt, shaped at the shoulders and open down the front. They may have hoods or vestigial or even functional sleeves, may be embellished with felted-in designs or embroidery. Yet they are made by peoples across the plains and plateaus and worn by the shepherds as protection against wind, sun and rain, heat in the summer and cold in the winter, and a comfortable mattress to lie down on come night. The coats were much-prized during the seventeenth and eighteenth centuries by noblemen, who lined them in silk and had them covered with buckles or embroidery, and by soldiers who wore them while riding to cover both themselves and their horses, like a modern oilskin duster (Turnau 1997, 103).

Felt mantles and coats come from a historic tradition of making a shaped garment out of a large single sheet of fabric or animal skin. Unlike skins or woven fabrics, however, which require seams that become points of weakness in the garment and cannot be easily manipulated into the desired shape, felt is particularly well suited for making thick, tough outerwear. The basic process is much the same from culture to culture: a large piece of felt that has not yet been hardened is folded in half to form the front and back, cut to provide sleeves if desired, and then felted a second time to close the seams into one continuous fabric. During the second felting, a hood or extensions to the sleeves or shoulders can be added. Once finished, the bottom edge and front center opening may need to be cut open. However, issues such as the shape of the coat, whether it has a hood or sleeves, how these are achieved and whether the sleeves are functional or decorative, as well as the nature of any embellishment, are dependent on the needs and aesthetics of the cultures that produced the cloaks.

While patterns and motifs in embroidery and other kinds of embellishment may be one of the easiest ways to tell rugs or woven textiles apart by the culture that made them, the presence and kind of sleeves separate the felt coats of Iran from those of Turkey. The felt mantles produced in Iran and Afghanistan generally have sleeves of some kind but show a wide range in sleeve types. Around Shiraz, functional sleeves are preferred and people wear the coats with their arms through the sleeves. When the coat is first made, however, the sleeves may be too stiff to wear, especially if the coat was made of strong wool by a good maker. In this case, the mantle may just be worn over the shoulders with the sleeves hanging until they soften enough to become useable. Far to the east, such sleeves are also common in Tibetan examples of felt coats, where the front panels are extended to overlap rather than left simply to hang open. Such innovation shows adaptation to both the clothing styles worn by the people and the cold winters typical of Tibet (Gervers in Burkett 1979, 33–6).

In the area surrounding Isfahan and eastern Iran, on the other hand, the sleeves were clearly never meant to be worn, even once softened, as they are made with closed ends. In parts of Afghanistan, the sleeves are even less functional, being no more than large, flat flaps, which serve as a ground for rich ornamentation in embroidery or cut work (Gervers in Burkett 1979, 32–3). The appearance of vestigial sleeves of this kind may be related to Turkmen and Uzbek weaving traditions. Among these groups, as well as down through Iran and Pakistan, some women's headdresses appear as full mantlelike coats with long, narrow sleeves that may stretch to the bottom hem of the coat and are often tied together at the back. Similar styles in felt appear in Iran among the Kurds and historically were worn by the Ottomans, who introduced them throughout their empire. In felt, unlike in woven cloth, the mantles are intended to be worn over the shoulders and often even have slits for the arms, so that they become a kind of caftan in felt (Gervers in Burkett 1979, 35).

In Turkey and further west, felt sleeves are virtually unheard of, but hoods begin to appear. Veronika Gervers suggests that the kepenek may be unique among felt mantles in appearing to have been developed solely through the benefits of felt rather than adapting felt to a model based on woven cloth or animal skins (Gervers in Burkett 1979, 36). Like all felt mantles, they are constructed of a single felt sheet, folded to create the desired shape and with the seams felted shut. They have notably curved shoulders and are longer than many other cultures' cloaks, falling all the way to the ankles of the wearer. The front and back may be embellished with a felted-in design but more likely will bear only the mark of the maker and the weight on the front and possibly the name of the owner inside.

The kepenek also typically has a hood, which separates it from closely related mantles made in Iran and elsewhere. The hood is added during the felting process after the first period of hardening. At this point the shape of the mantle is in place but the wool is still unfelted enough to allow loose wool to be felted on and formed into a hood during the second hardening (Gervers in Burkett 1979, 36). Like the folded-over front of the Tibetan mantles, the hood on the kepenek is a similar adaptation to the local environment. Felt is the specialty of Anatolia with its wide, arid plateau and large herds of sheep, but nearer to the coast and in the hills that separate the sea from the plains, rain is common (Gervers in Burkett 1979, 36). The hood provides more protection than the traditional brimless caps of the region.

Generally with neither sleeves nor hood, the coats made by various groups in the Caucasus are the most simply constructed of all the mantles. Called *burka,* or *bourka*, from the Turkish word for cloak, these coats were historically made from a large circle of felt, which became rectangular only during the nineteenth century. While most are simply a sort of cylinder of felt opening in the front and closed across the shoulders, the number of different ethnic groups inhabiting the area between the Caspian and the Black Seas is so large that the amount of variation is startling. Turnau comments that those from Dagestan were the most famous (1997, 103). These cloaks are of a single color. Veronika Gervers has stated that the men wore black while the women preferred white burka, but Robert Chenciner, writing twenty years later, suggested that black was for everyday wear, while white was reserved for special occasions. Similarly, Gervers states that these mantles are made not of sheepswool but goathair, while Chenciner suggests the reverse (Chenciner 1997, 84–5; Gervers in Burkett 1979, 33).

It seems probable that they are both right, depending on which groups of people they talked to.

Like the Hungarian brushed hats, the Dagestani burka is brushed with flax stalks after the final felting and drying to give it a hairy appearance – a practice that Gervers suggests has developed from using skins with the fur left on (Gervers in Burkett 1979, 33; Turnau 1997, 104). Some cultures singe the teased-out wool as a last step, which would again smooth the surface of the felt having removed any loose fibers through the brushing process. A link between the hairy, felted mantles and skins seems possible, however, in consideration of the Hungarian and Bulgarian mantles made of skins, which look very similar in appearance to their felted cousins to the east.

The felt burka is extremely important symbolically and practically in Dagestan. The mantle not only serves the usual purposes of providing protection from wind, rain and snow in the arid mountain pastures, it has also traditionally played a role in personal relationships. Felt burka were symbols of the connections between men – both through kinship and argument. To give someone a burka or to share one with another person expressed a close relationship and high esteem. However, knife fights to settle blood feuds were carried out on top of the fighters' two mantles, or a cloak might be shoved between the fighters to stop their knives (Chenciner 1997, 84). So much a standard part of everyday wear, mantles even appear in local Dagestani folktales.

Hungary also has a felted mantle called the *szür*. This cloak is always thrown over the shoulders despite its practical-looking sleeves. It may also have a folded-back collar. Szür are made by specialist tailors, although they may be embellished by women in the owner's household. Generally they are embroidered, called "flowering," in red and black, with accents in yellow and blue, although appliqué may also be used. The motifs typically represent plants: roses, tulips, cherries and tobacco leaves. The szür is associated with the shepherds of the plains or *puszta* around Debrecen, Kecskemét and Szeged, just as other mantles are associated with the herders (Gink 1971, 107).

Felt hats seem to make the world go around, taking on specific shapes and designs to best fit the people who make them and the culture and climate in which they live. Felt mantles, on the other hand, are rare in Central Asia and rarer still in central and western Europe. The lands of felted mantles stretch only across the plateaus of the Middle East and the hills of southeastern Europe. For all of their importance, however, hats and mantles make up only one half of the story of traditional felt from Central Asia westwards to Hungary. They are the felts that keep our individual bodies warm and well protected. But felt has another equally important role, as we have seen, in helping to warm us as families and communities. These are the felts of the home – the rugs and wall hangings whose types and patterns similarly show how felt has passed between cultures and bound them together.

FELT RUGS AND HOUSES

The felt yurts of Central Asia are much less common in the western half of the band of felt that girds Asia but they are not completely unknown. Felt as a relatively inexpensive and quickly produced covering could hardly be missed for its architectural properties in a region already familiar with its qualities of insulation and water resistance. Northern Afghanistan and Iran once made up part of the larger pasturing lands for some of the nomadic Kyrgyz and Kazakh tribes. As they moved, they brought their yurts with them. From the early Soviet era, however, borders became closed, and while politics may see nations as geographically separate, cultures are never so easily defined. Some Kyrgyz tribes remained in Afghanistan and are still there today, carrying elements of greater Kyrgyz culture including the yurt. Yurts were also adopted by the other tribes that the nomads traveled among, and were adapted to these tribes' own aesthetics. As a result, the yurts found in Afghanistan and Iran look like neither Mongolian nor Kyrgyz yurts.

Yurts in this desert climate are clearly adapted to suit the heat and aridity. They generally appear to be taller than either Kyrgyz or Mongolian styles, sometimes with a high, steeply pitched roof. The walls are straight, as in Mongolia, but they are covered with reed screens to help provide both shade and air, as among the Kyrgyz. Pictures of these studied for my researches rarely revealed walls of felt on the outside of the screens, which might simply be due to the time of year the images were taken. Interestingly, black felt seems much more common than white for covering the yurts in this area, in contrast to the yurts from further north. The color may simply be the result of the type of sheep available, but black might be preferred for covering yurts as a way to absorb the hot sun, providing shade during the day and warmth at night, in keeping with the large black tents used throughout the region (Burkett 1979, 10, 42, 59, 62). The Shahsavan people of Azerbaijan and northern Iran also use felt tents, but not full yurts. These tents are domed, with panels of felt hung vertically from the center crown rather than wrapped around the sides.

While yurts were used in Afghanistan and northern Iran, Turkey had its own felt house tradition. Called *keçeden evler*, these felt houses were similar to yurts with the felt "stretched over roped, staked frames" and forming a dome for the roof, but they were left permanently in one location rather than moved and were not considered tents (Glassie 1993, 634). The last of these houses were destroyed in the 1920s as people moved first into earthen houses and later into modern buildings, but at one time they appear to have been common throughout western Anatolia. Since the people in the west claim to have come from the east, it seems probable that keçeden evler were once used throughout Turkey. The felt houses' adaptation to settled life, however, is reflected in their sometimes being joined one to the next to provide multiple rooms of a single house (Glassie 1993, 635). More common in Turkey are stone or earthen houses with flat felt roofs, although now the felt is generally being replaced with tiles (Glassie 2007). All of these houses, whether felt-walled or felt-roofed, need furnishing, and in the simple form of the rug, this region's felt artists express some of their most beautiful and intricate designs.

Rugs and wall hangings are probably the most common use for felt in this region. These namad/namda grace the floor of many a home and have found their way into the tourist markets from northern India through Turkey. Embroidery and appliqué make their appearance on felt rugs throughout this region more often than felted-in designs. Each culture adapts the designs of their rugs and the style of embellishment to speak to the rest of their art, forming a whole aesthetic. In the eastern regions of Afghanistan, Turkmenistan and Iran, many felt rugs follow the patterns of the locally produced knotted carpets with repeated diamond- or octagonal-shaped motifs, like the gol on a Persian carpet. One rug, collected in 1947 in northern Iran near Takht-e-Soleyman, bore just such a design, with a large lozenge in the middle divided into quadrants, like many gol, and surrounded by multiple borders.

Many of the Turkmen designs feature a spiral motif and are double-sided, with the back covered in dots or a lattice (Burkett 1979, 27, 43). Some of the Yomud felts can look similar to the Kazakh and Kyrgyz ala-kiyiz designs with tulip and birdlike motifs, while others follow the heavily spiraled designs of the Turkmen. Among the Qashqa'i, who rarely if ever make felt now, the motifs are again like the guls of the knotted carpets, with central motifs repeated in adjoining lozenges and set off by lattices or smaller patterns. The Uzbek and Lakai felts of northern Iran, like those in Uzbekistan and Turkmenistan, are often embroidered with ram's horn and tree motifs forming into dense spirals. Similar patterns adorn their camel headdresses and horse blankets.

To the south, in northern India, felt rugs are almost exclusively embroidered with floral patterns in a chain stitch, although my nursery wall was decorated with an Indian namda embellished with an English alphabet and associated pictures – specially produced for the tourist market. The manufacture of these rugs was traditionally centered in what is now the northern Indian state of Jammu and Kashmir, particularly in the towns of Anantnag, Rainawari and Baramula as well as in the Ladakh region. The tradition of making these rugs is at least 200 years old, but as an industry, it reached its peak during the Second World War. Namda are made from the wool left over from, or not fine enough, for use in other textile processes. The wool is mixed with cotton, creating a somewhat softer finish, although this mixed-fiber felt is not as sturdy as felt of pure wool. The mixture of fibers also helps to keep the cost of the rugs down: the greater the quantity of wool, the higher the price. Historically, plain felt rugs were produced in Yarkand, which were then embroidered locally in Kashmir, Jammu and Ladakh. While in Srinagar, both plain and fully embroidered rugs were available for sale. Often the ground felt was dyed before embroidery, typically in shades of light brown, green, blue or yellow (Jaitly 1990, 73). The ground would then be embellished in floral patterns using a chain stitch filled in with either satin or buttonhole stitch. In India as well as Iran, patterns are sometimes now printed onto the felt using wooden blocks and dye. Although this method is an extremely fast way to embellish a textile, the printing wears off quickly from felt's rough surface (Burkett 1979, 45). While to the north, in Georgia, another tradition of quilted felt rugs once flourished, producing bold abstract designs. Felt rugs are also made in Armenia, although I was unable to find any examples or information on them.

Designs in Turkey fall into two categories – the abstract and the floral. The abstract patterns are closer to those made by the Turkmen, but feature geometric motifs such as spoked wheels, zigzags and close circles. More common now seem to be the floral designs, with bold flowers repeated across the central field of the rug or intertwined. All of these patterns are produced by felting in both loose wool and colored felt, cut to the desired shape. Many of the Turkish rugs also bear the name of the maker or the place made, all felted into the pattern. Rugmaking has also survived in Hungary, although not as strongly. The Hungarian rugs continue to resemble traditional rugs and embroideries, featuring designs of flowers and plants in felted-in designs.

CONTEMPORARY FELT ART

As in Central Asia, as felt has moved away from being a major necessity in daily life, it has found a new life in all kinds of art. By the 1970s, felt namda/namad were commonly sold to tourists in Iran and Afghanistan. They were exported to the West for sale in shops that specialized in folk and ethnic art and gained a certain amount of popularity. Today, small felt saddle pads embellished with felted-in flowers make up a portion of the textiles available for sale in tourist shops throughout Turkey. Like tourist art everywhere, these felts are both part of the tradition and something new. They carry on traditional methods of making felt and traditional designs, but not traditional functions, and often their colors and patterns slowly become adapted to the aesthetics of the tourists who buy them.

Yet alongside the tourist art, fine art made of felt also flourishes. Some of it clearly comes from playing with old forms, such as the tall hats, shaped like dervish hats but whimsically decorated in multiple colors that filled the window of a gallery I visited in Istanbul. Some came quite organically from the tradition of making felt. Mehmet Girgiç is an artist. While he learned to make felt traditionally and insists upon the importance of using traditional techniques, much of the work done by him and members of his workshop shows beautiful new designs. They produce rugs in traditional designs as well as patterns based on mosaics and images collected from a myriad of sources, plus scarves and shawls that use felt to form incredible textures and contrasts. Each is a challenge to felt's utilitarian reputation of old.

One group of Iranian feltmakers has also turned their craft to new designs by working in conjunction with an artist in California and selling the results to the West. Melina Raissnia became interested in felt in the late 1990s after her husband brought her a small felt rug from a visit to his native Iran. In 2002, on a return trip, the couple began trying to find feltmakers, only to discover the art had nearly died out completely. After a few years of collecting rugs and talking with feltmakers, Melina set up a felt workshop in Iran, making rugs based on both new and traditional designs. The rugs from this shop have been featured in design magazines around the world (Raissnia 2007). Poised between the traditional and the new, feltmakers of this region have shown that mixing both together can keep tradition alive.

In Hungary, Mari Nagy and Istvan Vidak not only create their own works in felt, but they have also helped to build ties between feltmakers from around the world to promote the art of feltmaking and the knowledge of its rich cultural history. Both come from a tradition of making felt. Mari learned to make felt balls from her grandfather. In 1984, the couple organized the first International Felt Symposium, in Keckskemet, Hungary, gathering feltmakers from around the world to learn from one another and exchange ideas. The symposium offered the first chance that many feltmakers had had to meet fellow artists from the other side of the political divide created by the Soviet Union's relationship with western Europe and America. They organized a second symposium in 2004, featuring a wide range of felting workshops and speakers. Meanwhile, they have continued to pursue their own artistic work and teaching. Their work clearly shows both their skills as feltmakers and their knowledge of feltmaking traditions around the world. While they teach everything from making felt toys to traditional Hungarian-style felt rugmaking, their work incorporates other traditions as well. One piece, entitled *Fest*, builds on the form of a traditional Central Asian horse and camel blanket, with squares of felt connected by their corners into a kind of patchwork and draped across the animal for celebrations. *Felt the World Together* draws on the images painted on shamanic drums in Finland. Artists like Mehmet, Melina, Mari and Istvan help to connect felting's past to the future through their own work and through their teaching. Not only do they build on their own cultures by embracing a traditional technique, but through their teaching and their artwork they help to gain recognition for this art form and build a worldwide community of feltmakers.

Moving gradually into the region covered in this chapter by sweeping westward and southward from Mongolia through Kazakhstan, Kyrgyzstan and Afghanistan, we start to see a symbolic felt girdle that connects many different peoples. Felt houses change in shape and begin to give way to other materials, mantles and cloaks gain or shed sleeves and hoods to accommodate the amount of rain and the local dress styles; rugs take on the designs of each group in turn, highlighting their way of life and of seeing the world. While the tradition of making felt remains comparatively vital in Central Asia, in the Middle East and Turkey, it is rapidly losing ground to modern manufacture and other textiles in these lands between the steppes and Europe. In this region, felt is beginning to transform. The tradition remains but it is moving more and more towards either tourist art or fine art. Moving westward still further, to the factories of western Europe, the tradition of making felt presents a very different story, one intimately tied to the history of industry and mechanization.

5.
FELT IN EUROPE

In much of Central Asia, the tradition of feltmaking remains an integral part of everyday life for many people. Even as the nomadic cultures have settled, felt not only continues to be an important textile around the home for many of the same uses that it has served for centuries, but has been turned to new purposes as well. In Turkey and the Middle East, felt was never quite as pervasive as in Central Asia, but it has also held its own in the modernizing world. While the textile is no longer to be found throughout the region or in every house, and feltmakers can be difficult to find, some still carry on the tradition and work hard to pass it down to future generations of feltmakers to provide beautiful rugs and coats and the hats for the dervishes.

In Europe, the story of felt is very different, for it is not so closely tied to home manufacture or, for the most part, to traditional culture. Instead, the story of much European felt is one of large-scale economic systems, of the move from individual craftsmen to guilds and then to capital-driven factories, producing quantities of hats often made of imported fibers and ready for export markets. These traditions, surrounding the learning and practicing of a craft, are tied to economics, politics and the prehistory of workers' unions. This is also a story of the hat fashions that dominated from the fifteenth to the mid-twentieth centuries, for in much of Europe during this period "felt" was simply another word for hat. Yet this is only one role of felt in Europe. While this bustle of growing industry describes much of western Europe, the countries in the far north have a slightly different tale to tell.

6 Map of Europe.

In Sweden, Norway, Finland and across the Baltic Sea into Estonia and Russia, felt is both a homemade fabric for making particularly warm boots, and increasingly works of art, and a factory-produced hat material. This region, then, combines the continuous traditional manufacture of felt for personal use found in places like Central Asia, the manufacture of felt both in the home and by specialized craftsmen as in Anatolia and parts of the Middle East, and the large-scale, fully automated felt factories of the contemporary West. Encompassing all of these felt traditions, northeastern Europe poses a special category that displays both the spread northwards of feltmaking from its roots in Central Asia and the full array of feltmaking technologies. Since the history of felt in Europe is different from that in the other feltmaking regions, it calls for a slightly different treatment. The tradition of felting is largely a mechanized one, so the traditional and the modern are not so easily separated. As a result, it is easier to think in terms of each country – moving through local histories from around the thirteenth through to the nineteenth century.

THE TRADITION OF EUROPEAN FELT

We know from the archaeological finds of felt discussed in the first chapter, as well as from Roman records, that felt was made in Europe at least since the reign of the Roman Empire and most likely long before. As we saw earlier, however, most of the archaeological record dates from after the seventh century CE. One writer on the history of hats claims that felt disappeared from most of Europe after the fall of the Roman Empire, only to be reintroduced in the early twelfth century by knights who returned from the Near East with armor padding and saddle blankets made of it following the First Crusade (Harrison 1960, 69). Yet, archaeological evidence suggests otherwise. Scraps of what are believed to have been hats have been found in England, and what appears to be English-made felt has been found in Poland along with felt of native manufacture. As mentioned before, the Polish not only used felt for the more common hats and boots but also for children's toys in the shapes of animals. Felt finds dating from the seventh to the sixteenth centuries are located across the countries bordering the North Sea. Certainly the Vikings had knowledge of feltmaking, possibly through their connections with Central Asian and Islamic traders. Curiously, however, no felt is known to have survived in the Baltic countries, where it would be expected. The Baltic states, especially Estonia, have long traditions of using felt for making men's hats and women's headdresses, and they are surrounded on all sides by cultures that both made and wore felt during this period. The old Ladoga region, in what is now northern Russia, also had felt, but Irena Turnau suggests that it may have been imported from Turkic peoples in Central Asia through trade (1997, 24). Although felt was never as common a material as woven and knitted cloth in Europe, what the archaeological finds across northern coasts do show is a consistent use of felt, especially for hats and boots and more likely for coats, mantles and padding since at least the seventh century CE.

After around the twelfth century, the record of felt becomes easier to follow and closely tied to the rise of modern capitalism and manufacture. During this period, we begin to find textual evidence to support the archaeological scraps of felt. In England, for example, late fourteenth-century bills recorded the sale of English felt to the Polish court. By the sixteenth century, there were 3,000 documented feltmakers in London, while scraps of felt have been found preserved both in London and in Newcastle-upon-Tyne from the same time periods (Turnau 1997, 24, 29). According to the written record, by far the greatest use of felt was for hats, although boots were also produced, especially across northern Europe where they were useful during the long, cold winters. Other forms of textile production, such as weaving and knitting, took precedence in Europe over felt for most purposes, but felt did appear occasionally in coats and was certainly used for all kinds of padding, especially in saddlery (Turnau 1997, 28). A large part of the historic record for felt from this time onwards comes from the records of the guilds. Considered a skilled craft, the making of felt was closely regulated by the medieval guild system.

GUILDS AND FELT

The guilds arose largely during the thirteenth through early seventeenth centuries as Europe moved out of the feudal system into early forms of capitalism. They remained until their dissolution by governments during the Industrial Revolution, although some have survived in Germany. The guilds were often originally formed as social, political or religious organizations rather than around a specific craft and in these looser forms date far earlier, but they gained much of their power and their connection to felt in the early modern period (Seligman 1887, 9). It is possible that various land reforms, including the early Enclosures in England, which moved commonly held arable land into privately held pasture, pushed people towards the cities and its trades. This urban migration increased the importance of the guilds during medieval times as the newcomers sought communities to provide the social and economic networks they had lost. The guilds served a wide variety of functions: controlling the quality of the products; serving as a cartel for buying materials and setting prices; providing a financial and social support network for members; supplying joint bargaining in the face of legal constraints as well as administrative functions for the governments; and probably most importantly, assuring a standard for training apprentices in the craft (Epstein 1998, 685–6). To what extent the guilds fulfilled each of these purposes is a continued subject of debate and probably depended largely on the individual guild.

One good account of guild activities for felting comes from Paris. The earliest record from 1292, notes that hatters should not mix glue in with the wool and that pure lambswool was preferred, although beaver and camelhair were allowable. These were apparently taken as suggestions rather than regulations since forty-seven out of fifty-four hatters were found not to follow them (Turnau 1997, 26). In its 1578 publications, the Paris feltmakers' guild displayed the importance of the guild in training. The apprentice spent five years studying the craft and four years working for the master as a journeyman. By the eighteenth century, a journeyman was expected to make two hats per day. The treatment of these journeymen, many of whom were only paid for 180 days out of their full year's work and received limited benefits from the guild, resulted in multiple revolts over the centuries, including several in France. Similarly in England, the apprenticeship term listed in 1348 was seven years (Turnau 1997, 28, 30). By the end of this period, the feltmaker should have been skilled indeed.

France provides a good case study for the importance of felt and the extent of the guild system, especially during the sixteenth through eighteenth centuries. Felt guilds existed throughout France, with important centers primarily in the south at Cévennes and Languedoc. Yet Chartres, Rouen and Sedan also held concentrations of felters and hatmakers, and Paris and Marseilles each had large felt industries. The sheer numbers of hats and caps produced by these guilds is stunning. The Paris felting guild was listed as the third most important in the city in the early sixteenth century and nearly 200 years later, the felt industry had grown exponentially. Records indicate 320 felt factories in 1776, while the number of journeymen hatters alone working in these factories increased nearly nine times to almost 5,000 men during the fifty years leading up to the French Revolution, resulting in three million hats produced per year (Sonenscher 1987, 45–54).

The Marseilles guild also grew rapidly, employing as many as 20,000 by 1789 and producing 360,000 caps and hats per year, mostly for export to Spain, South America and the Ottoman empire (Turnau 1997, 31). This last locale is especially interesting given the Ottomans' home production of felt. It could be that Marseilles was supplying specific kinds of hats or only selling in certain areas. While the guilds' records list the masters and their journeymen and apprentices, they do not take into account the large number of women who were also engaged in the industry, often in cleaning the sheep wool and the fur of rabbits and beavers. This division of labor is among the first evidence in Europe of the kind of specialization that made the Industrial Revolution possible – though it was well known that such labor divisions existed in ancient China, Egypt and India – as well as being an early implication of the limitations affecting women workers. In Normandy, the Huguenots had largely controlled the felt trade, and when they emigrated under persecution during the sixteenth and seventeenth centuries, they took their craft with them, becoming specialists in the countries they moved to.

At the beginning of the guild system, feltmakers rarely had their own guilds. Instead, the craft fell under various guilds, depending on the location and the era, and the ability of different guilds to make felt for one purpose or another was often under dispute. Most typically, though, general feltmaking was carried out under the auspices of the hatters. This was the case not only in France but also in the Baltics and in Gdansk, Poland, where guilds were established during the fourteenth century. Italy, which called its guilds "colleges," had an establishment of hatters in Florence by the same time. In Sweden, the hatters' guild was charged with making felt horse blankets. In Germany, the wool dyers formed the first guild known to undertake some feltmaking as early as 985. The hatters were not established until the end of the thirteenth century (Turnau 1997, 26–7). The carding bow is featured in the crests of multiple different guilds, including dyers and hatters, which implies that they were both making felt. Unusually, many German felters managed to strike out on their own over time and create their own guilds.

Though perhaps strange to the modern felter for whom fulling is the final step in making felt, felting and fulling were generally considered separate crafts and so had separate guilds. Usually, the fullers were in charge of finishing woven cloth while the hatters and felters made their felt from raw materials, but the two crafts often overlapped and some fullers were allowed to make felt for some purposes and not for others. The same was true of the haberdashers guild, which could make some felted hats but not others. The closeness of the three guilds' trades to each other sat at the root of a long and acrimonious fight in seventeenth-century England (Unwin 1963, 132–6).

The history of the Feltmakers' Guild of London shows a peak in the history of English felting and encapsulates the trends that would eventually be the standard for modern manufacture – the gradual specialization of guilds towards individual crafts rather than larger conglomerates and the division of makers from sellers. The seal of the journeymen hatters in 1820 provides the history of English hatmaking quite succinctly: "Hats first invented 1456. First made in London 1510. The Feltmakers' Company were first incorporated in London 1604; and again by charter 1667. Blanks first instituted 1798" (qtd. in Unwin 1963, 215). The text is accompanied by an image of a journeyman "who has just arrived in town and is receiving the refreshment and relief due to him by the rules of the union" (Unwin 1963, 215). While we know that hats were made well before 1456, even in London, these dates had obviously become part of the lore of hatters and are possibly tied to changes in fashion that promoted the felt hat over the cap.

Until the sixteenth century, the majority of felt hats made in England were rough, intended for daily use by laborers and farmers. Fine hats were almost exclusively imported from France and Italy – thus Chaucer describes the merchant with "Uppon his heed a Flaundrisch bevere hat" (Unwin 1963, 131). Only through the arrival during the 1500s of the Huguenots and other immigrants from northern France and the Netherlands did England begin to have its own feltmaking industry to rival those of the continent and start to assert its dominance through a guild of its own.

The making of felt, mostly for the less well-made caps, started out in England under the Drapers Guild in 1367, and the guild controlled all elements of textile production and monopolized trade. At this point, the guilds focused more on the sale of their wares than production. Sometime later, the Haberdashers and Leather-Sellers gained the upper hand from the drapers to control both the selling of textiles and the making of felt. With the rise in fine hatmakers, however, to around 400 workshops by 1576, the Feltmakers set out to form their own company separate from the Haberdashers. Needless to say, the Haberdashers fought back, seeing a loss of control over a profitable segment of the market, but the Feltmakers persevered and managed to form their own corporation in 1604 (Unwin 1963, 79). Part of this split focused on a division of labor between those who made hats and those who sold them. While most textiles were retailed by their makers, hats were standardized enough in their sizing, early on, to ensure that they did not have to be sold by someone who could also perform fittings and tailoring. Further, the necessity of a nearby water source dictated where hats could be made (in London, Southwark was known for its large population of hatters), restricting where hats could be sold if they were sold only by their makers (Corner 1991, 157). Thus the Feltmakers mainly wanted control of production while leaving sales to the Haberdashers. Later, in the 1630s, a separate Company of Beaver-makers was established specializing in hats of beaver fur, which was then very much in vogue. This new company managed to unite the Haberdashers and the Feltmakers against it and was soon disbanded (Unwin 1963, 145).

Like many guilds, the Feltmakers not only provided quality control and pricing of their products but also bargained on behalf of their members for the raw materials they required to make their hats. The company employed two men, Bradford and Caunton, to lobby on their behalf – originally for the initial founding of the guild, but later against the wool merchants. The Feltmakers desired that wool be sorted and cleaned before being sold to the felters, thus saving them this step and reducing the weight of the wool before purchase. Since wool was sold by weight, the felter did not want to have to pay extra for the dirt and lanolin which he would then have to remove before making his hats. The merchants responded negatively to the Feltmakers' request, "Bradford and Caunton, the parties that make this complaint, are two of very slender credit and of the worst sort of felters, haunters of taverns where they enter into devices, not to do any good to the commonweal, but to maintain their idle life with other men's goods" (qtd. in Unwin 1963, 132). The problem lay deeper than the preparation of wool, however.

Getting into the hatting business required a high investment of cash. The wool, and more particularly the beaver pelts, required for felt were expensive. The best materials were imported, which resulted in a very small number of merchants having control over the supply of raw materials. These merchants could extend credit to a hatter but then demand all of the proceeds of the product, resulting in a high level of debt among hatters throughout the seventeenth century. Even in the mid-eighteenth century, a hatter needed between 50 and 1,000 pounds to start his business, which was far higher than most textile trades and out of reach of many journeymen wanting to establish their own workshops (Corner 1991, 158). Perhaps because of these high start-up costs, the Feltmakers' guild was one of the first companies to go outside of its members for supporting capital and for people to serve on their board, both now standard practices of modern corporations (Unwin 1963, 157).

Since relatively few could afford to set up their own shops, English hatters may have remained as journeymen longer than in other trades, and England, like France, had its share of journeymen's strikes. The journeymen hatters are recorded as having acted in concert for their collective good since nearly the beginning of the Feltmakers' Company. In 1667, the journeymen had petitioned for a variety of by-laws that directly related to their duties and their treatment (Unwin 1963, 216). The Huguenots again had a great influence on the craft after the Edict of Nantes was revoked. This law had granted them equality in France, which they had not enjoyed previously. Facing potential persecution and heavy restrictions on their daily lives, large numbers of Huguenot hatters moved to England. They set up workshops outside of London that attracted English journeymen, especially those from the countryside. Protectionism set in and the Feltmakers chose to exclude the Huguenots by insisting that the journeymen train only with "qualified masters," i.e. English hatters. This move, in combination with a series of attempts to keep wages down and other controls, led to a journeymen's strike in the 1690s (Unwin 1963, 216–18). During the next 150 years, the journeymen continued to organize in support of their own interests against their masters, so that not only does the history of felt hats show the history of the move towards capitalism but it is also a history of the trade union.

The influx of the Huguenots and the actions of the journeymen affected the entire English hatting trade. The workshops in Southwark moved to Manchester and other smaller cities in search of cheap labor during the 1700s, but as the workshops moved, so did the journeymen, which strengthened ties between local journeymen's organizations. This movement caused concern among the Feltmakers of London, who tried unsuccessfully – through restrictions – to stop the Huguenot shops and the increasingly strong journeymen's groups (Corner 1991, 165). Eventually, the English hatters, who had flourished in the seventeenth and early eighteenth centuries, began to lose ground in exports to Europe under pressure from the resurgence of the French felt workshops and a small but rising Spanish industry, as well as to North America due to rising production there (Corner 1991, 163). With the Industrial Revolution making strides in other types of textile production, and the invention of large-scale carding machines just around the corner, the small workshops that formed the basis of the guild systems of England and France were becoming obsolete.

HATTERS AND HATS

Much of the history of feltmaking in Europe is closely tied to the history of the felt hat. We tend not to wear hats in daily life anymore, but this trend has taken root only in the last part of the twentieth century. For at least the previous 500 years, however, felt hats were an important part of attire, and their history extends much further when we consider the Phrygian caps of ancient Greece and Rome. Hats provided necessary head covering and protection against the elements, but they can also reveal much about their wearers. Although the story of hats can and has filled volumes on its own, including hats of many different materials and the entirety of costume history, we will stick to the highlights of felt hats.

The date of 1456 inscribed by the London journeymen Feltmakers for the invention of hats may be apocryphal but the mid-fifteenth century was firmly marked by English hatters as the beginning of hats. One 1829 writer of a monograph on hatmaking tells this story:

> Hats, however, are first mentioned in history at the time when Charles VII made his triumphant entry into Rouen in the year 1449. In F. Daniel's account of that splendid pageant, he says, that 'the prince astonished the whole city by appearing in a hat lined with red silk, and surmounted by a plume of feathers; from this period their general use is dated, and henceforward they gradually took place of the chaperoons [*sic*] and hoods that were worn before...' (Qtd. in Pufpaff 1995, 21–2)

With such kingly approval, hats started on their rise to prominence in France, overtaking the previous popularity of the hood by the end of the fifteenth century (Harrison 1960, 72). In Flanders, tall-crowned felt hats had already been in style for at least 100 years before this, which may be where Charles VII picked up the style along with Chaucer's merchant (Harrison 1960, 57).

Through the fifteenth century, felt hats were mostly reserved for travel and then almost solely worn by men (McDowell 1992, 7). As they grew in popularity through the sixteenth and seventeenth centuries, however, both regional and individual styles developed, most notably in the size, shape and styling of the brim. The seventeenth century marked a turning point in felt hats: as their price fell throughout the century they became more generally available, and the tricorne became symbolic of men's dress for the period. The tricorne was predominantly associated with the military. By 1750, it was part of the uniform of nearly all British troops, with the exception of the dragoons (Harrison, 1960 108). This style developed slowly from a wide-brimmed hat, whose wearers initially pinned up the right side of the brim to allow more free use of the sword without risking damage to the hat. This is the type of hat we associate with the French musketeers. While one side of the brim was practical for fighting, it was not particularly efficient for fast riding on horses or wearing at sea, and additional folds were made to streamline the hat into the full tricorne (McDowell 1992, 12).

The seventeenth century also marked the rising fashion for hats made of beaver pelts. The rage for such hats was so strong that it helped to drive the European expansion west into North America in search of new sources. Interestingly, although trapping was the primary source of beaver furs, hatters had a preference for old pelts that had been used in native coats, since the older fur felted better, possibly because the natural grease had been worn out of it and the fibers broken down enough to require less carrotting (McDowell 1992, 49). By the time the tall top hat reached high fashion in the nineteenth century, beavers were becoming increasingly endangered, but hats had taken full possession of fashion as they began to replace the wigs previously favored by the aristocracy. The first tall "silk" hat, which would hold its place as the height of men's fashion for the next century at least, appeared in the 1790s and was made, naturally, of highly polished beaver felt (McDowell 1992, 14).

With their increase in popularity, hats came to be understood symbolically as markers of religion, profession or status. Hats and headwear had held religious significance for centuries. Red hats were made requisite for cardinals by Pope Innocent IV in 1245 as a reminder of the blood of Christ. Among the Quakers of England in the 1600s, hat etiquette provided an important symbolic and political point. The Quakers did not believe that men should distinguish rank between one another as they were all the same to god, contrary to the system used in court at the time:

> In 1669 [William] Penn wrote a treatise against raising the hat to any but the Lord ('No Cross, No Crown; or Several Solid Reasons Against Hat Honour...'). One 'solid reason' ran as follows: 'The hat choketh because it telleth tales; it telleth what men are ... it is blowing of a trumpet.' A story is told that when Penn kept his hat on in the presence of Charles II, the king removed his own. When he asked why, the king reminded Penn that only one person might keep his hat on in the royal presence. (McDowell 1992, 27)

In a period when hats were used to show wealth and status within the court, Penn's stance would have been shocking. Nonetheless, the issue of whether the head should be covered inside or out, in church or places of business, by women or men, in felt or fabric, continues to be a matter of religious strictures to this day.

The extent to which hats "telleth what men are" is exemplified throughout nineteenth-century literature as integral parts of any man's description. Yet no one sums up the importance of the hat or is quite so concerned about their own headwear as Raskolnikov in *Crime and Punishment*:

> And yet when a drunken man ... shouted at him as he drove past: 'Hey there, German hatter!' bawling at the top of his voice and pointing at him – the young man stopped suddenly and clutched tremulously at his hat. It was a tall round hat from Zimmerman's, but completely worn out, rusty with age, all torn and bespattered, brimless and bent on one side in a most unseemly fashion. Not shame, however, but quite another feeling akin to terror had overtaken him.
> 'I knew it,' he muttered in confusion. 'I thought so! That's the worst of all! Why, a stupid thing like this, the most trivial detail might spoil the whole plan. Yes, my hat is too noticeable... It looks absurd and that makes it noticeable... With my rags I ought to wear a cap, any sort of old pancake, not this grotesque thing. Nobody wears such a hat, it would be noticed a mile off, it would be remembered...' (Dostoevsky 1987, 3)

Going through the dry run of the murder he will soon commit, Raskolnikov fixes on his own hat as the one flaw in his plan, the one object that people are sure to notice, not because of its shabbiness but because it does not fit with the rest of his clothes. His clothes mark him as poor, and the poor mostly wore caps. Further, he is wearing a German-style hat in Russia at a time when things that were noticeably German were a source of some derision. On the other side of the crime scene, Sherlock Holmes, at the end of the century, is noteworthy for wearing a cloth deerstalker cap rather than a felt hat, showing the extent to which his mind was on greater things than fashion.

In western Europe, class distinctions show up not only in the style of the hat but also the color. The round-crowned, curled-brim hat known as the bowler was designed in 1850 by the Bowler family of Southwark, England and sold for 12 shillings. William Coke of Norfolk had originally ordered the new design for his gamekeeper to replace the traditional soft hats which wore out quickly. Coke wanted something more durable and rigid but fitting close to the head so that it would not be caught by tree limbs and bracken. Although made by Bowler, Coke ordered his hat at Lock's in London. James Lock and Company has been in operation since 1676 and supplied hats to the Duke of Wellington. They remain open today (Sutherland 1982). The company called it the Coke hat, but the name never stuck. Instead, the hat became extremely popular across classes as the bowler. In England, however, the color of the bowler marked the style of the man, as gentlemen wore black while tradesmen, and more particularly racecourse bookies, wore brown. In the United States, the same hat took on the name derby and gained a greater following in brown (one of the Brown University men's singing groups is still called The Brown Derbies and dresses to suit), but some of the class-color associations remained (McDowell 1992, 14).

At least since the times when Romans used the felted cap as a symbol of the free man, while the aristocracy went hatless, hats have been political symbols, just as they have been religious and economic markers. Napoleon expressly chose a large felt bicorne trimmed in gold as a symbol of both his military prowess and power and the legitimacy of his rule. While most cavalrymen also wore bicorne hats, they wore theirs with the points at the front and back, maximizing the streamline of the hat so it would not be lost during a charge. Napoleon, on the other hand, wore his sideways, emphasizing his status and drawing attention to his position to encourage his soldiers.

Later revolutionaries also espoused unique hat styles as political symbols. Garibaldi in Italy adopted a tall, soft, large-brimmed hat that some attributed to his travels in South America and others to the Italian peasant farmers (McDowell 1992, 29). Either way, such wide-brimmed hats became symbolic of radicalism and independent thought in the nineteenth century as they came to be closely associated not only with politics but with artists and writers. This connection has lasted into contemporary film depictions of about any period from 1800 to 1950, with the broad-brimmed hat in felt or straw the constant companion of the free-thinking artist. Hungarian nationalist Lajos Kossuth also embraced a soft felt hat, which his tour of the United States in 1851 threw into vogue. The same style was later adopted by the Irish Fenians (McDowell 1992, 29). All of these soft hats contrasted with the stiff top hats that were part of a gentlemen's attire according to social mores, thus directing attention to the radicalism of the wearer. Yet as McDowell points out in his history of hats:

The old adage that 'You cannot lead a revolution in a top hat' is undoubtedly true, but equally so is the fact that once the revolution is over, you cannot lead a government in a Phrygian cap. (McDowell 1992, 29)

Napoleon's move into his bicorne proves the point. What is remarkable about hats, however, is that, despite Europe and North America's general preference for woven and knitted fabrics, felt has nonetheless been able to assert a profound influence on society in the guise of the hat, becoming one of the primary ways of telling prince from pauper and patriot from priest. Hats remain an important marker of social status at the Ascot races in England, where the hat trade, and with it the felt market, continue.

FELT IN NORTHERN EUROPE

While much of Europe focused its felt production on hats, this was not the case in the northern countries of Sweden, Norway and Finland, as well as parts of northwestern Russia. Here, the cold climate and long winters made felt an eminently practical material, providing the necessary warmth and resistance to weather that made the fabric popular across the steppes. These regions have a long history of making felt not only in the home but also in workshops and factories. While hats were certainly part of the felt output of the northern countries, they also specialized in felt boots.

As we know, felt has a long tradition in the north. Archaeologists have found fragments of felt throughout Scandinavia and Finland, northern Germany and Denmark, that point to widespread use of felt by the Vikings. The oldest felt found in Norway consisted of two pieces used to wrap the body in a funeral pyre in Hordaland in southwestern Norway and dates to the fifth century CE. Felt animal masks are also associated with Viking sites, such as the bear or sheep mask found at Haithabu in northern Germany. Inga Hägg has suggested that such masks served magical and symbolic functions for their wearers during tournaments (Sjöberg 1996, 17). It is also possible that they were used either for shamanic purposes or else for celebrations, as in Dagestan. Although felt was vital in these northern areas, it did not stretch into Denmark after this early period. Similarly, references to felt are found in Icelandic sagas and archaeological sites but the tradition of making felt had not survived there until it was recently revitalized.

From the nineteenth century onwards, northern Europe provides an interesting blend of felting traditions: on one hand, felt hats and boots were often made in factories like those in

7 Felt boots from northwestern Russia.

Britain and France, on the other, felt was also being made in the home, especially in northern districts. That said, this division was by no means rigid and local hat- and bootmakers persisted in some areas through the early twentieth century. Geography also played a role: since the southern parts of Sweden, Norway and Finland are closer to the larger cities and the trade routes of the Baltic Sea, it was easier for people there to simply buy – rather than make – their felted hats and boots. In the north, felt was both more necessary due to the cold and often easier to make at home with wool from the family's sheep. While the factories were traditionally run by men, women performed much of the home production, although there seems to have been some give and take between professional male felters and local women.

Knitting and spinning may have been among the tasks of every housewife, but producing felt was considered difficult and skilled labor – only a few women in any village may have possessed the knowledge to make it (Sjöberg 1996, 19). These women could use their felting skills to turn a profit for their families, not only by making boots for their husbands and children but also by traveling among the nearby farms and providing boots for all of the inhabitants, much like the itinerant weavers common in colonial America. A good pair of felt socks was valued enough to command a higher price than their knitted counterparts, and tales are told of poor families who made their fortunes on carefully guarded felting know-how (Sjöberg 1996, 19). Such cottage industry was seen as profitable enough to attract government attention. Felt socks require much less time to make than knitted ones, but they also need more wool. The true premium, however, was not on materials but on the knowledge of how to make felt. In the early twentieth century, the Norwegian government developed local employment schemes around Haus, near Bergen on Norway's southwest coast, encouraging families to make felt socks and shoes at home. A factory was set up to process the wool in 1911. Women would get wool from the factory to make their shoes and then return the shoes to the factory for sale. At its height, the project employed around 100 people (Sjöberg 1996, 21).

The knowledge of feltmaking has risen and fallen in northern Europe with the fortunes of the people. During and after the Second World War, for example, many families who had abandoned the craft returned to making felt because of the shortages and poor economy caused by the war (Sjöberg 1996, 21). As the economies of the countries improved, people once again began to leave the difficult work of making felt to others. Felt production in Finland, for instance, had nearly stopped by the 1960s. Felt saw a resurgence, however, in the 1970s and 1980s, as part of the more general interest in craft and natural materials and cultural traditions following the 1976 publication of Katarina Ågren's book on felt in Sweden.

Unlike much of the rest of Europe, felt hats were not as important as an industrially produced commodity in the northern countries, but they were certainly worn all the same. Part of the reason hats never became the industry they were elsewhere is because a portion of them were produced at home or by local feltmakers. Felt historian and artist, Gunilla Paetau

Sjöberg, remarks on two hats made of felt in the mid-nineteenth century by Östen Olofsson Sundberg, in Västerbotten, Sweden, and a woman in Vilhelmina in the 1920s who made women's felt hats. Most interestingly, she records that felt hats became common in the 1850s in the town of Multrå, because a "hat man" had moved to the town and popularized felt hatmaking (Sjöberg 1996, 19). This story implies that in smaller towns, fashions in hats were largely dependent on the styles made by the local hatter. Felt hats were sometimes referred to in Swedish as *tovhatt* or *hattov*. Both of these terms appear in estate inventories of the early nineteenth century, and Katarina Ågren suggests that the use of *tova*, a dialect word, in the first term implies homemade felt rather than a factory product (Sjöberg 1996, 19). While felt hats and caps were common, and professional hatmakers were to be found in towns across northern Europe, the lion's share of felt, both factory and homemade, is found in socks and boots.

Felt socks were generally worn underneath leather work boots or ski boots as a removable liner. They could be added in winter for extra warmth and easily removed if they got wet. These socks are made of a single piece of felt, formed around a wooden shoe last, which allows for a good strong covering with limited places for snow or ice to sneak in. Felt socks go under a wide number of names, depending on local dialects, from *tovesockar* in Västerbotten in northeastern Sweden to *tossen* in Hälsingland, further south along the coast. In Norway, felt socks are called *labber*, while the Finnish call them *huopasylingit*, *sylingit* or *sylingar* (Sjöberg 1996, 18–22). They are still made and worn today across the north and have become a fun project for home felters around the world, since it is possible to felt them directly around the intended owners' feet. A Russian acquaintance told me that her American husband insisted on buying new felt boots whenever they were in Russia since nothing else kept his feet warm around the house in winter.

Some of the tradition of feltmaking in northern Europe can be traced to Russia. The Russians are partly responsible for introducing felt boots into northern Europe. The Finns claim to have learned the technology of making felt socks from the Russians who occupied southern Finland from 1809 to 1917 and established the first felt factories there, in the south. The Russians were particularly known for their tall felt boots, which could be worn outside the house with or without a leather shoe covering. Not only were they made by the Russian-built factories in Finland, but they were also popular in the north of Norway, under the name *russekatankerna* (Sjöberg 1996, 21). Felt boots hold a special place for northern Russians – they helped keep the troops warm along the Western Front during the Second World War, not to mention during several other military campaigns. Aleksandr Solzhenitsyn's bricklayer, Ivan Denisovich, laid great store by his boots in the gulag.

Today, felt continues to be used for shoes and liners in ski boots, and these felted socks have made their way from home production back into the factory. Following this progression, the A. Lahtinen Huopaliike company of Finland has been producing felt boots and socks or slippers since 1921 and remains possibly the only maker of tall felt boots left in Finland. The company still makes their boots entirely of wool without the addition of synthetic fibers. Interestingly, they also still use a two to three percent sulphuric acid solution to prepare the wool for felting (Lahtinen 2007). The company has diversified their product lines, however – they now also supply hats, waistcoats and even insulated sleeves for mugs, as well as raw wool ready for home feltmaking in addition to traditional boots and slippers. Although the number of felt factories has decreased, a few do remain. Alhon Huopatehdas specializes in felt shoes and is located in the same town as Lahtinen.

Marketing outside of northern Europe, the Haflinger shoe company of Germany have recently popularized clogs with felt uppers and cork soles in the United States. Other companies have followed suit with similar felt shoes. Although the fiber has changed from wool to synthetics, alpine ski boots continue to be lined with thick felt. These needle-felted liners provide necessary warmth and padding for skiers. The shift to synthetic fibers for ski boot liners helped to reduce the weight of the already heavy boots and to keep skiers' feet drier, since synthetics dry faster than wool, allowing the liner to dry completely overnight.

FELT IN MODERN NORTHERN EUROPE

As it has historically, the modern industry of feltmaking continues to coexist with home production, though much of the latter is now carried out by dedicated artists working to produce wearables and gallery works. Felt as a medium for art has become as important in northern Europe as it has in Central Asia and Anatolia. Like the Central Asian feltmakers, northern European feltmakers have drawn upon the long history of felt in their cultures and turned it to new and interesting patterns and designs. In Kyrgyzstan, the traditional methods of making felt have changed very little, although makers now produce a wider variety of items and have moved much of their production into their courtyards and houses. In Anatolia, what is made, mostly rugs, has remained traditional while the method for making it has changed, becoming more mechanized. In northern Europe, we see a wide range of relationships with traditional feltmaking. To return again to Glassie's discussion of tradition, he offers this final definition, which is helpful here: "[we] understand tradition as a process, an integrated style of creation" (Glassie 1995, 408). The northern European artists working in felt are drawing on cultural traditions that stretch back centuries. They may choose to make traditional items, such as hats or boots but they may make them to modern tastes and in innovative shapes. They may choose to use traditional methods of felting, rolling their felt by hand, or employ a machine to speed the process, but whatever they choose, much of their work shows both an acknowledgement of the feltmakers before them as well as individual creativity.

One artist engaged with the traditional in interesting ways is Finnish artist Eija Pirttilahti. Pirttilahti learned first to knit and take care of the Finnish-breed sheep that her family kept before learning to felt. She trained in both agriculture and art, settled on a farm in 1992 and began the company Sammallammas, predominantly weaving rugs. Gradually, feltmaking took over the business. Today, she makes a range of clothing and gift items for sale, but much of her work takes its inspiration from the natural world around her. Her three-dimensional works depict foxes, bears and horses. However, her background as a rug-weaver and the tradition of *ryiji* (also called "rya") rugs also influences her work. Traditional in northern Norway, Sweden and Finland, ryiji rugs are made by knotting yarn to produce a deep, shag-like surface, a similar process to that used for Persian carpets but often using striking abstract patterns. The rugs date to at least the fifteenth century. In Finland, such rugs were used for wedding ceremonies – the couple would kneel on the rug as they exchanged their vows and would then use the rug either as bedding or on the wall of their new home. Pirttilahti has imported the tradition of ryiji rugs into felt, making large wedding felts, designed after the patterns of the ryiji rugs, to be used as part of a wedding (Pirttilahti 2007).

Karoliina Arvilommi, another Finnish feltmaker, also incorporates traditional ryiji weaving into her felt. Arvilommi also began as a professional weaver, creating art weavings for independent designers in addition to her own pieces. After five or six years, she discovered felt, and produced her first felt work – a hat that combined her interests and included both felt and ryiji techniques. Since then, the felt "took over." Reflecting the same sense of constraint in the structural nature of weaving, Arvilommi found a release in felt. She discovered that she could work the felt by feel, rather than through the intense mathematics required for weaving. She finds inspiration in the fibers themselves and the colors that are created as she makes the felt. Her wall hangings use rich colors, frequently blending from dark to light, and curved organic shapes, often seemingly drawn from nature, that require the viewer's contemplation.

Arvilommi has also continued her work with her ryiji and felt hats, and they have since been added to the collection of the National Design Museum in Helsinki.

The history of feltmaking in Europe shows the wide variety of manufacture used for felt, from the home to the factory. Except in the north, where felt has been an important fabric for helping people to keep warm and thus was a tradition of home production, felt in most of Europe displays a very different kind of history than it has undergone in other parts of the felting world. Many scholars have seen felt as a fabric of necessity, one made by people who have limited weaving technology. The history of felt in Europe proves instead that there is simply nothing better than felt for some purposes. No other textile provided quite such warmth and water resistance before the advent of synthetic fibers, and certainly no other textile can be shaped and molded like felt. Moreover, the history of felt in Europe gives a window into the rise of industrialization and with it the debates over imported goods and labor rights. The story of felt is bound up with the history of the cultures in which it is made and it has influenced each of these cultures in different ways. Having covered the lands of the feltmakers from the east in Mongolia to the west, with Great Britain and France, we have seen the wide variety of traditions that have shaped felt. Yet in this age, when many of the nomads have settled and hats are no longer part of everyday wear for most people, we find that felt is still around, perhaps in greater quantities than before, but it appears in different places. Felt has become part of other traditions – those of fine art and engineering, of crafts and home décor.

6.
FELT IN WESTERN ART

With modern technology come modern methods of making felt and modern feltmakers and users. Since it first appeared in the Western art world in the 1960s and 1970s, felt has gained a wider appeal as an artistic medium. This introduction of felt into art coincided with a burst of experimental and avant-garde art that broke down the barriers of who an artist was and what defined "art" – work that had begun with the Arts and Crafts movement of the late nineteenth century and continued through Art Nouveau and the Bauhaus. As a result not only of these ongoing conversations about art but also the advent of new materials, art could no longer be confined to marble or bronze sculptures and oil paintings – plastics and fibers of all kinds began not only to be incorporated, but also to become the basis of whole new genres. Fiber arts, as distinct from the use of textiles and fibers in design, began to appear in galleries and museums, offering new ways of looking at both art and fiber. The importance of felt was furthered by the rising interest in craft and the return to natural materials and handmade objects that accompanied the social movements of the late 1960s and 1970s. Although felt has only ever been espoused by a few artists, it has nonetheless come to be respected as a material for more than utilitarian hats and boots.

In the preceding chapters, I have sought both to give the history of felt and to show how it has shaped and been shaped by the cultures that have produced it; how each has turned this simply made textile to their own needs and their own aesthetics. Moreover, I have shown how felt continues to be important as an art form within these cultures. Yet, as noted above, all of these cultures have some sort of tradition of feltmaking – for houses, rugs, hats or boots. In modern Western society, our tradition of making felt is largely an industrialized one. Felt has only recently graced the gallery and the museum and its appearance there is the result of at least two trajectories of Western art, one that has asked what we mean when we say something is art and one that has sought to make art more inclusive.

In this chapter, I am interested in felt as an artistic medium, one that has specifically engaged with the tradition of art as it appears in those galleries and museums and as it is studied by art historians. This art is influenced by the aesthetic traditions of the West, of Europe, America and Australia, and participates in a conversation with all of the art that has come before it. This art is also influenced by the tradition of craft, by the history of trades and guilds and skilled workmanship, and by the discourse between art and craft that began in the nineteenth century. And finally, this art is influenced by and influences the culture in which it is created, viewed and discussed. We have seen some felt artists from the traditional lands of felt, those who, according to Henry Glassie, have learned to make a traditional thing using traditional methods but marked it with their own creativity. What is important here is felt's rising role in another cultural tradition – the tradition of Western art from the statues of the Greeks through van Eyck, Monet, Picasso and Warhol. The new felt artists made something to fit within this tradition but their creativity led them to use a non-traditional material for their purpose.

THE BEGINNING OF FELT AS ART – JOSEPH BEUYS AND ROBERT MORRIS

Before we can talk about felt's role as art, we must first clarify what is meant here by the word art itself. Needless to say, there are books written on that subject alone, and many more on how art includes or diverges from craft. To understand how groundbreaking the emergence of felt into the art world was, it will be necessary to describe some of the ways in which art and craft have stood in relation to each other. Ultimately, however, the lines between art and craft (and kitsch, as discussed later) are not significant here; we are concerned with felt foremost, and secondarily, with traditions rather than terminology. The role of felt in the Western canon of art follows one tradition, while the role of felt for poodle skirts and around the Christmas tree follows another. Both traditions are important parts of Western culture, both express creativity through felt, but they do so in different ways, they are seen in different venues, and we bring to each different assumptions. For that reason, I have separated the art made with felt that we see in galleries and museums from the felt art we encounter every day.

Felt has been used in the world of art for centuries for utilitarian purposes. In printmaking, felt helps support, cushion and clean the plates. Similarly, textiles have been respected as an art form for even longer – tapestries and embroideries were highly valued during the Renaissance – but in the past few centuries, they have rarely been ascribed the same status as painting and sculpture. For these arts, felt has long formed a ground fabric for embroidery and other surface designs. But it was not until the mid-twentieth century that felt came into its own, taking pride of place as a sculptural medium. In order for this humble textile to make its appearance, some of the strictures that had governed what Western art is needed to be questioned, and felt was to play a small but important role in that questioning. Much of the credit for this early use of felt in Western art, and in the politics of art itself, lies with the German artist Joseph Beuys.

Born in 1921, Joseph Beuys studied and later taught art in Düsseldorf. Although primarily a sculptor, he was also a forerunner of modern performance artists, staging "actions" in galleries and other public venues. These incorporated the spontaneous production of his art, his philosophies about art as typically expressed through lectures (although such lectures might be directed not at the audience but, for example, at a dead hare cradled in his arms), and often elements of ritual. The last helped to earn him the name the "Shaman of Düsseldorf," underlined by his signature fur-lined greatcoat and felt trilby-style hat. He was eventually fired from his job for allowing everyone who applied to the university to attend his classes regardless of their status with the art institute itself. Beuys believed that everyone was an artist and that art needed to engage with "elementary forgotten knowledge" (Borer 1996, 15).

Beuys began using felt after a personal crisis in the 1950s that made him question how people's interactions with, and discussions about, sculpture revealed a deep misunderstanding of how sculpture reflected and provoked thought. He turned to what he saw as "the 'poor' materials...: felt, fat, dead animals, copper, sulfur, honey, blood, bones ... all things that hitherto had been unworthy of art" as a way of returning to elemental objects that could then become transformed through thought into art (Borer 1996, 15). Through the use of these very organic materials, Beuys believed that he created art that did not represent the material world around him, as earlier realist artists did, but rather give form to ideas and beliefs. Moreover, by using materials that were familiar to everyone in their daily lives, he felt that he could speak to everyone, even if they only understood the thought he was expressing with reflection. As a critic of Beuys' work, Alain Borer, puts it: "Beuys [used] his felt, copper, or animal fat because of their ability to reveal to *everyone* a basic truth, but one that would only be made manifest *later*, after much striving" (Borer 1996, 21; ital. in original). The debates about what art is and to what extent it should be easily comprehended are often said to have begun with the work of artists such as Wassily Kandinsky and Marcel Duchamp in the early twentieth century. Certainly, these issues have an even longer history – writers since Plato and Aristotle have been engaged in defining what is and is not art. Kandinsky and Duchamp's works, however, brought these debates into the realm of modernism and its engagement with the shocking.

By the time Beuys chose to work in felt and fat, therefore, these discussions had been circulating for decades, but art schools and museums often remained rooted in older forms of teaching and artistic expression that excluded both the kinds of work Beuys was engaged in and fiber art as a whole. The first was questioned for its departure from traditional forms and subjects; the second was dismissed as either craft or women's work. At stake was the accessibility of art. At least since the nineteenth century, when English artist William Morris sought to elevate craft to the level of art and make the ownership of art available to all, artists and critics have been engaged in discussions that blurred the lines between art and craft and suggested that all people should have access to art. The Bauhaus school of the 1920s had brought together a group of artists, including Kandinsky, in an attempt to merge art and design – the fine arts and the applied – and thereby partly continue William Morris' ideals. The school is noteworthy for having taught textile design, particularly weaving, as part of its offerings, and thus helped to create the space for fiber art. The Bauhaus dissolved in 1933 due to political pressures, and the Second World War restricted the activities of many artists. As part of the German avant-garde of the 1950s and 1960s, Beuys was in a position to argue that the earlier attempts to break down the barriers of art, from multiple perspectives, had not been successful and to challenge the establishment through his use of felt and other "elemental" materials.

Beuys' work was intensely philosophical, commenting on art, politics, the environment and culture. Like Kandinsky before him, Beuys' philosophy was drawn in part from Rudolf Steiner, who believed that spirituality should infuse all human thought and action – a state achieved through a closer connection to the natural world. For Beuys, felt was both a natural product and resembled the natural world, as his sculpture from 1965, *Snowfall* (Schneefall), demonstrates. The piece consists of three rough pine branches sticking out on one side from beneath several layers of grey felt. Caroline Tisdall, a journalist and critic who spent significant periods of time with Beuys during the 1960s, explains his use of felt:

> Snow has much the same effect as felt. Like felt it absorbs from the atmosphere...
> It is a warmth-preserving insulator, and the principle of the Eskimo igloos made of snow is the same as the felt yurts of the Mongolian nomads. It is a sound insulator, too, and a great inducer of silence. (Tisdall 1979, 78)

Felt stands simultaneously for snow and shelter, cold and warmth, and insulator of the body and of sound. Referencing the Mongolian yurts, the artist notes the ancient lineage of the felt, using it to draw analogies between natural coverings, snow and skin, and humanmade ones: tents, blankets and clothing. Beuys returned again and again to the idea of felt as an insulator – as a material that soaks up the air around it while providing a barrier between that air and the thing within. He brings this idea of felt as an insulator of sound to its height in *Infiltration-Homogen for Grand Piano* (1966), which displays a piano entirely encased in felt – the manifestation of what Tisdall calls "an intensified atmosphere of silence" (Tisdall 1979, 83).

For Beuys, felt was not only elemental and everyday, and thus more accessible to viewers, but it was also symbolic. Beuys used felt to represent or allude to warmth and the protection from weather and cold that all humans require – thus the textile itself was elemental but it also represented the fulfillment of an elemental need in humans as hinted at by *Snowfall*. He made this idea most obvious in one of his "warmth sculptures," a 1967 piece that combines felt with a heating element and was part of his *FOND* series. The felt becomes an electric blanket, storing heat. Beuys continued to play with the idea of felt as a receptacle for energy, in the form of heat or sound or even electricity, throughout this series. Perhaps one of the best examples of the necessity of felt as integral to life, however, is in his 1969 piece entitled *The Pack* (das Rudel). In the work, a number of wooden sleds spill from the back of a Volkswagon bus, seemingly heading away into the wilderness beyond. Each is laden with a rolled felt blanket, a ball of fat and a heavy flashlight. Each sled offers the essentials for human survival and comfort – warmth and protection, food at its most basic and warming and light (Borer 1996, 25 and plate 107). Beuys' belief in felt and fat as basic to life lies in part in his own autobiography:

> According to the story, Beuys, who was flying for the Luftwaffe, crashed in the Crimea in 1943; Tatar tribesmen 'brought him back to life' by covering him with felt and salving his wounds with fat. (Tsouti-Schillinger 2001, 158)

Although some art historians argue that this story is apocryphal, others note that it performs a symbolic function by providing Beuys with a kind of "myth of origin," which, given the artist's interest in the spiritual, would have been vital.

One of Beuys' most famous works containing felt, a piece of performance art, remains only in photographs. The action, *Coyote*, took place in May 1974 in the René Block Gallery in New York City as part of his series "I like America and America likes me." The artist locked himself into an open gallery space with a coyote, two large felt blankets, a walking stick and a pile of *Wall Street Journal*s for a week. During this time, the felt became central to the interactions between Beuys and the coyote. On a basic level, it provided bedding and warmth – the very things that felt has been providing people with for centuries and that is so integral to much of Beuys' work. But it also became a form of disguise and protection, as Beuys covered himself with one blanket and slowly turned, allowing the coyote to come closer to this strange form, at once both human and iconic of the shepherd (Tisdall 1979, 230). The felt embodied the transformations Beuys undertook in his relationship with the coyote, and it became the literal fiber of their connection with each other.

Beuys was not the only artist to discover felt as a medium for sculpture in the late 1960s. Robert Morris also produced works of art made of felt that similarly employed the textile as a kind of wrapping skin, yet Morris' approach to felt and reasons for working in it were quite different from Beuys'. Unlike Beuys, Morris did not see his role as an artist as being bound up in the symbolic, the natural world or spiritualism. Instead, as one of the Process artists, his interest in felt portrays his larger concern with form, with the properties of different materials (he also produced landscape sculptures) and with the effects of chance and the simple physics of the earth, such as gravity (Tsouti-Schillinger 2001, 149). Some of Morris' pieces, such as *Untitled (Stacked and Folded)* (1967) seem to pay homage to Beuys, building on the basic beauty of layers of felt massed on the floor of the gallery. Like Beuys, Morris also used felt as a cover, a way of encasing and silencing, in *Muffled Sump* (1995). In this piece, Morris wrapped felt around a working water pump, so that the viewer, although seeing only a mountain of felt, hears the pump and the water coming from within, like a heartbeat (Tsouti-Schillinger 2001, 155). This work draws attention to the ability of felt to clothe on one hand and conceal and silence on the other – it becomes almost animate.

Most of Morris' works in felt, however, rely on the natural drape of textiles and the influence of gravity as it pulls against the tacks that hold it to the wall (ironically, the very problem textile conservators have fought against for years). The weight and thickness of industrial felt provided a resistance to the effects of draping – since a stiff piece of felt will not hang with the same fluidity as a fine piece of silk, for example – and also helped to speed up the effect of gravity. Morris described his attraction to working in felt as based in its mutability: "felt has anatomical associations; it relates to the body – it's skinlike. The way it takes form, with gravity, stress, balance, and the kinesthetic sense, I liked all that" (qtd. in Tsouti-Schillinger 2001, 149). Morris often draws special attention to the pull of gravity by slitting the felt or cutting it into bands, as in *Untitled (Six Legs)* (1969) or *Untitled (Inverted Shoulder)* (1978). Yet the very changeability that so inspired Morris to work with felt could also be a challenge for museum curators and gallery installations. One museum's installation staff apparently spent days failing to get one of Morris' works to look as it had in earlier installations. The effect was only achieved after Morris came in and kicked it a few times (Tsouti-Schillinger 2001, 149).

The artwork made in felt in the middle of the twentieth century reflected an important shift in the way we think about art in the West, and just as felt had a role in some of the social and economic developments that changed western Europe into a capitalist and industrial society, it was also quietly in the midst of this move into new forms of art. Beuys' incorporation of felt drew in part on his own reactions to German culture following the Second World War, including his imprisonment during the second half of the war in the Crimea. Through his work he displayed his concern about the sense of alienation resulting from the industrialism of modern life that seemed to him to pervade German culture. Beuys believed the solution to this malaise lay in returning to what he saw as the most basic needs of mankind. Yet the felt also tied Beuys to other artists engaged with ideas of seeing art in the everyday, such as Andy Warhol and Claes Oldenburg – making the familiar unfamiliar while at the same time giving everyone access to art. Robert Morris, on the other hand, saw felt as a place to experiment with the properties that govern us all – time, gravity and change. His work helped to open up the range of materials available to artists and encouraged us to look at art as expressions of form rather than necessarily as standing for something else. While Beuys was using felt as a primary material and Morris was employing it for studies in form, both were predominantly concerned with sculpture rather than with felt itself. Just as it had in the history of industrialization, felt would receive little fanfare or acknowledgement of its importance. It would take a combination of events and movements to bring felt out of the shadows, first of painting and sculpture and then of its woven and knitted counterparts, and into the world of fine art.

Felt's greatest liability in this process was its label as a medium not of high art but of craft and low art. The distinction between art and craft had come into place by the mid-eighteenth century, dividing painting, sculpture and architecture from all other forms of expression and manufacture. The premise that allowed this division between fine art and craft centered on the object's purpose. Immanuel Kant, the eighteenth-century philosopher, labeled fine art as anything that has no purpose aside from being a work of art – it was meant purely to be looked at. He referred to craft as "mercenary art," the product of work rather than play, diminished because it was intended for use in daily life (Kant 2001, 531). Thus painting and sculpture could be art, but weaving, resulting in rugs and clothing materials, and cabinetry were craft. Over time, this hierarchy came to dominate the way we thought about creative expression in Western culture. Terms such as highbrow, associated with fine art, and lowbrow, assumed for most craft as well as popular culture, determined how objects were received and where they appeared. So ingrained were these ideas, at least in the popular mind, well into the mid-twentieth century, that the word culture itself became synonymous with fine art, even in the face of intense questioning of this hierarchy by scholars, critics and artists for several decades (Levine 1988, 224–5).

By the 1960s and 1970s, artists had begun to approach this boundary from various directions, and it would take all of their efforts, in addition to larger social changes, to finally collapse the distinction. Continuing to build from earlier periods in art, ethnic art generally and textiles specifically were garnering new interest during this time. Possibly for the first time in the Western world, they were being looked upon as art rather than specimens of natural science, and museums themselves were changing their layouts in response (Arnoldi 1992). As we rethought our relationship with other cultures, so too did we reconsider those cultures' aesthetics. Some precedence for engagement with non-Western art existed in the works of artists such as Picasso, who was deeply inspired by African art – also an influence in many textile designs of the 1920s and 1930s. Other artists of the period, notably Degas and Gauguin, traveled in the South Pacific and drew on both the places they saw and the local art in their works. The ultimate effects of these new views of non-Western art, however, took at least until the 1970s to be more fully embraced, with the refashioning of museum displays and a move away from the use of the word "primitive" to describe them. Using similar arguments for opening up the definition of art, some of the feminist artists saw in craft a distinct tradition of women's creativity, and fiber arts in particular as an example of that creativity. These artists built on the momentum of the feminist and equal rights movements to challenge the high/low distinction that had favored white male artists.

Fiber artists often approached the art/craft division from other angles as well. Some attempted to distance their work from craft by insisting that the medium used did not necessarily make the product useful. This argument positioned their work as art rather than craft according to Kant's definition; thus the arguments from all sides served to break down Kant's insistence on the inability of art to be useful. Further, people were beginning to see value in crafts in their own right, as we shall see, throwing the hierarchy into uncertainty. Unfortunately, though fiber arts are more accepted than they once were, the debates over high and low art persist not only in the academy but also in politics, as the discussions about funding for the American federal programs like the National Endowment of the Arts and the American Folklife Center show – both have been threatened with cuts following exhibits that are deemed "controversial," such as Robert Mapplethorpe's photography (Will 2001).

FELT ASCENDANT – CRAFTSMANSHIP, A SHRINKING GLOBE AND THE INTERNATIONAL FELTMAKERS' ASSOCIATION

By the end of the 1970s, fibers of all kinds had shot to prominence as their own artistic medium. Through the breakdown of the barriers of art by artists such as Beuys, Anni Albers and many others, fibers began to be taken seriously as a potential medium for fine art. Two other important influences – one a larger movement within Western society and one a single event that lasted less than a year – also helped to bring felt into the light. The first was the crafts movement of the 1960s and 1970s, and the second, Mary Burkett's exhibition *The Art of the Feltmaker* in 1979. Following the changes in how we think about art and what constitutes art, these two events helped to provoke new developments in the art world and provided a catalyst for more general acceptance of fibers, including felt, as an artistic medium and for a blossoming of felt art and a community of artists and scholars dedicated to the study of felt.

In many ways, the crafts movement of the 1970s drew its inspiration from the earlier arts and crafts movement of the late nineteenth and early twentieth centuries – represented by William Morris and Gustav Stickley – that combined social reform with artistic design. The earlier movement saw art and the handmade as an integral part of life, offering a return to craftsmanship as a way to provide ordinary people with objects of beauty and give the artisans a sense of worth for their skills. The interest in crafts in the 1970s encompassed this association between social reforms aimed at rectifying the problems of modernity and the importance of skilled craftsmanship.

The 1970s crafts movement was driven in part by a dissatisfaction with modern life. Many people felt that the industrialized modern world had produced a life that was consumeristic and fragmented – people were out of touch with one another and with the natural world. In the United States, this dissatisfaction was heightened by the failure of the modern world to prevent armed conflicts, such as Vietnam. Returning to making things by hand was one way to reestablish this lost connection. Hand crafts, from woodworking to knitting to macramé, gained increased attention as people moved away from the plastics, synthetic materials and prefabricated goods that had been one of the developments of the previous generation.

At the same time that artists were challenging the barrier between arts and crafts, crafts were beginning to make a comeback in larger society. The social movements of the late 1960s and 1970s helped drive this interest in craft because of its associations with the natural, individual creativity and cultural expression. Felt was seen as connected to, and symbolic of, both older technologies and the natural world, tying it to the return to agriculturally based lifestyles and smaller communities. Craft, as a form of personal creative expression, was not reliant on the formal institutions that had dictated the limits of art for centuries. Further, craft engaged with materials, like felt, that had been neglected by those institutions. Finally, felt was also representative of ethnic cultures around the globe at a time when ethnic identity and cultural diversity were seen as increasingly important.

The back-to-the-land movement in Europe and North America, like the crafts movement, expressed discontent with modern life and often more particularly with the suburban lifestyle that had arisen in the United States after the Second World War. Just as many of the new craftspeople focused on the process of their work as a means to reduce the pace of life, the back-to-the-land movement sought to slow down by leaving the cities and suburbs to return to a more agriculturally based lifestyle. Many people began small farms that focused on providing the immediate needs of the farmers rather than on producing large crops. A few sheep were often part of this, offering their wool for home textile production. On a practical level, however, few owners of even small flocks of sheep can keep up with the wool they produce. Felting uses up wool more quickly than spinning and knitting or weaving and thus is attractive to a new farmer looking at a pile of wool and watching as their sheep grow more – a path many modern Western felters have followed (including myself). But the discovery of felt as an artistic medium was hardly just a matter of using up wool. Part of returning to the land involved returning to preindustrial materials, such as wood, metal and wool. In the search for a more natural material, sheep's wool was an obvious choice. Meanwhile, fiber artists and craftspeople were attempting to escape the regimentation of the loom in part by searching out other technologies. Both farmer-craftspeople and artists were investing in using more natural mediums to make natural products, and both found an answer in felt.

A desire for self-sufficiency and personal expression was at work in both the back-to-the-land and the crafts movements as they attempted to move away from store-bought possessions. Some of the same ideas pushed the planting of family gardens and homemade blankets. This self-sufficiency was carried into dress: remaking old clothes with patches and embroidery or making clothes from scratch formed a major part of the 1970s crafts movement, as the title of *If You Can't Go Naked, Here Are Clothes to Sew on Fast* (Lawson 1973) sums up nicely. Felt, warm and versatile and needing no edge-finishing, became one of the mainstay fabrics for those wishing to make or embellish their own clothes, especially using appliqué (Laury and Aiken 1973, 63–6). It was as part of the crafts movement that artist Jean Ray Laury, along with co-author Joyce Aiken, provided guidelines for using felt for making and embellishing clothing in their 1973 book. She has continued to use felt over the years and still works with it today for its colors and texture (Laury 2007). It offered incredible potential for creativity in everyday objects, turning even the store-bought into an expression of individuality. Felt had one further advantage for the back-to-the-land farmer and craftsman – it could be made with readily available materials.

For all that felt seemed a perfect fit in both of these movements, however, one difficulty remained. Many people no longer knew how to produce it. At first, most people learned from other practitioners, as had been done for centuries and continues to be one of the most common methods of learning among feltmakers. Increasingly, however, books focused on individual crafts began to be published to fill the gap, with Mary Walker Phillips' 1970 book, *Step-by-Step Macramé*, among the first and most successful. Katarina Ågren's *Tovning* was first published in 1976 in Sweden. Ågren had been working as a curator at a regional museum in Västerbotten in central Sweden when she began investigating felt in the 1960s. Although felt had largely died out in Sweden by this time, with the increase of commercially made goods and central heating, Ågren was able to locate and talk with several people who knew the craft. Her book created a revival of interest in making felt across not only Sweden but all of northern Europe (Sjöberg 1996, 18). In the United States, Beverly Gordon produced one of the first books on felt in 1980, entitled *Feltmaking*. Gordon's book set the standard for most future books on felt: it offered a brief history, a look at current art and fashion made from felt by way of inspiration, and instructions for making your own felt along with project ideas (Gordon 1980).

As an artist, Beth Beede followed a path to felt through just such a focus on natural materials and the resurgence of craft. She had attended the Art Institute of Chicago and studied painting and sculpture, but then went on to have a family and homestead in Alaska. By 1975, Beede had become interested in using recycled or recyclable materials and making art that would be seen and used every day. Beth and her husband, Larry, soon discovered felt. Larry constructed a felting machine from found parts and shared the plans with other aspiring feltmakers, and the couple began to teach felting and host workshops in their Massachusetts home. Beede is now retired from teaching, but she continues to produce felt artworks. As a dedicated teacher and one of the earliest artists to work in felt in the United States, Beede has influenced or taught many of today's felters. Some even refer to her as the "'mother' of American feltmaking" (Westfall 2005, 31–2).

Ideas of craftsmanship, the handmade, and a return to the natural world during this time were not the only influences on felt. As in the fine art world, people were also taking on important political issues such as civil rights and equality. The push for equal civil rights in the 1960s, particularly in the United States, helped to increase awareness about social classifications such as race and ethnicity. People began to pay attention to how they identified themselves and others and sought to break down social barriers by celebrating diversity, often as expressed through textiles. Patterns that drew on specific ethnic designs became popular. Artists and designers turned to traditional cultural motifs and aesthetics for inspiration.

Certainly another influence was also at play here. During the 1970s, Afghanistan was opened to travelers from the West and became a destination for students of anthropology and art history as well as tourists. Many people have reported to me that they first encountered traditional felt while in Afghanistan during this time, and many brought felt rugs home with them, though few seem to have survived. Air travel and telecommunications were beginning to make the world seem a smaller place, and as people traveled they encountered both cultures and materials that had received little attention before from the West. Further, Westerners were no longer looking at the rest of the world in the same way. On the one hand, cultures like those in Afghanistan came to symbolize the very sense of personal connection and cultural identity that many Westerners felt they had lost. On the other, the Civil Rights Movement had, by extension, required that people approach cultures that were new to them with sensitivity and respect, and one way of doing so is to see value in the arts produced by those cultures. All of these factors led to a desire for a new kind of ethnicity – one that was inclusive, drawing on many traditions to create a new artistic expression that could characterize a generational rather than a racial or geographic community. As the introduction to one book, showing crafts mostly from around the San Francisco Bay area in the early 1970s, puts it:

> Many of us have hungered for a cultural identity strong enough to produce our own versions of the native costumes of Afghanistan or Guatemala, for a community life rich enough for us to need our own totems comparable to African or Native American masks and ritual objects.
>
> The native funk and flash in this book tell us something of that hunger and what we are doing to fill it, as well as something of the meaning of those artifacts from other places and times. (Jacopetti 1974, 5)

The author, Alexandra Jacopetti, sums up in these two sentences all of the dissatisfaction with contemporary Western life and the search for a way to confront it specifically through artistic expression. Much of this book, and dozens of others like it, focus on how readers can use their own creativity to decorate the everyday – from the clothes we wear and rework rather than throw away to the objects in our homes and even the homes themselves – to endow them with personal spiritual and creative meaning, combining some of the ideas expressed by William Morris and Joseph Beuys.

The crafts movement was in some ways a direct result of attempts by at least a century of artists and critics to make art and artistic expression accessible to all. As more people felt that they too had access to art and art was allowed a wider range of mediums, the desire for natural materials in everyday life led to the embrace of natural materials in art as well. Again, felt was an ideal choice. All of these social movements played into one another. Some artists responded more to one than another, were more conscious of one or another, and some found completely different paths to felt than anything outlined here. The awareness of felt as a potential artistic medium in Western art, however, can be seen as one outcome of all of these interwoven (or perhaps entangled?) influences throughout Western culture, creating the catalyst through which felt was recognized as important. Yet one other event proved to be of crucial importance for felt art and is often marked by artists working in felt as the beginning of felt art as a field of its own.

The second influence on the acceptance of felt as an art form was a single event. In 1979, the exhibition *The Art of the Feltmaker* opened at Abbott Hall in Kendal, England. This exhibition was the first known special exhibit dedicated to felt. Mary Burkett, the curator, had been collecting and studying felt for close to two decades, predominantly in the Middle East, but she went beyond this region to focus on felt traditions from across Eurasia and included a few pieces from artists who were working in felt. Burkett first became interested in felt during a trip to Iran in 1962, when she saw some women making felt near the roadside (Burkett 1979, iv; Thomas 2000, 252). This led to several years of travel, research and collecting – eventually leading up to the exhibit. The exhibit toured England, providing both inspiration for those who were new to felt and a way for those who had already begun working in the medium to meet and network. The importance of this single exhibit to felt art cannot be overstated, for not only did it provide the book that would become the basis for all future study of felt but it also became a jumping-off place for the group that would be felt art's biggest promoter – the International Feltmakers' Association.

Although some artists had already been working in felt in Europe and around the world, this exhibition gave prominent voice to both their artwork and the long history and broad cultural influence of felt as a textile. The exhibition helped to spur the already rising interest in felt that was part of the crafts movement, and from the year of the exhibit on, makers of felt around Europe, North America and Australia began to come together in one felt-centered event after the next. The year 1984 proved a landmark one in the felt world. Many artists and scholars working in felt met in Kecskemét, Hungary, at the invitation of István Vidák and Mari Nagy for the First International Felt Conference, in memory of Veronika Gervers. This conference was perhaps the first time that so many felters and scholars from a wide range of traditions, and across the political divides of western and eastern Europe and Soviet Central Asia, had gathered to share their knowledge (Thomas 2000, 253–4). During that same year, feltmakers in England founded the International Feltmakers' Association (IFA), representing a wide range of interests across the arts and education and even including some of the remaining hatters. The IFA sought to promote the study of felt and its use as an artistic medium and remains the largest felt arts organization to this day (International Feltmakers' Association 2007).

The founding of IFA kindled a steadily growing interest in felting. The community was kept together by the publication of various felt newsletters and journals, including *Felt Filt*, edited by Lene Nielsen, and IFA's own quarterly, *Echoes*. At roughly the same time as IFA was getting under way in England, North American felters were also organizing. The felters began as a subset of the weavers, meeting for the first time in 1978 at the Handweavers' Guild of America biannual conference, called Convergence, held in Fort Collins, Colorado. The next formal meeting as part of Convergence would not happen again for fourteen years, but the feltmakers kept busy and connected. Felt artist, Patricia Spark, began publishing the

North American Felters' Newsletter in 1992 and an international felt conference, separate from Convergence, was held in 1994 in Canada, at Castlegar, British Columbia. Since then, these international conferences have continued in the United States and Canada every three years.

In the last twenty years, felting organizations have arisen across the globe. At least three felting groups are active in Australia in addition to those who meet through the spinning and weaving organizations, and an active email discussion board helps to keep felters in contact across the country. Together with felters in New Zealand, they have organized the Southern Hemisphere Felters' Workshops. Organizations have also been started in regions where people have been making traditional felt for centuries, such as Filtti – the Finnish Felt Association, which was founded in 1998. All of these organizations support a wide range of people interested in felt, from scholars to those who make felt only for their own use or to give to friends (like the early felters of the 1970s crafts movement), to artists who produce magnificent works in felt for galleries and museums. They offer courses for those wanting to learn more and arrange exhibitions for those already skilled. It is to these skilled artists that we now turn.

FELT IN FASHION AND FELT IN THE GALLERY

Like many textiles, felt in art has tended to be used in one of two ways: either for fashion, including wearable art and hats, or else for sculpture. Because of felt's associations with floor coverings in many traditional cultures, however, it has also been used in a third category of large, flat works, intended for either the floor or the wall, with designs that go from the pictorial and realist to the abstract to the ruglike. The distinctions between these different types of forms are often fuzzy at best, and since feltmakers tend to define themselves more by their medium, felt, than by their product, one artist may choose the form that best suits her purpose, rather than working only in one or another, and experiment with new techniques and new forms as her work progresses. These distinctions are somewhat arbitrary, and much more important is the creativity that has shaped felt in new and exciting ways. Probably the largest published collection of works by felt artists across all of these areas is the book *Felt/Filz: Art, Crafts and Design* (2000), edited by German artist Katarina Thomas. The book displays works by artists from around the world, capturing the stunning variety of felt art – sculptural, pictorial and wearable – and shows some of the fascinating new directions that felt has taken. As one of the book's authors writes: "Felt has become definitively modern"

(Thomas 2000, 65). The pages that follow profile some of the artists working in felt today and attempt to provide some insight into the reasons they give for their attraction to felt as a medium. These artists are only the tip of the felt iceberg (or perhaps the doorway into the yurt?) but they, alongside the artists and artisans already mentioned, help to demonstrate the range of ingenuity being applied to felt today.

Jorie Johnson grew up around textiles. Her father was a wool and cloth merchant in the United States and was a strong advocate of natural fibers. Johnson studied art in college and in graduate school, focusing on textiles from the start. While studying textile art in Finland in the late 1970s, she discovered felt through learning to make traditional-style Finnish felt boots (Johnson 2007a). Felt not only sparked her creative interests, she also found that it could be easily produced in relatively small spaces and with equipment common to any kitchen or bathroom. Considering herself something of a nomad, these qualities made for a perfect artistic match (Westfall 2005, 35). Johnson does indeed move around from her studio in Kyoto, Japan, spending part of each year traveling for workshops, exhibitions and research, and she takes her inspirations from the traditions and histories of feltmaking and other arts around the world, drawing on "[the] functional in the United States, the naturalistic creative force in Northern Europe and the poetic tradition in Japan" (Johnson qtd. in Westfall 2005, 35).

Johnson makes a wide variety of felt pieces, from sculptures and wall hangings to wearable fashion, from thick and structural to thin and gauzy. She thinks of all of her works as sculptures, regardless of their additional function as jackets or scarves, rugs or wall hangings. Yet despite classifying them as art objects, she also desires her work to be useable, denying the historic separation between art and craft (Johnson qtd. in Aimone 2002, 30). Throughout her work, she develops the myriad properties that make felt so versatile, using color and form to augment each other and the felt itself.

Dutch artist Inge Evers describes her journey to felt as closely associated with several of the same paths that lead many artists to felt. She first encountered felt as a child during the Second World War. Clothing was scarce, and she remembers her mother making her a pair of shoes out of one of her father's felt hats. Later, she remembers writing stories on a chalkboard. The felt eraser became both the secret depository of her narratives and, in cleaning the board, an invitation to create more. Evers started making her own felt as an extension of her work in other fibers. During the 1960s, she was making textile murals and began to study different kinds of fabrics and more particularly the natural fibers. From there, Evers followed a path similar to the one outlined in this chapter describing the rise of felt: she found Veronika Gervers' articles on felt, then Katarina Ågren's book. She continued to experiment with wool and her own feltmaking through trial and error, while researching what little published material she could find. Mary Burkett's exhibit, *The Art of the Feltmaker*, made Evers realize that there was a whole vast history of feltmaking. She attended the first international symposium in Hungary, and from then on has continued to connect with feltmakers around the world through study and workshops and art. She went on to write her thesis on felt as a form of community art. Evers appreciates the double meaning of the word felt in English – referring to both the fabric and the idea of feeling or emotion – despite their different etymologies. Feltmaking allows for a sense of play, a way to explore the imagination and express one's feelings. For Evers, "feltmaking is a way of conscious living," but above all, she says, making felt makes her happy (Evers 2008).

At least since the 1970s, the United Kingdom has been at the forefront of the felt movement. From Mary Burkett's curated exhibition, *The Art of the Feltmaker*, artists and scholars in the UK have come together to promote felt and felt art. Artist and educator Sheila Smith has been one of felt's greatest promoters and one of England's premier felt artists. Smith enjoyed making things from her childhood and originally trained as a teacher of home economics. Although long interested and involved with textiles, she learned to spin and weave in the 1980s, and like many feltmakers, became interested in felt through these related crafts. Smith admits that her first foray into felting was not a terrific success, but she became intrigued by the fabric while studying for a degree in textile design. She wanted to make a fluid felt garment with good drape, unlike the thicker, stiffer felt she had mostly seen. After some work, she was successful. She has continued to perfect the technique; that first jacket seems thick and heavy to her now (Smith 2007b).

Since then, Sheila Smith has been making, showing and teaching felt across the UK and Europe. Most of her work consists of wearable felt pieces, although she has also made a large number of sample pieces demonstrating specific techniques, for example *shibori* felting or embroidered felting. Like many felt artists, Smith values the variability of felt. She appreciates felt's long history as a functional and decorative textile. In honor of this history, she prefers to make functional pieces herself. Yet, at the same time, she compares working with different colors of fiber to the way that a painter uses colors of paint – learning how different preparations and types of wool can be adapted to create specific finishes. In her teaching, Smith highlights the importance of having a basic understanding of how felt and dyes work. By learning the process, students are able to take control of their own work (Smith 2007b).

Although felt art has been made in the United States for many years, it only recently began to attract the attention it deserves, largely through the work of dynamic new feltmakers. Christine White is one of these felt artists. She discovered felting less than ten years ago, when a friend, looking at her three-dimensional knitting, suggested that she skip the needlework and go straight to felt. She found a simple instructional book to try it out, but was so taken with the process that she began felting every day and had soon turned it into a full-time profession. Now, White divides her time between making felt for galleries and commissions, teaching felting and selling raw materials through her store, New England Felting Supply, located in an old movie house in Massachusetts.

Unlike many of the other feltmakers who discover felt through a long-term interest in art, White began her career as a metamorphic geologist, studying how mountains form from rocks that change their composition over time. Her interest in change and variability gained from her work in geology is a large part of what has drawn her to felt: the creation of a huge range of fabrics – from gossamer cobwebs to thick, heavy wall hangings or rugs – out of a loose pile of wool. Like Smith and Johnson, White sees felt as "deceptively simple." The process can be carried out by any age group or skill level, making it welcoming to newcomers, but the apparent simplicity of the technique can be developed to make works of great complexity. Building on her scientific background, White has released a book on feltmaking that not only provides instruction and sample projects, but looks deeply at the technical aspects of felt (White 2007b). White is thrilled to be helping to shape many people's first impressions of felt, as interest in the medium grows in the United States through her work, her store and her writing.

Many American felters reflect White's sense of experimenting alone, developing techniques as they go along and only then meeting with other felters. Ruth Walker, a Missouri feltmaker, talked about her experiences learning about felt as she made it. After being introduced to felt by a friend, Walker had developed her own method for making hats by building up layers of differently colored wool and yarns, almost like a papier mâché technique. Her first hat won her a prize at a wool festival, but only after meeting other felters did she begin to realize that her method for making felt was unusual. Walker enjoys the challenge that comes with experimenting with different dyes and types of wool. Walker is glad to see the increased attention that felt is receiving in the United States but is also cautious that those new to felt recognize the difference between knitted felt and true felt straight from the fleece as the single term felt gets applied to both.

Felt is often made for wearable art, but by artists such as the ones we have discussed so far, these pieces are typically one-of-a-kind items. Nonetheless, in the world of international fashion, a few big designers have been picking up felt and using it for more than hats. While fulled woven fabrics had long been used for coats, the fabric shortages of the 1930s led to experimentation with a wide variety of textiles, including felt. The Italian designer Elsa Schiaparelli produced a long coat with a patchwork design as part of her spring collection for 1939. This coat was meant to play on the eighteenth-century *commedia dell'arte* harlequin while at the same time evoking folk dress, rather than the harlequin's silks, through its materials. Felt waned in popularity for fashion after the Second World War, but it has made regular appearances since then, first in the 1960s and later in the 1990s. Comme des Garçons featured jackets and trousers made of felt in their Autumn/Winter collection of 1995. Chief designer, Rei Kawakubo, studied fine arts and literature rather than fashion design, and her background comes through in the highly structural pieces that she creates. Felt's variable thickness and unique drape make it perfect for such experiments with form and structure. One sweater in the 1995 collection seems to represent the idea of a favorite large sweater more than the sweater itself. The sleeves are especially large and set into huge armscyes [armholes] well off the shoulder and the hem drops to just above the knees. The piece is made of white felt with red and pink splashes. The use of felt heightens both the structural feel of the sweater and its size. Reminiscent of Claes Oldenburg's large sculptures of everyday objects, we are drawn to the sweater as a sculpture. Japanese designer Issey Miyake included felt in his Autumn/Winter collection for 1997, "Prism Collage." He designed coats and other clothing constructed from white felt that had been needle-felted with layers of colored, gauze-like fabric to produce a textile with the colors seemingly resting just under the surface. Like Beth Beede, Miyake was drawn to felt as a way of recycling materials – combining fabrics in layers through felting to create new textiles with their own levels of interest (Simon 1999).

Designers – such as Miyake and Comme des Garçons – are drawn to felt for the properties it offers: the unique ways in which the wool can hold and display colors; the ability of felt to consist of layers of color or fabric that seem to transform the individual components into something greater than a sum of parts; and, just as Beuys and Morris found, felt's ability to be sculptural in ways that few other textiles can, because of its highly variable density and drape. Few designers use felt and those that do use it only infrequently, but when they do, they create remarkable fashions that highlight felt's amazing versatility, from yurt walls and practical boots to the catwalks of Paris.

7.
FELT EVERYWHERE

We have seen felt's long history from the steppes of Central Asia to the hat shops of Europe. We have seen felt made by peoples who have produced this fabric for centuries, its techniques passed down from mother to daughter, father to son for generations; felt that is so central to life that it has its own festivals, songs and blessings. We also have seen felt made by people who learned to make it in art school or from colleagues: felt that asks those who see it to reflect on what they see and on the felt itself. We have seen felt made by hand and the industry of felt. But for all that these ways of felting help to shape what felt is and what felt means, we have nonetheless missed some of felt's most pervasive and least-lauded roles: the felt of the everyday Western world. In knowing how felt is made and who makes it, we only know one part of felt's story. This chapter tells the other part. It tells the story of how Western felt is used.

Felt is everywhere. It literally keeps our machines moving and us safe. We use felt and other nonwovens every day, often without even being aware of it. To list all of the tasks that felt has performed would require a book of its own and years of research. Instead, five general categories help to give a sampling of how we now use felt and where it appears – crafts, retail clothing and home goods, kitsch, industry and engineering, and a final category for everywhere else. Felt is a staple of home crafts, the handmade embellishments on clothing, picture frames, small toys and finger puppets. These crafts are different from the felt art we have seen in earlier chapters largely because they rely on store-bought felt but they are different in other crucial ways as well – in how they are produced and dispersed and in the forms they take. In recent years, in particular, felt has made a comeback in the retail world as "folk" styles have become popular. Suddenly felt is no longer a souvenir from Central Asia, the work of an artist or something made by a favorite aunt; pillows and decorations of felt are available for sale from large chain stores. Yet this fashion is likely to come and go, and as it does, today's popular felt may, like many of those felt crafts, end up as kitsch. Moving from the handmade to retail to wholesale, I will look at why felt is prized both for industrial uses and in engineering and glimpse some of the unexpected places you can find it.

FELT CRAFTS

Not only have the traditional feltmakers found new methods and new ways to show their skills, but "felt" itself has changed. Acrylic nonwovens appear in lurid, multicolored piles of paper-sized sheets in every craft store, fabric store and primary school art room and go by the name of felt. This is the new "felt," what we often think of when we hear the word. Its stability and strength make it the perfect craft material, and as such, it has appeared in count-less Halloween and pageant costumes, holiday centerpieces and *Better Homes and Gardens* projects. Away from the glamour of the art world, the industry of the workshop and factory and the traditionality of the felt culture, I will investigate some of the more mundane uses of felt, from the poodle skirts of the 1950s to the hundreds of homemade felt Christmas decorations.

The felt used in artworks such as those in the last chapter forms part of the traditions of Western fine art and fashion, but this covers only one area of felt use. Homemade crafts are another, not entirely separate, tradition. These crafts are certainly creative and they may draw their inspiration from some of the same places as the works of art or even from those works themselves. The history of making home crafts is difficult to follow, but it has existed at least since the nineteenth century. Crafts arose out of the needlework that women once did to embellish their clothing, accessories and furnishings. By the mid-nineteenth century, craft or needlework projects were a staple of the new women's magazines such as *Godey's Lady's Book* and *The Ladies' Home Journal*, along with advice on cooking, fashion and childcare. The craft projects gave women ideas for hand work to occupy their time in a ladylike fashion and decorate their home. Although the styles have changed, the magazines and their projects remain the staples of every grocery store checkout aisle and have expanded into television with Martha Stewart and the Home and Garden network.

Some of these crafts were reinvigorated as an extension of the 1970s crafts and fiber arts movements. Creativity as expressed through the embellishment of everyday objects and through the handmade were central tenets of both these larger social movements, with their ties to specific philosophical ideas and to the project-based craft tradition of ladies' magazines. At this point, crafts also began to splinter into different paths. Some crafts and craftspeople remained true to the project model of the women's magazines, focusing on relatively simple handmade items aimed at either adults or children and typically using premade felt as a starting material. This type of craft was centered more on the production of a specific object rather than the material. Others moved more towards the model of developing a single skill through books and workshops, and these often began with the wool itself and proceeded through making felt. This craft tradition focused on the process and the medium more than the product. Ultimately, where the borders lie between these different forms of craft is difficult to define, but what is important here is the coexistence of the two and the acknowledgement that, although stretched, the term "crafts" must serve to cover all of those things made of felt and made by hand. These crafts are generally made by people who do not consider themselves professionals or artists and typically are not intended for display outside the home, although they may appear for sale in craft fairs.

Many of the crafts that involve felt are not oriented towards making the felt from loose wool but rather with using premade felt as a material. The Aetna Felt Corporation carries multiple lines of these felts, specifically made for the craft market. They come in both the small, paper-sized sheets and rolled yardage, in everything from 100 percent wool to blends of wool and rayon to 100 percent acrylic or polyester, and in upwards of sixty different colors (Aetna Felt Corporation 2007). Interestingly, synthetic felts tend to be recommended for use in crafts on the basis that they can be more easily washed than wool felt. Felt's properties are precisely what make it so prized by craftspeople. Not only does it come in such a wide range, but it can be cut easily without tearing or needing to be hemmed and it responds to a wide range of treatments: it can be sewn, glued, painted, stamped, shaped or almost anything else you can think of (Kirby 2003, 4).

By far the majority of felt-related crafts, and by extension felt-related craft books, are aimed at children. Felt is perfect for many children's crafts: it is soft and easily worked, even by younger children. Many of us remember making puppets and stuffed animals from sheets of felt, cut to shape and sewn or glued together, at school, home, church or camp. Mobiles and decorated cards are also popular, but perhaps one of felt's most lasting locales is in Christmas decorations. Our tree was decorated with felt soldiers made by one of my brothers, and almost everyone I spoke to about this project had a story to tell about making felt ornaments or cards for relatives. We also had felt stockings that we had made ourselves, and I have been told of felt wreaths, felt Santas, felt tree decorations and a large felt skirt wrapped around the base of the tree. Felt is nonsectarian and appears in decorations of all kinds, for every holiday and season: a felt dreidel and menorah wall decorations in honor of Hanukkah, felt leaves to celebrate autumn, flowers for spring, and American flags for the Fourth of July. Because of its wide uses, felt often becomes a ground fabric for teaching children other skills, such as sewing or appliqué quilting (McAllister 2003).

Felt crafts for adults, especially those found in the pages of many women's magazines, can be more complex – requiring more careful cutting or delicate manipulation of the fabric and assuming a greater knowledge of basic sewing and construction skills (Feldman 1980). The craft books for adults also provide a bit more information on the textile. They may begin with the story of St. Clement walking on the wool until it matted and thus discovering felt (although one book attributed it to St. Feutre) and include some information on the properties of felt or wool. The basis for these books, however, lies in the projects more than the history, and the projects are designed to provide useful items for the home or for friends and family. These books almost always contain a large section of projects for toys and clothing to be made for children. While the books are representative of the kinds of crafts being made from felt, they do not cover the ingenuity of the many people who work in felt. Their products, including felt dolls, felt outfits for teddy bears and felt doilies of every description, can often be found in church sales and craft fairs, if they are for sale at all.

Many of the objects listed above are intended for display only, but another related and perhaps more ubiquitous use of felt has been in clothing and costumes. Probably the most well known clothing made of felt was the poodle skirt of the 1950s. These circle skirts were intended to be fairly stiff so that the fabric would stand out in wide folds around the woman's legs. Felt's relatively high density and thickness made it perfect for the desired effect, which could be augmented by the addition of crinolines underneath. Moreover, felt was easily cut out in interesting shapes, such as poodles or music records, and appliquéd onto the skirt at home allowing for the personal embellishment of store-bought skirts, whether they be felt or woven. Such felt appliqué on clothing has been a standard of children's clothes for decades, with felt trains, flowers and animals embellishing the bodices of many girls' and boys' outfits. I, myself, sported pinafore-style dresses decorated with cut-out felt stars in my early youth. During the 1970s crafts movement, felt appliqué, especially when combined with embroidery, offered a way for many people to show their own creativity on their clothes using techniques and materials they had worked with before. Felt appliqués and patchwork were used to individualize jackets, blankets, dresses and skirts, bags of all shapes and sizes and the cuffs of blue jeans, to name only a few, in patterns of rainbows, spiders, letters, flowers and ethnically based designs reminiscent of eastern European motifs or even the *mola*s of the Kuna Indians (Laury and Aiken 1973).

For the same reasons that felt is such a good material for crafts and appliqué, it is also one of the easiest and most common materials for homemade costumes. Whether they be for Halloween or children's pageants, costumes are typically made with the intention of wearing them only once or twice. Thus the ideal fabric for costumes must be quick and easy to work, be able to take on any number of shapes, come in a wide selection of colors, and be inexpensive. Yet again, felt fits the bill, especially since it is readily available and does not need its edges hemmed. Felt can also be adapted to almost anyone's skill level, being simply cut, glued and wrapped or sewn into complex patterns. Better still, the thermal properties that have kept countless shepherds warm around the world also keep American children warm on cold Halloween nights. Felt offers such unique properties for costumes – because of its drape, the variety of thicknesses available and its texture – that it has even been used in Hollywood for certain costumes in *Star Wars*.

While the crafts and costumes discussed so far have made use of manufactured felt, the art of feltmaking is becoming more popular. Many of the new feltmakers are introduced to felt through other crafts, such as knitting. Starting about ten years ago, knitting attracted renewed interest, particularly among college students in the United States. Some of these knitters had learned to knit from their mothers or grandmothers, but many were learning from each other. Knitting was seen as a profoundly social activity – a chance to get together and chat with friends while still doing something – and "stitch and bitch" sessions arose across campuses and in local communities. These younger knitters wanted patterns that provided a contemporary look, and since many were beginners, projects that were fast, easy and used large yarn and needles were even better. A host of books on how to felt knitted pieces, such as *Knit One, Felt Too* and *Felted Knits,* responded (Taylor 2003; Galeskas 2003). The popularity of felting knits is so strong that in knitting stores about half of the book inventory is given over to knitting for felt. Obviously, this is not felt in the true sense of fibers interlocked purely through heat, moisture and agitation, but rather it uses the fulling process on knitted instead of woven fabrics. The felting is achieved by putting the finished knitted piece into a regular clothes washer and filling it with hot water, allowing the washer to do the work. Felting knitted items not only provides a stronger, denser final fabric, which is particularly good for sturdy bags or hats, but it also gives a different texture and finished look than either straight knitting or felting, and makes use of skills and equipment that many people already possess. Felting knitted items was marketed in particular towards beginner-level knitters, since the fulling process would help to hide mistakes and integrate the fibers around lost stitches that might otherwise come undone (Malcolm 2005).

Felt can be a means of getting children interested in making things or helping people to learn new craft skills, but more and more often, the felt itself is what children are learning to make. Many feltmakers are involved with teaching feltmaking to children either as part of school or summer camp programs. Its relative ease, accessible and limited materials, and quick process make it a good classroom or outdoor activity. In England, feltmaking programs have been developed specifically for use in schools. English feltmaker and scholar Stephanie Bunn combined feltmaking with theater and worked with a group of children to create a story yurt.

Perhaps as an extension of the knitting-to-felt phenomenon or perhaps simply as people seek new ways to express themselves creatively, feltmaking is gaining in popularity among adults. Many of the artists discussed in the previous chapter have published their own how-to books on making felt, including Chad Alice Hagen and Jorie Johnson's recent *Fabulous Felted Scarves* (2007) and Sheila Smith's *Felt to Stitch* (2007). While books aimed at using felt as a ground fabric typically do not include much history or cultural information about felt, these texts by felt artists revel in felt as an artistic form in its own right, giving details of where it came from, who has used it and the many forms it has taken.

No doubt this only scratches the surface of the extent to which felt is used in crafts. Any local library contains a wide selection of books that cover everything from making your own felt, to felting your knitted projects, to sewing felt into every conceivable shape. Some of these crafts are made by adults and some by children, some are made from patterns or out of books and some are entirely the product of their makers' imaginations, but all show the creativity and skills of the maker. Yet just as people have gained interest in making felt, they have also become interested in buying it.

RETAILING FELT

In the past five years, felt products have lined the shelves of stores ranging from the boutique to the chain megastore. While felt is predominantly found amidst the house wares, covering pillows or sewn onto bedspreads, or among the toys, it has also made forays into ready-to-wear clothing. The extent to which felt has appeared on the market seemed to reach its height in 2006, but it continues to have an important presence in the market at multiple market levels. Felt covers a huge range of styles, from the nature-inspired to the "artsy" to the "hip." It purveys hominess and worldliness, simplicity and creativity.

Go to the toy section of any good store and you are almost guaranteed to find felt. Felt dolls and puppets can be bought as well as made at home, and felt provides a good, soft, non-toxic material for making toys such as soft blocks. Felt is also ideal for making soft books for toddlers. The felt is sturdy, not easily torn like paper, and turning the pages becomes a silent activity. Also, if the book is thrown, no one is hurt. Felt storyboards were a major part of my own childhood. These sets consisted of a piece of stiff card flocked with fiber, or a larger roll-out piece of felt, and a wide variety of shapes cut out of different colors of felt. The child can then create scenes, sticking the felt pieces to the board and rearranging them. My personal favorite was a sea-themed board in blue with fish, grasses, a diver, and even a shark. Story felts are still made and, if anything, are more complex. Many now print images onto the pieces of felt, so they are no longer simple, one-color shapes, and at least one set consists of a large piece of felt that folds up into a suitcase shape, with four pockets to hold the differently themed pieces.

In housewares, felt has much larger representation. The large, one-stop American shopping chain, Target, carried felt pillows. US catalog companies, including Viva Terra, Sundance and Garnet Hill, have all carried pillows and other interior décor in felt during the last few years. However, boutique-style mall chain, Anthropologie, perhaps tops the list for its use of felt. Not only does it regularly carry clothing items either made of or containing felt, as well as felt pillows and seasonal decorations and toys such as hand puppets from Nepal, but it even sported a huge wreath made of felt at the entrance of one of the mall stores for the 2006 holiday season. The wreath was purely store decoration and had been made by the staff out of hundreds of squares of white and cream-colored felt, sewn together. It was not for sale but did hint at the many felt offerings inside. Interestingly, Viva Terra carried a similar wreath the following holiday season, made not of felt but of felted sweaters, along with felt slippers, bags and pillows.

Felt products highlight the soft texture of felt's surface and make use of both the creaminess of undyed white felt and the depth of color that can be achieved in wool. Earth tones and deep reds, greens, oranges and blues are popular, pastels are extremely rare. Pillows typically have felted-in patterns, often consisting of a few stripes, while other décor items may be decorated with stitching or beads. Felt products are almost always relatively simple in their patterns, consisting of a few large, abstract motifs. Bags may be more complex, and more than other felted items, their marketing includes information about their makers – "Hand-scrubbed and pounded by Nepalese and Tibetan villagers" (VivaTerra, Holiday 2007, 76–7). Both the design of these felted items and their marketing seems a nod towards "authenticity."

Just as the crafts movement of the 1970s found inspiration in the handmade and in arts of non-Western ethnic groups, objects that appear handmade and/or have a provenance in non-Western ethnic groups are popular once again. This could simply be fashion, but it is worth viewing it in conjunction with other current trends: those that look to the environment, such as the green movement, and cultures based on the search for self-improvement or wellbeing, as proven by the popularity of yoga and tai'chi, for example. Perhaps the vogue for felt is partly the result of some of the same dissatisfactions with modern life that led people to these practices – rooted in other, seemingly more "authentic," cultures – in the first place. At least a portion of the felted goods carried by the catalogues are made in Central Asia by women's craft co-operatives such as Altyn Kol and Altyn Oimok and have been marketed through the Central Asian Craft Support Association in Kyrgyzstan and Aid to Artisans in the United States. At least five years ago, several of the individually owned gift shops around the United States began carrying Nepalese-made felt bags and coin purses in modern designs. These kinds of small felted items, and particularly fulled wool products from Nepal, have been on offer in such shops since the 1970s, especially from companies focused on aid and fair-trade practices, like Oxfam. In fact, the concept of craft-based aid extends at least to the Reconstruction Era following the Civil War, with the establishment of the first African-American and later Appalachian craft schools (Whisnant 1983). Many of the retailers make use of this pedigree by mentioning the makers in their marketing and product descriptions. By emphasizing the Central Asian makers, the retailer can offer the buyer a sense that they are helping the makers through their purchases. The buyer's sense of the world and their position as a humanitarian becomes symbolized by the objects they purchase through such fair-trade organizations – in this case, felt. Yet the buyer is also saying something about their own sense of style and their ability to create a home environment through the use of presumably handmade objects. The overall aesthetic may have changed, but what the crafts movement sought to produce, modern companies now offer for sale.

Felt, perhaps in part because it was something so many people made crafts from in their childhood, carries associations of home and the handmade. In a pillow or decoration, it gives the sense of a personal touch, a connection not only to other people but to creativity as well. This creativity may be expressed through actually making felt objects, as described in much of the rest of this book, but it may also be shown through decorating. Felt offers the decorator, professional or otherwise, a soft, warm finish that feels like home. By feeling handmade, even though they may not be, felt décor items suggest the homeowner's personal creativity and style, and their ability to take time to express it despite the fast pace of modern life. In other words, the felt can imply that the house is a kind of haven.

Just as the 1970s crafts movement sought the natural, the current expression of dissatisfaction with modern life often focuses on simplicity as a cure for modern ills. The search for simplicity is based on a belief that we have overly complicated our lives, and the use of the words simple and natural in everything from foods to magazine titles proves how pervasive this desire is and how well marketers have made use of it. Felt has been a part of this move towards the simple and the natural, partly because of its association with the handmade. To make something by hand shows that the maker possesses the required skills but also has the time to do things by hand. Yet we cannot forget the extent of felt's association with childhood, at least in North America. This connection to childhood may be partly why felt items are particularly popular in the winter displays and catalogues as they strive to promote buyers' nostalgia about Christmases past. Not only do companies sell the wreaths described above, but a wide selection of ornaments in shapes of Santas, snowmen and angels are available largely, though not exclusively, through catalogue outlets specializing in holiday décor. Such felt holiday decorations can provide a sense of remembered childhood, of looking back on crafts projects done as a child that you no longer have, yet made with a skill level that few children possess.

In the case of some of the felt decorations, however, the fact that they were not made at home may be more important. Many of these felt decorations are made in Kyrgyzstan, which rather ironically is a predominantly Muslim country. Nonetheless, various catalogues have been selling nativity scenes made of felt with a yurt for a manger and Mary, Joseph and the Wise Men looking distinctly Kyrgyz, complete with traditional Kyrgyz dress. The yurt nativity not only provides the owner with memories of childhood connected to felt, but also symbolizes her awareness of the world. Displaying something made in another culture marks someone as the sort of person who travels, who is conscious of living in a global community. Even if the person has not been to Kyrgyzstan, they show that they are nonetheless knowledgeable about the world and committed to drawing connections with other people in it.

Felt's popularity and appearance in the marketplace will rise and fall with fashion trends. As "ethnic" styles came into fashion during the last few years and felting gained some popularity as a craft, felt products made a resurgence as a way to achieve a homey, natural look without necessarily having to learn how to make or work with felt. One of the great benefits of knitted felt and the growing interest in making felt is that it is no longer viewed exclusively in connection with children's crafts. Felt has grown up, as its appearance in many different kinds of retail markets proves, and people are learning just how versatile and stylish felt can be.

FELT KITSCH

One other area of felt products in the home and market remains to be explored – felt as kitsch. At times, felt has been turned to mimic a more prestigious or expensive item, either seriously or with a sense of irony and fun. At other times, as tastes change and styles come and go, some of the felt objects bought or made for home décor or apparel become kitsch. In some ways, many of the objects described above may be or may become kitsch, but they are not inherently so, since kitsch is dependent on the eye of the beholder. Certainly felt is no less subject to being used for or becoming kitsch than any other medium, yet I have discovered that when I tell other people about my interest in felt, they often think first of felt kitsch. Interestingly, this connection seems much stronger in North America than elsewhere, and so this section deals predominantly with the American association between felt and kitsch.

Kitsch is difficult to define, since it has been used so variously and with such loaded meanings. At its most broad, kitsch refers to any kind of popular art – mass-produced or handmade, referential or ironic. At its most cynical, it implies debasement and sentimentality and is associated particularly with the middle class. Art historian, Denis Dutton, describes kitsch as something meant to symbolize the good taste and status of the owner by reworking images from recognized works of art to produce objects like Leonardo da Vinci's *Last Supper* in embroidery (Dutton 2007). Such objects imitate works that have high art status ascribed to them but are not themselves considered high art; they thus attempt to depict good taste but fail (Dutton 2007). Here, neither of these extremes will do.

As I have said in the previous chapter, these distinctions between high and low art, good and bad taste, are often not useful to make, since they imply hierarchies of taste that arbitrarily declare some things art and some not. Kitsch, like art and craft, is a matter of who is looking and their personal ideas and standards, though it has become a battleground on which definitions of good and bad taste are demarked (Bourdieu 1984). So, instead of relying on such heavily fraught definitions, it is more helpful to think about kitsch not in reference to taste but rather in terms of the meanings that each piece possesses for the person who owns and displays it (Miller 2006, 235). As scholar Judy Attfield explains: "kitsch is a valid category of popular taste that communicates a pleasurable, aesthetic, genuine experience" (2006, 201). Following Attfield, then, kitsch here refers to two major categories of objects. First, it includes all of the objects that mimic elements of the maker's ideas of what good art is or should be and remake it in the maker's own milieu. For this kind of kitsch, a sense of fun, of playing with images, can be more important than the overall aesthetic. Kitsch may be referential to high art without being reverential of it. Second, some kitsch is specific to a generation, era or place. This type of kitsch references the aesthetic elements that were iconic of that era or place. Such objects become kitsch at a distance, when we can look back and see how those aesthetics are reflected in the object. In these terms, felt has certainly been a major component of kitsch of both categories.

Within the first category of kitsch, Western art has provided a rich ground for felt. Searching for felt kitsch, I found two variations of da Vinci's *Last Supper* in felt – one made out of pieces of felt sewn together and another that was a *Last Supper* felt storyboard for children. The same company makes a range of biblically themed felt storyboards complete with instructions about how to set up the scenes accurately. Van Gogh's *Starry Night* has not only been replicated in felt but directions on how to make your own can be found on the internet. Many of the souvenirs found in holiday-town gift shops make use of felt for place-specific kitsch. The child's waistcoat made of felt is virtually all-purpose, using only color to distinguish it: with fringe and a gold star it adorns a cowboy; in brown, a Native American; in black, a pirate. Yet felt coin purses, or bags emblazoned with the name of a resort or embroidered with an image of a major local sight, both serve the functions of a souvenir by prompting memories of the holiday and of kitsch by reproducing in felt and thread the original object, whether artistic, architectural or natural.

Embracing and collecting kitsch has become its own field within crafts, and one in which felt often comes to the fore as a marker of what is kitsch. For example, "kitschy kitty" is available for sale online. Meant as a gift item, a small handmade felt cat with embroidered highlights rests in a decorated matchbox. What makes the kitty kitsch is partly its purpose, as being entirely for pleasure and viewing, and partly its use of felt. Another fabric might be equally kitsch but would not have the associations with crafts and childhood. The use of felt plays off the idea of kitsch as something intended for fun but it can also be used to reference earlier design trends, particularly the 1950s, when felt was a popular fabric for homemade clothes and accessories. One such item was a felt coin purse appliquéd with a Bambi-style deer found on a British site advertising kitsch for sale. Here the felt connected the purse to both the past, through the design of the large-eyed deer, and to a sense of childlike play. It was popular enough that the catalogue carrying it, aimed at alternative youth style, sold out quickly. Playing with ideas not only of kitsch but of femininity, the same company offered a black felt bag embellished with a pink felt skull and crossbones.

Whether it mimics fine art or artifacts of other eras, all of these objects use felt as a way to comment on their own status as kitsch. In doing so, they draw attention to the felt they are made of, juxtaposing it with the images they depict, to comment on our expectations of both art and felt, often with a sense of fondness and good humor. Because the connection between felt and kitsch is so strong, at least in the United States, it would be remiss not to mention it, but it must also be remembered that kitsch, as a concept, is heavily debated. One person's kitsch may not be another's. Regardless of whether they are kitsch, craft, home décor or fashion accessory, however, the majority of the objects discussed in this chapter are constructed of commercially produced felt. While the fabrics we see in stores may be what most consumers think of as felt, these represent only a small portion of the output of the large felt manufacturers. Many of the end-uses of felt we never see or simply do not think about as we go about our daily lives. These are the industrial uses of felt, the places that engineers have found where no other textile or material will do.

FELT IN INDUSTRY AND ENGINEERING

Felt covers our pool tables and our mattresses, it pads the breaks in our cars and the carpets in our houses, and, vibrantly dyed, it still makes hats, for cowboys and church ladies. The properties that make felt perfect for life in the Gobi Desert also make it perfect for use in cars and airplanes and even space shuttles. Nonwovens are important industrial textiles that influence and affect our lives, often without our knowledge. The technology of felt, applied to synthetic fibers, has created a new breed of textile: inexpensive and sturdy. Both true wool felt and synthetic nonwovens have helped create the modern world.

Felt played a major part in the construction of the New York subway system. In 1900, William Barclay Parsons was the chief engineer on the project to build the first section of the subway, from City Hall to West 145th Street. Parsons wanted to use the same method that had been employed in Boston a few years before – cutting into the street to dig the trench for the subway and then recovering it. However, Manhattan lies just at sea level on a bed of hard rock, leaving it with a high water table. Somehow, Parsons needed to dig through the rock and seal the tunnels to make them as waterproof as possible for the trains. The first task could be accomplished with a large imported labor force from as far away as South Africa, but the second required felt. Water was known to seep through concrete and block constructions, wearing them down over time. At the time, oilcloth and felt were the two most water resistant fabrics available. Parsons chose felt. Once the tunnel was dug and walls of brick and ceramic blocks were erected, the felt was soaked in tar and laid over the top of these blocks to seal out the water. Concrete finished the wall surface. The roof was constructed similarly. Concrete was poured over giant arch-shaped molds and put in place then topped with tar-soaked felt, which was in turn covered from above by the fill for the road bed (McKendry 2004, 17). The builders of the subway turned to the same technology that the Vikings had relied on centuries before to keep water out of their ships – felt. The subway opened its first line on October 27, 1904. Without felt's ability to resist water which has made it so prized for houses and coats for centuries, one of the most extensive subway systems in the world might not have been able to overcome the basic problems of its environment.

In the 1940s, felt was integral to the war effort and the Felt Association, a trade group of industrial felt producers, published *Felt Facts* to advertise the many uses the military might find for their products. Clearly felt was already an important fabric for the war. The authors give this assessment: "In current war operations, designers of parachute troops' uniforms and harness specify it, also employ it as cushioning for gun turret mounts, insulation against vibration in fighting planes and tanks; gas mask gaskets for infantry and other fighting branches" (The Felt Association 1943, 5). Felt was clearly being used in some capacity – as padding, insulation, polishing or filtration – in every branch of the military during the Second World War. The authors proclaim that "Felt Will Help Win the War Against the Axis," in part by providing insulated boots for the Russian Army on the Eastern front, "while their unlucky enemies, wearing nondescript, inadequate footwear, froze to death" (The Felt

Association 1943, 5). The boots were made in the United States, which seems particularly poignant set against Russia's long history of felt bootmaking on the one hand and the Cold War, which would come years later. During the Second World War, felt was one of the best insulators available and thus lined aviation helmets and provided crucial warmth to the US Army Arctic research team.

8 Washing felt industrially in the 1940s, for use in the Second World War.

The Felt Association's book provides a fascinating look at the felt industry at a crucial time as they try to assert their place not only in war machines but also for "post-war industrial reconstruction" (The Felt Association 1943, 4). Felt has been used for reducing vibrations on machines and padding moving parts since the first industrial machines were built in the late eighteenth and early nineteenth centuries. Because felt is already well compacted, felt pads do not suffer from further compaction by machine parts pushing together. It was precisely this quality which made felt perfect for car brake pads and in airplanes. Felt literally keeps us safe. The Felt Association, however, also remarks on the importance of felt in medicine. In the 1940s, felt was used in "splint pads, head halters and fracture appliances … short wave diathermy apparatus and precision instruments" (The Felt Association 1943, 6). Felt was used in the equipment for blood transfusions and anesthesia. Although most medical products are now made of synthetic nonwovens, they continue to rely on the specific properties that felt had to offer. Felt and nonwovens are still important as cushioning, for gaskets in machines and pumps, and most of all for air filtration systems. Even the air filters in homes are based on felt, as are the filters in woodworking and dust masks found in every hardware store.

Felt continues to be vital in the printing industry. In an offset printing press, the etched or carved image is printed first onto a large rubber sheet. The paper is then printed from that sheet using a heavy roller to press the paper into the sheet. Developed from lithography, offset printing allows greater control of the image as it prints onto the paper and the rubber provides a smoother surface than the etched printing block, making for a smoother and more even-looking print. Furthermore, because the image reverses each time it is transferred, offset printing allows the artist to etch the block right side up rather than as a mirror image. Just rolling the paper directly on to the rubber, however, would damage the fibers of the paper, because of the size and weight of the rollers. Instead, a blanket of felt or fulled woven wool is inserted between the paper and the rollers. The felt helps to distribute the weight of the rollers more evenly, again creating a smoother image, and protects the fibers of the paper from being damaged. Purely woven fabric would not have worked as well, since the interstices of the yarns would create thicker and thinner areas, just like the lines reveal a fabric's weaving pattern if you press your hand down on it for several minutes. Furthermore, the felt acted like a sponge. In old presses, the paper was wetted before it was printed. Like all fibers, the paper picked up the inks better if it was already damp. The water in the paper, however, could dilute the inks and damage the image if it was squeezed from the paper onto the rubber sheet bearing the image. So the felt helped to soak up the excess water from the paper and draw the inks into the paper fibers (Hegarty 2007). Felt, as we know, is especially stable when wet, making it ideal for the job. Because of its uses in printing, felt has even been used to track counterfeiters by tracing their shipments of felt padding for the presses (Jani 2007).

The uses for felt have only multiplied as technology has advanced. Some have been longer lasting than others. Felt continues to be used as padding in helmets, beyond the scope of the military. Felt padding could once be found in horseback riding helmets, though it has now been largely replaced with foam padding, and was also used to line American football helmets. In the 1980s, felt was even turned to curing male pattern baldness. Remnants of clean white felt were ground extremely fine and dyed. This felt powder was put under pressure in aerosol cans and could be sprayed to cover the bald spot (Bryk 2007). The technology has apparently improved over the years and remains available, though often only through late-night television offers.

FELT EVERYWHERE

As we have seen, felt is literally everywhere, in places we might least expect it. Perhaps no other textile is so taken for granted as humble felt and yet used so much. Nearly every machine we use relies on felt in some way. It is vital in medicine, printing, industry, every kind of vehicle and most ships. Many sports use felt for padding or protection – it is the basis of saddle pads for horseback riding. Music also makes use of felt. Felt lines drums and cymbals to achieve the right tone and level of sound and to quiet vibrations. It also pads the hammers in a piano and can be used for sound absorption in recording studios or on the instruments themselves.

We have covered many of felt's infinite uses, but just in case some were forgotten, Aetna Felt Corporation offers the following A to Z:

Absorbers	Auto Harp Parts
Acid-resistant Packing	Automotive Parts
Acoustical Materials	Bags
Adhesive "Dots"	Ball Bearing Strips
Air Compressor Lubricators	Banners
Aircraft Parts	Base Padding
Air Fresheners	Baskets
Alphabet Letters	Bass Drum Beaters
Anti-Rattle Strips, Pads and Gaskets	Bearing Pads
Anti-Squeak Strips and Pads	Beater Balls
Apparel	Beveled Laps
Appliance Parts	Billiard Cloth
Applicators	Bins
Athletic Letters	Blankets
Athletic Pads	Bobs

Brushes
Buffing Felt
Bumpers
Burnishers
Cabinet Bumpers
Capillary Mats
Capsule Wipes
Card Table Pads
Carpet Pads
Carrier Heads
Chairs
Chalkboard Erasers
Chamois Buffs
Chandeliers
Channel Felt
Chassis Strips
Chisel Honing Felt
Clamp Cushioning
Coasters
Cones for Polishing
Construction Felt
Corn and Bunion Pads
Costumes
Covers
Craft Felt
Cushions
Cutlery Box Liners
Cylinder Felt
Dash Liners
Deburring Felt
Decorations
Dental Felt
Deodorizer Wicks

Die Cut Shapes
Die Maker's Felt
Discs
Door Seals
Dots
Drum Beaters
Dryer Seals
Dust Filters
Dust Seals
Elbow Pads
Electrical Felt
Embossing Felt
Engineered Parts
Engraving Blankets
Engraving Roll Covers
Equestrian Felt
Erasers
Etching Felt
Felt Feet
Felt Shapes
Filters
Flags
Flame Resistant Parts
Flares
Flexible Parts
Fluid Transfer
Fuel Oil Filters
Furnace Insulators
Furniture Pads
Gameboards and Pieces
Gaming Tables
Gaskets
Glass Polishing Felt

Glass Protectors

Grain Mill Seals

Granite Polishers

Grease Retention

Grinding Felt

Griptape

Gun Butt Pads

Gun Cleaners

Handbags

Hangers

Hats

Helmet Liners

Hobbies and Crafts

Holiday Decorations

Horse Blankets

Horse Collars

Horse Leg Wraps

Impregnated Felt

Industrial Wipes

Ink Feed Felts

Ink Pads

Insoles

Insulation

Ironing Felts

Isolators

Jeweler's Felt

Key Fobs

Kiln Insulators

Knee Pads

Knife Edge Felts

Laminated Felt

Lamp Bases

Lapidary Felt

Lapping Felt

Letters (Die-cut)

Leveling Pads

Light Seals

Linings and Liners

Lint and Air Seals

Lithographer's Felt

Locomotive Lubricators

Lubricating Felt

Machine Oilers

Mallets

Marble Polishing Felt

Marker Tips

Mechanical Felt

Medical Felt

Metal Working Felt

Mil. Spec. Felt

Miniature Split Laps

Mirror Polishing

Mold Polishing Felt

Motor Mounts

Munitions

Murals

Musical Instrument Felt

Nibs

Noise Control

Oil Filters

Oil Retainers

Oil Seals

Oil Skimmers

Oil Wicks

Oilers

Organ Felt

Orthopedic Felt

Oven Insulators

Packing Felt

Padding

Pads

Parachute Strap Liners

Pen Nibs

Pennants

Percussionists' Pads

Piano Felt

Pigeon Nests

Pipe Covering

Pipe Hanger Felt

Placemats

Plastic Polishers

Plugs

Plush

Pneumatic Tube Seals

Podiatry Pads

Polishing Cloths

Polishing Wheels

Pool Table Felt

Precision Seals

Pressure Sensitive Felt

Printers' Felt

Promotional Items

Protective Pads

Quake Absorbers

Quilting Felts

Ring Buffs

Rings

Roll Felt

Roller Bearing Seals

Roller Felt

Rotating Shaft Lubricants

Rubbing Blocks

Rugs

Saddle Pads

SAE Felts

Sander Platens

Satin Finish Bobs

Satin Finish Wheels

School Supplies

Scratch Removers

Seals

Seamless Felt Belts

Shaped Felt

Sheet Felt

Shims

Shock Absorbers

Silversmith Buffs

Sleeves

Slippers

Smoke Generators

Sound Insulation

Spacers

Spill Absorption

Spilt Laps

Stain Applicators

Stainless Steel Polishers

Stamp Pads

Steel Mill Wipers

Steno Machines and Repair

Story Boards

Strainers

Table Cloths

Table Pads
Tadpole Gaskets
Tannery Felt
Tape
Taxidermy Felt
Technical Felts
Theatrical Felt
Toys
Traction Rollers
Transmission Felts
Trophy Bases
Tube Felt
Tumbling Media
Turntable Mats
Tympani Beaters
Typewriter Pad Felt
Unmounted Felt Bobs
Unmounted Felt Buffs
Upholstery Felt
Vacuum Felt

Vibration Dampers
Vibratory Finishing Media
Wall Coverings
Washers
Weather Stripping
Welding Pads
Wet Process Felt
Wheels
Wicks
Wiping Strips
Wood Hub Brushes
Wood Rubbing Pads
Wood Stain Applicators
Woodworking Tool
Polishers
Xerography Light Seals
Xylophone Bed Felts
Yard Goods
Yoke Pads
Yuletide Decorations

8.
THE MEANINGS OF FELT

This book has been an exploration into an often overlooked textile through the various peoples who have created traditions producing and using it. Looking at traditions requires focusing on shared cultures, created through ethnicity, geography, or even, as in the case of industrial felt, shared skills. We have moved back and forth between physical things made from felt – archaeological artifacts and works of art – and felt's appearance in written and oral histories, including trade records, inventories and personal accounts. We have also looked at cultural evidence, at the works of anthropologists and ethnographers, and early historical records documenting travelers' narratives. Most of these have been Westerners visiting Central Asia, but more recently important research is being produced by the people who grew up in felt cultures giving insider perspectives. Felt has been particularly well storied, perhaps because it is so old and so much a part of so many cultures. Understanding the remarkable nature of felt requires pulling together all of these stories. Yet we also need to consider some of the assumptions that have been made about felt. We have looked at how felt has been honored in Mongolia and Kyrgyzstan and historically in Iran. We have also seen the respect it is given among printers, hatters and engineers. And we have examined how it helped to break down the barriers of Western fine art. Yet as I worked on this book, I became fascinated with what people said to me when I told them about my project. The first part of this chapter, then, looks at some of those assumptions – the meanings ascribed to felt.

I have told so many stories of felt, that it only seems fair to tell my own. I cannot remember how I first encountered felt, though I believe the Indian namda that hung on my wall as an infant is probably a good place to start. Perhaps it established the narrative for what followed, since one of my favorite childhood toys was also felt – a storyboard with a sea theme – and I remember being fascinated by the pink felt wings on the stuffed dragon that was my constant companion. I had Halloween costumes made of felt and can remember elementary school projects involving it, but it was only much later that my interest in felt really developed. Felt insinuated itself in my life from multiple directions. First, my mother and I began to keep sheep, and while I learned to spin and weave, neither of us could possibly keep up with the sheep's production of wool. On a whim, I took a hatmaking class at a wool festival – a gathering of sheep-owners to show their sheep and wool and learn from one another. Felting uses a lot more wool, much faster, than spinning, weaving and knitting. A few years later and more fiber-obsessed, I found myself at the end of my coursework for my master's degree in textiles and in need of a thesis topic. Piling all of my textile books full of glossy photographs around me, I determined that I would write my thesis on whatever textile struck me as I paged through them. At the Pazyryk saddle, I stopped. That was the beginning. I have never made another hat. Instead, I discovered a global community of feltmakers dedicated to upholding traditions and creating innovations in felt, who share ideas and techniques with incredible openness. The rest of this chapter is dedicated to them.

Given the prevalence of felt in our lives, it is not surprising that we should have formed ideas about it without necessarily being aware of it. Most of these ideas are developed through our exposure to the fabric and thus reflect the ways in which our specific culture uses it – whether as material for building and furnishing houses or for making childhood crafts. Much of this book has been dedicated to looking at how felt is viewed in other cultures, such as in Mongolia or Iran, but we have also glimpsed the assumptions that surround felt in the West, that have influenced how felt art has been received by the larger culture of Western fine art. When I told people here in the United States that I was writing a book on felt, the most common response I received was, "Felt? You mean the stuff we made puppets from at camp?" or, dishearteningly, from someone in the felt industry, "But it's so boring!" I can only hope I have proven them wrong. Despite felt's prevalence in our lives, in brakes and computers and insulation, as hats and boot-liners, we think of it primarily in terms of the one place where we encountered it head on, manipulating it with our hands and turning it to our own purposes – the elementary school arts and crafts room. As I researched this book, particularly the later chapters, I discovered that this association between felt and children's crafts revealed several other Western assumptions about felt. Many of these assumptions can be seen as both positive and negative, depending entirely on the context and the worldview of the speaker. Yet they are also the very assumptions that have both spurred people to embrace felt as a medium, pushing it to new purposes and forms through their creativity, and caused others to scorn it, condemning it as too "boring" or utilitarian. Needless to say, I think felt is fascinating, but by uncovering some of the ways that felt is thought about in the West, we may gain insight into why felt has not received the attention it deserves.

Beyond its industrial uses, most people think of felt either as a children's material, as the comments I received show, or else as a women's medium. The first association is obvious. Felt is one of the first textiles we knowingly work with as children, learning to cut and sew. With its edges that require no finishing and its ability to be shaped, glued and printed, it is a perfect medium for children. Unfortunately, many people stop making things early in their lives and so these puppets and costumes and ornaments are as much as they see of the textile. It becomes relegated to memories of their youth. As we grow older, our ideas are more firmly shaped by our culture, often leaving felt behind. Giving felt its due may require us to look on it as we did in elementary school, as a fabric with great potential for creativity and ingenuity.

The second association – between felt and women – is more problematic and requires more examination. For better or worse and often in the face of historical evidence to the contrary, the processing of fiber in fabric has often historically been considered women's work in the West. This relationship is reflected by the majority of women students in almost any fiber arts course and many of the textiles programs at universities around the United States. It is also at work in the arguments that divide art from craft, or fine arts from applied arts, which began in the nineteenth century but focused on fiber in the mid-twentieth century. According to the logic of these arguments, women can make applied art in their own milieu, fiber, but it cannot compete with the fine art produced by men in painting or sculpture.

As described earlier, such gendered divisions were challenged during the 1960s and 1970s by both the women's liberation movement and the rise of fiber arts. Yet, they sometimes persist in other forms: "...felt seems to have an inherent quality which causes many women to recognize in it a medium which suitably reflects their situation" (Schmitt qtd. in Thomas 2000, 26). Such statements assume that women are biologically predisposed towards felt. Making a connection to felt an essential part of womanhood runs the risk of implying that women are less able to work in other mediums or that felt does not speak to male artists; it can unintentionally reintroduce the very hierarchies that the fiber arts and feminist movements worked to break down. It cannot be disputed that many artists working in felt are women, yet this must also be taken within the context of Western art and the challenges to the artistic canon of the last fifty years. On the one hand, part of the critique of the art/craft divide offered by feminist artists of the 1970s centered on establishing that women did have a longstanding artistic tradition represented by weaving, sewing and even feltmaking. On the other hand, fiber artists trained in weaving strove to move beyond the confines imposed by weave structures and the limits of the loom (Auther 2009). By suggesting some sort of essential and unknowable relationship between the women artists and felt, such statements can belie the complex and diverse reasons behind artists' choices to work in felt.

Our ideas about felt not only focus on who makes it but also the materiality of felt. Felt is often considered elemental. This association comes from its very construction. Wool is among the first fibers used by humans to construct cloth and was the standard fiber for much of our clothing before the mechanization of cotton processing. The importance of felt's ancient history must not be underestimated – we know it to have existed for thousands of years. In part because of this history, we think of wool, and by extension of felt, as serving our basic human needs for warmth and protection. It is this very line of thought that led Joseph Beuys to begin using felt and that the felt blankets in *The Pack* are meant to convey, as discussed in chapter six. Wool is also a natural fiber. As a culture, we associate it with our own presumed past as farmers and shepherds, which evokes images of a utopian past before the contamination of pesticides and modern industrial methods. This relationship is prevalent enough that felt companies are beginning to market their felt as a green textile, drawing on the current rising interest in the environment and green consumerism. The elemental nature of felt is increased as the wool is processed. Felt relies on little or no specialized equipment, making it seem a more basic technique than weaving or knitting, despite a similar level of specialized skill and knowledge being required to make it well. Further, felt goes from fiber to fabric in a single step. Unlike other techniques, felt does not require that the fibers be spun into yarn before the yarns can be combined and manipulated into a cloth.

Because of the weight of these associations, felt has frequently been symbolic of the body, in particular as an extension of the skin or even as organs (in Thomas 2000, 99, 103, 113). Scholar Peter Schmitt suggests that it is this connection to the skin that makes felt such a desirable medium for women artists in particular, referencing works on motherhood and sexuality as well as the use of felt for clothing and wearable art. At the same time, however, he also comments that Robert Morris was "among the first" to remark on felt's skin-like qualities (Schmitt qtd. in Thomas 2000, 25–6). Certainly, Schmitt is correct at one level – felt, with its long history, soft surface and use for covering and containment, can resemble skin and does suggest the fulfillment of basic human needs for warmth and shelter. Many of the artists I spoke with and read about cited ancientness and simplicity among the qualities that drew them to work in felt in the first place. In itself, this assumption of felt as elemental makes sense. It becomes complicated, however, when it is taken in conjunction with some of the other assumptions about felt, such as its connection with women and children.

Historically, Western society has emphasized a connection between women and the body as a way of maintaining male power structures, often by suggesting that women, because they are more connected to the body, are thus less intelligent or somehow less evolved than men. Writing in the late eighteenth century, Mary Wollstonecraft expressed this connection: "women are not allowed to have sufficient strength of mind to acquire what really deserves the name of virtue" (Wollstonecraft 2001, 586). As an early feminist, she goes on to attempt to prove this wrong, but the idea has been remarkably persistent, gaining momentum with the application of social Darwinism in the nineteenth century and underscoring much of Sigmund Freud's writings on women in the twentieth. Given the treatment of women in this culture and more specifically in the tradition of Western fine arts, drawing a direct correlation between felt as elemental and the prevalence of women felt artists has the potential to reiterate the very ideas that many of these artists have sought to break down. Instead of focusing on this as a cause and effect, it may be more productive to see how something as weighted with associations of simplicity and history as felt can inspire such complexity and sophistication. German artist, Margarete Warth, describes the creativity involved in making felt as she argues against these very assumptions, which lead many to discount the textile. She comments that felt is often "derided as 'housewives' art," but goes on to remark that making felt in one's kitchen requires the repurposing of both kitchen and tools. Her work embraces the possibility of multiple interpretations. She challenges the viewer to look at their own assumptions about the object they are viewing, about felt and its relationship with nature and women (Warth in Thomas 2000, 175).

We must think beyond our assumptions about felt as simple and basic to recognize the skill and artistry of Central Asian feltmakers. Much as women artists must negotiate the history of gender politics, so must we remember the legacy of orientalism – the assumption that other cultures are caught in the past and unable to become modern (hooks 1992, 27)

– when considering art by non-white artists. Felt is strongly connected with many of the cultures of Central Asia and the Middle East. Yet, rather than fix on felt as an essentializing marker of these cultures' link to the natural world and to the basic needs of humans, we gain more by seeing the work of the feltmakers from these regions as deeply engaged in modern conversations about art and culture, drawing on their specific traditions and experiences in many of the same ways as artists everywhere do.

Assumptions such as these can color the ways we perceive felt and felt art, pushing our perceptions into preformed ideas or challenging us to think in new ways about both felt and the world around us. By questioning our ideas about felt, we may be able to see it anew. Much of this book has focused on the products made from felt, betraying my own assumptions about art as a physical thing that exists in a specific place. However, many of the feltmakers I spoke with referred not to the elemental nature of felt or to the meanings of their own pieces but rather to the pleasure gained by having direct contact with the materials, with the warm, damp wool, focusing not on the product but on the importance of the process itself (Smith 2007b; Johnson 2007b). Discussing her own realization that the process could be the most important part of her work, especially when teaching, Jorie Johnson explained:

> It is too easy to focus on the final product, and how many can be made in so many hours, instead of the attraction to the material and all the images that such a fluffy wonderment called the sheep brings to help the existence of mankind on earth. (Johnson 2007b)

Perhaps it is this knowledge, more than anything else, that has created a special bond among feltmakers around the world, forming them into their own community.

Despite often being a solitary endeavor, the production of textiles seems to create communities. Most of this book has been organized around looking at these communities on a local level – by ethnicity or geographic region or job description. We first encounter felt and form ideas about it as children from the community that immediately surrounds us, whether it be in a felt yurt or a craft class at camp or school. Such local communities have clear cultural traditions, allowing us to see how felt has developed within that culture over time, keeping some elements of the process or design the same while changing others to maintain its relevance in the culture, thus we can follow the progression of felt from Pazyryk to contemporary Kyrgyz shyrdak. Local cultures do not keep each form of artistic expression they use separate. Instead, each form is informed by other aesthetics, beliefs and ways of going about daily life within the culture and in turn also impacts the rest of the culture. Feltmaking incorporates the full ecology of the culture, reflecting the culture's ideas in addition to the maker's, as in the blessings, riddles and events that are all part of large-scale feltmaking in Mongolia. Centering on local communities helps us to see feltmaking as a product of a culture rather than a discreet entity.

Focusing on local cultures also creates a means for comparison between cultures. For example, Iranian feltmaking is clearly related to Anatolian feltmaking in the methods used and the way that designs are felted in to create floral patterned rugs, even though they are each coming out of different cultures and may use these rugs differently. We can similarly track migrations and paths of influence by combining the history of felt and the kinds of patterns and methods of production with the history of trade. The history of the European feltmaking guilds of former centuries clearly illustrates another kind of community – one based on employment and skill. Yet even these guild communities came from and operated in specific cultures. The anxieties expressed by the protectionism (especially the restrictions placed on who was allowed to train journeymen) of the London Feltmakers' Guild in the face of an influx of Huguenot felters demonstrated the level of cultural difference perceived between the two groups, as well as their economic interests. Further, I have argued that Western fine art is also a kind of community, though it is less localized geographically. The fine art tradition evolved alongside the guilds and in awareness of them. This created the climate for the distinctions between art and craft that designated some skills – painting or sculpture – as arts, and others – feltmaking or woodcarving – as crafts. These cultural traditions and structures migrated with the Europeans into the lands they colonized in the Americas and beyond. Similarly, when these hierarchies were broken down, they affected the entire fine arts community around the world. What took place in the culture of fine arts, however, marks greater shifts both in how communities can interact in the age of technology and in the kinds of communities that can exist now in the age of the global. Certainly much information can be found about felt on the internet, but as I researched this book, I was struck repeatedly by felt's ability to bring people together.

Inge Evers coined the phrase "felt the world together," and it has become an unofficial motto of the many feltmakers and artists that form a global community of felt. This community does not live in a single place but is tied together through a love of felt and a strong belief in its value as a textile. They have joined as a community through the networks of groups like the International Feltmakers' Association, through courses in one another's workshops, travel and word of mouth. These feltmakers have often made felt their lives, and they actively work to promote their art through teaching it to others and constantly continuing to learn, either from each other or through research trips, particularly to the centers of traditional feltmaking in Central Asia, Anatolia and northern Europe. Many consider this connection to be one of the greatest parts of their work (Johnson 2007b). Through this movement and outreach, they broaden the community, bringing feltmakers and felting techniques together from a wide range of traditions and combining them in innovative ways. Many of these artists have also returned to the local level and used felt to help foster communities at home and abroad. Making large pieces of felt is, by its nature, a collaborative activity – it requires working literally side by side. This is part of the reason that feltmaking has often led to celebration, as in Mongolia and Dagestan. New feltmakers from around the world are now drawing on those properties to help teach feltmaking in ways that strengthen ties between the makers both locally and globally.

While most books on textiles, and many that are on unrelated subjects, prefer metaphors of "weaving together knowledge" and "piecing stories like quilts," it seems more appropriate for us to think of the histories, cultures and meanings of felt as a piece of, well, felt – a complex textile made up of single but enmeshed threads of fiber and tradition. What I hope has become clear throughout this book is that there are no discrete stories of felt. Unlike threads in a woven cloth, each culture that produces felt shares elements of its technique or design motifs with those cultures that surround it, creating a continuum of felt from Central Asia to western Europe and beyond. Especially now, feltmakers are meeting one another to exchange ideas and expertise, blurring political and cultural boundaries. Yet while all of these feltmakers participate on this global level, they also bring to their felt the distinctly local, blending into it their own surroundings and cultures. This felt meshes together both geographical cultures and historical ones – connecting the mountains and steppes, the past and present. Because of its unique properties, felt has lent itself more to some end-uses than to others, and so we have felt cloaks, felt hats and felt boots used around the world and through thousands of years. These ancient felts, from the saddle blankets of Pazyryk to the Phrygian caps, form ever-renewing sources of inspiration. The stories of felt move through and between each other, like individual wool fibers. At times they go in opposite directions, letting felt be both new and old, traditional and modern, but such contradictions serve only to create a firmer fabric. It is easy, especially in modern, Western society, to forget about felt or to discount it, but like the Central Asians, we could not live without it.

GLOSSARY

Batt: A sheet of loose fibers, which may or may not be oriented in the same direction. A batt is usually made of fibers that have been carded but not yet felted. In feltmaking, the batt represents the stage just prior to when felting begins. Batts of loose wool or other fibers are made of cleaned, carded wool that is then moistened and felted.

Bow: A length of wood strung with a taut string used for carding wool in parts of the Middle East, Central Asia and eastern Europe. The body of the bow is struck with a wooden mallet, causing the string to vibrate and loosen the fibers surrounding it. Carding bows are often several feet in length and require skilled use.

Carding: The process of combing fibers to release dirt and grease and orient the fibers. Carding can be done through a number of methods: with a bow, a wooden rake, or cylinders or paddles covered in tines (called cards). Carded wool is then laid in the batt to be felted.

Carrotting: A process for making animal fur – particularly rabbit, nutria or beaver – ready for felting. The fur pelts are soaked in a solution of hydrogen peroxide and nitric acid to create scales on the fibers. This solution, however, leaves the fibers a reddish color.

Creep: The ability of the fiber to move towards the root when pressure is applied. The direction of creep is caused by the orientation of the scales, so that they provide friction when rubbed from the tip towards the root but creep when pressure is applied in the opposite direction. Only scaled fibers, such as wool, have creep.

Crimp: Spiraled coil that appears as waviness in locks of wool caused by the two different types of keratin cells in the cortex. In one set of cells, the paracortex, the keratin is matured and hardened and the cells are larger, but the keratin is soft and pliant in the smaller orthocortex cells. The two bundles of cells lying next to one another cause the fiber to bend both back and forth and to twist on its axis, with the paracortex generally on the inside of the bends, forming the characteristic coil of wool fibers.

Felt: Any fabric made directly from wool fibers that are entangled by mechanical means without the use of a binder or adhesive through the introduction of heat, moisture, pressure and friction.

Full: To apply the felting process to a previously produced woven or knitted textile to give it the properties and finish of a nonwoven. Fulling woven wool fabrics is a common technique for creating sturdy, water-resistant textiles for outerwear. Fulling mills were known to have existed at least since Roman times.

Nonwoven: A textile made of synthetic fibers, such as nylon or polyester, that replicates the structure of felt but is made through other techniques since these fibers do not have the natural scales of wool and thus cannot be felted. Needle punching and heat melting are the most common methods for producing nonwoven fabrics.

Shyrdak (also shirdeg): A large felt rug from Central Asia. The Kyrgyz and Kazakh piece these rugs together from two differently colored pieces of felt; in Mongolia, the rugs are heavily embroidered.

BIBLIOGRAPHY

Aetna Felt Corporation. Company website [accessed 2007]. Available at www.aetnafelt.com

Agren, Katarina. 1976. *Tovning*. Vasteras: ICA-forlaget.

Aimone, Katherine Duncan. 2002. Jorie Johnson: Coaxing Fashion from Felt. *Fiberarts* Mar/Apr, 28(5): 30–3.

Arnoldi, Mary Jo. 1992. A Distorted Mirror: The Exhibition of the Herbert Ward Collection of Africana. *Museums and Communities: The Politics of Public Culture*. Eds. Ivan Karp, Christine Mullen Kreamer and Stephen Lavine. Washington, DC: Smithsonian Institution.

Arvilommi, Karoliina. LiinaLommi Felt Designs. Web page [accessed 2007]. Available at www.4felts.com

Atasoy, Nurhan. 1992. Dervish Dress and Ritual: The Mevlevi Tradition. *The Dervish Lodge*. Ed. Raymond Lifchez, pp. 253–68. Berkeley: University of California.

Attfield, Judy. 2006. Redefining "Kitsch," The Politics of Design. *Home Cultures* 3(3): 293–306.

Auther, Elissa. 2009. *String, Felt, Thread and the Hierarchy of Art and Craft, 1960–1980*. Minneapolis: University of Minnesota.

Bacon, Elizabeth E. 1966. *Central Asians Under Russian Rule: A Study in Cultural Change*. New York: Cornell University.

Barber, Elizabeth Wayland. 1999. *The Mummies of Ürümchi*. New York: W. W. Norton.

Bascom, William R. 1954. Four Functions of Folklore. *Journal of American Folklore* 67: 333–49.

Batchuluun, L. 2003. *Felt Art of the Mongols*. Ulaan Baatar: Institute for the Study of Arts and Culture, Mongolian University of Arts and Culture.

Beaton, Clare. 1994. *The Felt Book*. New York: Sterling.

Borer, Alain. 1996. *The Essential Joseph Beuys*. New York: Thames & Hudson.

Bourdieu, Pierre. 1984. *Distinction: A Social Critique of the Judgment of Taste*. London: Routledge and Kegan Paul.

Brown, Victoria. 1996. *New Crafts Feltwork*. London: Lorenz.

Bryk, Nancy. 2007. "Felt." Web page [accessed November 1, 2007]. Available at www.madehow.com/Volume-7/Felt.html

Bunn, Stephanie. 2004. Lecture on Central Asian Felt.

Burkett, Mary. 1977. An Early Date for the Origin of Felt. *Anatolian Studies* 27: 111–16.

Burkett, Mary. 1979. *The Art of the Feltmaker*. Kendal: Abbot Hall.

Bush, Nancy. 2001. Nalbinding – From the Iron Age to Today. *Piecework* 9(3): 28–32.

Catholic Forum. Web page [accessed 2007]. Available at www.catholicforum.com

Chenciner, Robert. 1997. *Dagestan – Tradition and Survival*. Richmond, Surrey: Curzon.

CIBA Company. 1958. Felt. *CIBA Review* 129.

Corner, David. 1991. The Tyranny of Fashion: The case of the felt-hatting trade in the late seventeenth and eighteenth centuries. *Textile History* 22(2): 153–78.

Cooper, Merien and Schoedsack, Ernest (directors). 1925. *Grass: A Nation's Battle for Life*. (Documentary) DVD, 71 minutes. Paramount.

Diba, Layla S., ed. 1998. *Royal Persian Paintings: The Qajar Period, 1785–1925*. Brooklyn, NY: Brooklyn Museum of Art.

Dostoevsky, Fyodor. 1987. *Crime and Punishment*. New York: Bantam.

Dutton, Denis. 1998. Kitsch. Web page [accessed 2007]. Available at www.denisdutton.com/kitsch_macmillan.htm

Emery, Irene. 1966. *The Primary Structure of Fabrics: An Illustrated Classification*. Washington, DC: The Textile Museum.

Epstein, S. R. 1998. Craft Guilds, Apprenticeship, and Technological Change in Preindustrial Europe. *The Journal of Economic History* 58(3): 684–713.

Evers, Inge. 2008. Personal interview.

Feldman, Annette. 1980. *Fun with Felt*. New York: Van Nostrand Reinhold.

Felt Association. 1943. *Felt Facts*. New York: Korbel and Colwell.

Floor, Willem. 2003. *Traditional Crafts in Qajar Iran, 1800–1925*. Costa Mesa, CA: Mazda.

Foley, John Miles. 2002. *How to Read an Oral Poem*. Urbana and Chicago, IL: University of Illinois.

Forbes, R. J. 1964. *Studies in Ancient Technology*. Vols II and IV. Leiden: E. J. Brill.

Galeskas, Beverly. 2003. *Felted Knits*. Boulder, CO: Interweave.

Gervers, Michael and Gervers, Veronika. 1974. Felt-Making Craftsmen of the Anatolian and Iranian Plateaux. *The Textile Museum Journal* 4(1): 14–29.

Gervers, Veronika. 1982. *The Influence of Ottoman Turkish Textiles and Costume in Eastern Europe, with Particular Reference to Hungary*. Toronto: Royal Ontario Museum.

Gervers, Veronika. 1983. Construction of Turkmen Coats. *Textile History* 14(1): 3–27.

Gink, Karoly and Ivor Sandos Kiss. 1971. *Folk Art and Folk Artists in Hungary*. New York: Hastings House.

Girgiç, Mehmet. 2007. Personal interview.

Glassie, Henry. 1993. *Turkish Traditional Art Today*. Bloomington, IN: University of Indiana.

Glassie, Henry. 1995. Tradition. *Journal of American Folklore* 108(430): 395–412.

Glassie, Henry. 2007. Felt Houses in Turkey. Personal e-mail, August 29.

Gordon, Beverly. 1980. *Feltmaking: Traditions, Techniques, and Contemporary Explorations.* New York: Watson-Guptill.

Grousset, Rene. 1970. *The Empire of the Steppes: A History of Central Asia* (trans. Naomi Walford*)*. New Brunswick, NJ: Rutgers University.

Hagen, Chad Alice and Johnson, Jorie. 2007. *Fabulous Felted Scarves.* New York: Lark Books.

Harris, Jennifer, ed. 1993. *Textiles: 5,000 Years.* New York: Harry N. Abrams.

Harrison, Michael. 1960. *The History of the Hat.* London: Herbert Jenkins.

Harvey, Janet. 1996. *Traditional Textiles of Central Asia.* London: Thames & Hudson.

Hegarty, Donal. 2007. Personal interview.

Herodotus. 1958. *The Histories* (trans. Aubrey de Sélincourt). London: Penguin.

hooks, bell. 1992. Eating the Other. *Black Looks.* Boston: South End Press.

International Feltmakers' Association. 2000. *Felt.* Lanark: International Feltmakers' Association.

International Feltmakers' Association. 2007. Website. Available at www.feltmakers.com

Jacopetti, Alexandra. 1974. *Native Fund and Flash: An Emerging Folk Art.* San Francisco: Scrimshaw.

Jaitly, Jaya, ed. 1990. *Crafts of Kashmir, Jammu, and Ladakh.* New York: Abbeville.

Jani, Frank. 2007. Personal interview.

Johnson, Jorie. 2007a. JoiRae Textiles. Web page [accessed 2007]. Available at www.joirae.com

Johnson, Jorie. 2007b. Personal interview.

Johnson, Sarah. 2002. The Relationship Between the Feltmaking of Ancient Asiatic Tribes and the Origin of Early Chinese Papermaking. University of Oklahoma.

Justin, Valarie Sharaf. 1980. *Flat-woven Rugs of the World: Kilim, Soumak, and Brocading.* New York: Van Nostrand Reinhold.

Kadolf, Sara J. and Langford, Anna L. 1998. *Textiles.* Upper Saddle River, NJ: Merrill.

Kalter, Johannes. 1997. *Heirs to the Silk Road: Uzbekistan.* London: Thames & Hudson.

Kant, Immanuel. 2001. The Critique of Judgment. *Norton Anthology of Theory and Criticism.* Ed. Vincent B. Leitch. New York and London: W. W. Norton.

Kirby, Hughette. 2003. *Crafts from Felt.* Mankato, MN: Bridgestone Books.

Lahtinen Felt Company. Web page [accessed 2007]. Available at www. huopaliikelahtinen.fi

Lau, Kimberly J. 2000. *New Age Capitalism: Making Money East of Eden.* Philadelphia: University of Pennsylvania.

Laufer, Berthold. 1930. The Early History of Felt. *American Anthropologist, New Series* 32(1): 1–18.

Laury, Jean Ray. 2007. Personal correspondence.

Laury, Jean Ray and Aiken, Joyce. 1973. *Creating Body Coverings.* New York: Van Nostrand Reinhold.

Lawson, Donna. 1973. *If You Can't Go Naked, Here Are Clothes to Sew on Fast.* New York: Grosset and Dunlap.

Leix, A. 1941. Turkestan. *CIBA Review* 40: 1434–40.

Levine, Lawrence. 1988. *Highbrow/Lowbrow: The Emergence of Cultural Hierarchy in America.* Cambridge, MA: Harvard University.

Levine, Louis D. 1977. Notes on Felt-Making and the Production of Other Textiles at Seh Gabi, a Kurdish Village. *Studies in Textile History: In Memory of Harold B. Burnham*. Ed. Veronika Gervers, pp. 202–13. Toronto: Royal Ontario Museum.

Lewis, Tedford. 2004. Personal interview, Webster Groves, MO, March 23.

Londos, Eva. 2006. Kitsch is Dead – Long Live Garden Gnomes. *Home Cultures* 3(3): 293–306.

Malcolm, Trisha. 2005. *Vogue: Felting on the Go*. New York: Sixth and Spring.

Maksimov, V., Diadiuchenko, L., Sorokin, E. and Usubalieva, B. 1986. *The Kyrgyz Pattern*. Bishkek: Kyrgyzstan.

Mayhew, Bradley, Plunkett, Richard and Richmond, Simon. 2000. *Central Asia*. Oakland, CA: Lonely Planet.

Mazzawi, Rosalind. Metallic Bronze, Old Gold. Web page [accessed August 13, 2002]. Available at www.silk-road.com/artl/maslow.html

McAllister, Buff. 2003. *Sewing with Felt*. Honesdale, PA: Boyds Mill.

McDowell, Colin. 1992. *Hats: Status, Style and Glamour*. London: Thames & Hudson.

McGavock, Deborah and Christine Lewis. 2000. *Feltmaking*. Marlborough: Crowood.

McKendry, Joe. 2004. 2004. The New York Subway. *New York Times*, October 23, sec. A, col. 2, p. 17.

Miller, Daniel. 2006. Things that Bright Up the Place. *Home Cultures* 3(3): 235–49.

O'Bannon George. 1974. *The Turkoman Carpet*. London: Gerald Duckworth.

Olschki, Leonardo. 1949. *The Myth of Felt*. Berkeley, CA: University of California.

Oxford English Dictionary online. Felt. Web page [accessed 2007]. Available at www.oed.com

Phillips, Mary Walker. 1970. *Step-by-Step Macramé*. New York: Golden.

Pilin, Alexander. n.d. *A Tale of Felt*. No publisher.

Pinner, Robert. 1998. The Turkmen Wedding. *HALI* 100: 104–6.

Pirttilahti, Eija. "Sammallammas." Web page [accessed 2007]. Available at www.sammallammas.fi

Polo, Marco. 1958. *The Travels* (trans. Robert Latham). London: Penguin.

Pufpaff, Suzanne. 1995. *Nineteenth Century Hat Maker's and Felter's Manuals*. Hastings, MI: Stony Lonesome.

Raissnia, Melina. 2003. Felt Rugs from Iran. Web page [accessed December 2007]. Available at www.turkotek.com/salon_00104/salon.html

Raissnia, Melina. 2007. MelinaRaissnia.com. Web page [accessed December 2007]. Available at www.melinaraissnia.com

Rudenko, Sergei. 1970. *Frozen Tombs of Siberia: The Pazyryk Burials of Iron-age Horsemen* (trans. M. W. Thompson). Berkeley, CA: University of California.

Ruyak, Jacqueline. 2003. Jorie Johnson: Felt as Matrix. *Surface Design Journal*: 39–43.

Ruysbroeck, Willem van. 1900. *The journey of William of Rubruck to the eastern parts of the world, 1253–55: as narrated by himself, with two accounts of the earlier journey of John of Pian de Carpine*. London: Haklyut Society.

Scott, Richard. 2002. Personal interview. Estes Park, CO.

Seligman, Edwin Robert Anderson. 1887. *Two Chapters on the Medieval Guilds of England*. Baltimore: American Economic Association.

Shamir, Orit and Baginsky, Alisa. 2002. Medieval Mediterranean Textiles, Basketry and Cordage Newly Excavated in Israel. *Towns and Material Culture in the Medieval Middle East*. Ed. Yaacov Lev, pp. 135–58. Leiden and Boston, MA: Brill.

Shohat, Ella. 1992. Notes on the "Postcolonial." *Social Text* 31/32: 99–113.

Simon, Joan. 1999. Miyake Modern – Japanese Designer Issey Miyake (interview). *Art in America* Feb.: 78–83

Sjöberg, Gunilla Paetau. 1996. *Felt: New Directions for an Ancient Craft* (trans. Patricia Spark). Loveland, CO: Interweave.

Smith, Sheila. 2007. *Felt to Stitch*. London: Batsford.

Smith, Sheila. 2007b. Personal interview.

Smith, Sheila and Walker, Freda. 1995. *Feltmaking: The Whys and Wherefores*. UK: Dalefelt.

Sommer, John L. 1996. *The Kyrgyz and Their Reed Screens*. Fremont, CA: The Author.

Sonenscher, Michael. 1987. *The Hatters of Eighteenth-Century France*. Berkeley, CA: University of California.

Starostin, Sergei. 2005. StarLing Project: Etymological Dictionary and Database. Web page [accessed 2007]. Available at http://starling.rinet.ru/cgi-bin/main.cgi?flags=eygtmnl

Stirling, Polly. Wild Turkey Feltmakers. Web page [accessed 2007]. Available at www.wildturkeyfeltmakers.com/PollyStirling.html

Sumner, Christina and Feltham, Heleanor. 2000. *Beyond the Silk Road: Arts in Central Asia*. Sydney: Museum of Applied Arts and Sciences.

Sutherland, Douglas. 1982. Lock's of London: Gentlemen's Hatters. *New York Times*, October 3, sec. Travel.

Sydykova, Gaukhar and Ruzieva, Dilia (directors). 2002. Red *Butterflies Where Two Springs Meet* (documentary). Produced by the Soros Foundation, The Network Women's Program of the Open Society Institutes and the Institute for Social and Gender Policy (Russia).

Taylor, Kathleen. 2003. *Knit One, Felt Too*. North Adams, MA: Storey.

Thomas, Katharina, ed. 2000. *Felt: Art, Crafts and Design*. Stuttgart: Arnoldsche Art.

Thompson, Jon. 2003. Early Safavid Carpets and Textiles. *Hunt for Paradise: Court Arts of Safavid Iran 1501–1576*. Eds. John Thompson and Sheila R. Canby. Milan: Skira.

Tisdall, Caroline. 1979. *Joseph Beuys*. New York: Thames & Hudson.

Trever, K. V. 1932. *Excavations in Northern Mongolia, 1924–1925*. Leningrad: (no publisher name listed).

Tsarev, Nikita. 2001. Ornamented Funeral Felts from the Noin Ula Necropolis Second Century BC to Second Century AD. *Oriental Carpet and Textile Studies* 6: 94–8.

Tsouti-Schillinger, Nena. 2001. *Robert Morris and Angst*. Athens and New York: Bastas and George Braziller.

Turnau, Irena. 1997. *Hand-felting in Europe and Asia*. Warsaw: Institute for Archaeology and Ethnology.

Unwin, George. 1963. *Industrial Organization in the Sixteenth and Seventeenth Centuries*. London: Frank Cass.

VivaTerra. 2007. Holiday 2007 catalogue. Pueblo, CO: VivaTerra.

Westfall, Carol D. 2005. Contemporary Feltmakers. *Shuttle, Spindle and Dyepot* 36(3): 31–7.

Whelan, Carolyn. 2004. Where Fashion Meets Farming: Wool – A Warm and Fuzzy Outlook. *International Herald Tribune*, May 29, sec. Money Report, p. 21.

Whisnant, David E. 1983. *All that is Native and Fine: The Politics of Culture in an American Region*. Chapel Hill, NC and London: University of North Carolina.

White, Christine. 2007. Personal interview.

White, Christine. 2007b. *Uniquely Felt*. North Adams, MA: Storey.

Will, George. 2001. "Art" Unburdened by Excellence. *Washington Post*, January 26.

Wollstonecraft, Mary. 2001. A Vindication of the Rights of Women. *The Norton Anthology of Theory and Criticism*. Ed. Vincent Leitch, pp. 582–93. New York and London: W. W. Norton.

Wulff, Hans. 1966. *The Traditional Crafts of Persia*. Cambridge, MA: MIT.

Zumwalt, Rosemary. 1998. A Historical Glossary of Approaches. *Teaching Oral Traditions*. Ed. John Foley. New York: Modern Language Association.

ACKNOWLEDGEMENTS

I have been extremely fortunate to be the recipient of much encouragement, kindness, aid and information while researching and writing this work. People who write about felt are few, and yet, despite all of this, there is a quiet sea of information. I am certain that I have left out artists and facts that I simply did not know existed due to the paucity of academic writings on the subject. For this, I am truly sorry, and I invite comment and exchange so that perhaps in a later edition – or another book – a more complete history may be written. Further, as the artistic world pays more attention to felt as a material, the information on felt will increase.

Much of the information for this book was gathered by simply talking with people, with makers and users of felt. Many people gave me their time, showed me techniques or shared their knowledge. They all deserve mention here as the least I can do to show my thanks. Michael Gervers, Mary Burkett and Stephanie Bunn kindly welcomed me into the scholarship of felt and offered their assistance, support and encyclopedic knowledge. Mehmet Girgiç graciously took me to the wool bazaar, taught me which wool is best for felting and why, showed me how to make felt, provided me and my husband with a fantastic lunch, a place to stay and numerous cups of sustaining tea. In Kyrgyzstan, I am grateful to the extensive networks of feltmakers who shared their expertise and their beautiful work. Particularly, I want to thank the staff at the Central Asian Craft Support Association and Janyl at Altyn Oimok. I wish them both great success for the women of Kyrgyzstan. Trent and Rejoice in Kochkor provided some good insight, conversation and a much-welcomed spaghetti dinner. All of the felt artists showcased in this book were gracious with their time and thoughtful answers to my wide-ranging questions.

My PhD committee deserves thanks for bearing with me as I pushed my dissertation off to focus on finishing this book and by being interested in a topic so far removed from their own studies and much of my other work. Similarly, my master's committee and Linda Welters, in particular, helped promote my interest in felt in the first place. Finally, Rebecca Hall and Shelley Ingram have given me sympathy, encouragement and close reading as required. Most of all, to Domhnall goes the credit for keeping me laughing and the beasts cared for as I roamed the world in search of felt, asking only an interesting hat in return.

ILLUSTRATION CREDITS

COLOUR PLATES

Plate 1 Copyright: The Hermitage Museum.
Plate 2 Copyright: The Hermitage Museum.
Plate 3 Photo: Willow G. Mullins.
Plate 4 Photo: Willow G. Mullins.
Plate 5 Photo: Willow G. Mullins.
Plate 6 Photo: Willow G. Mullins
Plate 7 Photo: Willow G. Mullins.
Plate 8 Photo: Willow G. Mullins.
Plate 9 Photo: Willow G. Mullins.
Plate 10 Photo and copyright courtesy: Altynai Osmovea.
Plate 11 Photo: Willow G. Mullins. Copyright courtesy: Raikul Ahmatova.
Plate 12 Photo and copyright: The Ashmolean Museum, Oxford (EA 2002:6).
Plate 13 Photo: Willow G. Mullins.
Plate 14 Photo: Willow G. Mullins.
Plate 15 Photo: Willow G. Mullins. Copyright courtesy: Mehmet Girgic.
Plate 16 Photo: Willow G. Mullins.
Plate 17 Photo: Willow G. Mullins.
Plate 18 Photo: Willow G. Mullins. Copyright courtesy: Mehmet Girgic.
Plate 19 Copyright: The Royal Ontario Museum.
Plate 20 Copyright: The Royal Ontario Museum.
Plate 21 Photo: Willow G. Mullins.
Plate 22 Photo and copyright courtesy: Eija Pirttilahti.

Plate 23 Photo and copyright: Arvilommi.

Plate 24 Photo: Art Resource, New York. Copyright: © 2008 Artists Rights Society (ARS), New York/VG Vild-Kunst, Bonn.

Plate 25 Photo and copyright courtesy: Jean Ray Laury.

Plate 26 Photo and copyright courtesy: JoiRae Textiles.

Plate 27 Copyright courtesy: Inge Evers.

Plate 28 Photo and copyright courtesy: Sheila Smith.

Plate 29 Photo: John Polak. Photography and copyright courtesy: Christine White.

Plate 30 Photo and copyright courtesy: Jean Ray Laury.

Plate 31 Copyright: The Metropolitan Museum of Art, New York, Gift of Ruth Ford, 2002 (2002.479.4).

Plate 32 Photo and copyright courtesy: Linda Welters.

FIGURES

Fig. 1. Copyright: Maine Historical Society

Fig. 2. Copyright courtesy: University of Kentucky Special Collections.

Fig. 3. Photo: Hedda Gjerpen. Content copyright: ©iStockphoto.com.

Fig. 4. Image credit: Domhnall Hegarty.

Fig. 5. Image credit: Domhnall Hegarty.

Fig. 6. Image credit: Domhnall Hegarty.

Fig. 7. Photo: Alexei Khromushin. Content copyright: ©iStockphoto.com.

Fig. 8. Image credit: Felt Association 1943.

INDEX